PEACE THROUGH PERSONAL GROWTH

PEACE THROUGH PERSONAL GROWTH

Sukhvinder Jutla

ARPress
ILLUMINATING IDEAS
EMPOWERING VOICES

ARPress
45 Dan Road Suite 5
Canton MA 02021

Hotline: 1(888) 821-0229
Fax: 1(508) 545-7580

Ordering Information:
Quantity sales. Special discounts are available on quantity purchases by corporations, associations, and others. For details, contact the publisher at the address above.

Printed in the United States of America.
ISBN-13:   Paperback   979-8-89330-669-9
              eBook   979-8-89330-668-2

Library of Congress Control Number: 2024902533

DEDICATION

To my father, late Tirlok Singh and late mother Pritam Kaur for their wisdom and all the sacrifices they cheerfully made in raising me.

To my wife and soul-mate Kulwant, my children Parupkar, Amrita and Jagtar and their soul-mates Jasmeet, Jaspaul and Kiranpal who provide me with all the love, motivation and support.

To my beautiful grandchildren Jovan, Diya, Rohan, Jiyo, Layla and Taara through who I experience once again the miracle of life.

To my relatives and friends who read this book and provided very beneficial and constructive feedback. I thank you all very much.

CONTENTS

Have we become numb to the increasing frequency of terrorist acts? They seem to happen in other countries and do not affect us directly.

There has been nothing to compare to the horrific magnitude of the 9/11 attacks, yet. But could something even more disastrous happen again? When?

We feel helpless at events seemingly outside our control. But what if we could individually contribute towards collective peace? And what if we grow personally and prosper no matter what happens?

This is a fictional story of the very wise Sheikh Umeed, the imam, living in New York, who has always been preaching for peace but discovers to his horror that his son has been involved with terrorist activities.

We follow his experiences from initial shock and deep dismay to really trying to understand what drives ordinarily peaceful humans to extreme violence—to acknowledge injustice without condoning terrorism.

He shares with us the lessons he learns along the way—how we can grow mentally and spiritually and live a life of peace and prosperity.

How can we learn from the lessons that terrorists are unknowingly teaching us, the lessons that we can teach to the terrorists, and the steps we and the terrorists can take to bring about lasting peace?

Is there an end to mindless violence? Are we being buffeted by a terrible, passing storm, or are we in a never-ending upward spiral of violence? Is there daylight after the end of the world's terrorist nightmare?

In answering these questions, we have the opportunity to grow mentally and spiritually and leave a legacy of peace and prosperity.

FOREWORD

Life is constantly presenting us with challenges. Most of these are unexpected, unwelcome, and arrive without warning- but some are catastrophic. However, each of these challenges contains lessons and opportunities that make us grow and transform our lives for the better.

One of the major challenges the world is facing is terrorism and the seemingly endless, unbreakable cycle of violence. How can this cycle be broken and peace prevail?

How often do we miss these opportunities because our anger and helplessness does not even allow us to benefit from the lessons hidden in the challenges?

Sometimes we learn these lessons accidentally. What if we were to embrace the challenges and consciously move from anger or passive acceptance of status quo to purposefully shaping of our lives? How can we transform ourselves from being passively peaceful to being actively peaceful? How much more peaceful and prosperous would our world become?

In this book, we learn how to benefit and grow from different types of challenges – some which are transitory like a meteorite shooting across the sky, some which are subtle and go unrecognized, some which persistently stare us in our faces and do not go away until we address them, and some which are beyond our individual influence and control.

In this book, you can learn how to navigate through vague, confusing, and contradictory situations that occur in our real lives.

You will learn about the multiple benefits in your life when you take on a specific challenge in your life. You will learn how your individual growth leads to your prosperity and collective peace.

You will find many parallels in your own life with the challenges faced by the characters in this fictional story. Highlight those that touch you and reflect upon them. Discuss them with someone you love and trust in order to reinforce the benefits.

My sincerest wish for you, the reader, is that you enjoy reading this book and apply some of the lessons in it. May your life become peaceful and prosperous and may you benefit personally and become an active contributor to a peaceful and prosperous world.

Sukhvinder Jutla

Return from Afghanistan

I was very happy to see Nasib as he came down for breakfast, still yawning. "Ah! Nasib, my son, it is so good to see you after more than a year. Come sit down. I hope you got a good rest after your long flight. Your mother is preparing your favorite breakfast meal. I bet you did not get this in Kabul."

Nasib still looked tired after a long journey. "Mom and Dad, it is so good to return home. Dad, you are right. I really missed Mom's cooking. You know, it is the simplest things in life that we take for granted and only appreciate them when we don't have them anymore."

My wife, Fatima, was fussing over Nasib as usual. "Fatima, my dear, you have really gone all out to spoil your son. I never got treated like this even on Father's Day. I wouldn't be surprised if you started spoon-feeding him."

"Do I sense a touch of jealousy, dear?" Fatima questioned teasingly. "You are a fine one to complain about favoritism. Shahnaaz is going to finish university this year, and you treat her like she was still your little princess. Whenever I say no to her, she comes running to you. I am the one who butters her bread, but in turn, she butters you up and you melt and give in. I tell you there is no justice in the world."

"Now, now, Fatima, I only agree with her if she makes sense. It is just that she has more freedom than you had back in our country. You had to wear the hijab, and she has a choice. I would have agreed with her if she had decided not to wear the hijab, and that would have upset you. I told her she can decide for herself, hoping that she would end up wearing the hijab. I must admit that I was as relieved as you when she did wear the hijab. Otherwise, being the imam at the mosque, it would have been difficult for me. However, I would have crossed that bridge if I had to. I am learning not to worry about things which may never happen."

Nasib interrupted with a wounded look. "Hey, you guys, this is getting very serious, let us just continue fussing over me. Shahnaaz will be here soon and start to get all the attention. Let me have my place in the sun!"

I am so thankful to Allah that we have such a close and loving family. Wecan exaggerate our differences and joke about them, I thought.

Shahnaaz made a grand entrance and went straight to give Nasib a big hug. "How is my long-lost brother? I am so happy to see you! I thought the Taliban had abducted you. Just kidding! But I am really happy to see you."

"Shahnaaz, I really missed you! What is this with the hijab?" asked Nasib. "You look very elegant. And what made you decide to start wearing the hijab?"

Shahnaaz did not answer his question but demanded, "Before I answer that, I have a bone to pick with you, brother. Why did you not phone me or e-mail me or text me even once?"

Nasib tried to defend himself, "Shahnaaz, do you think I was on a Club Med vacation? I promised myself that if I graduated with first class honors in computer sciences from the university in 2005, I will spend one year in Afghanistan before I start my job. I wanted to reconnect with my roots, culture, and religion.

"There were no cell phones or computers for miles around where I was. No electricity, no running water, nothing, just rugged, dry mountains. It was very rough and made me realize how spoilt you are."

Shahnaaz went on the attack as usual. "Me? Spoilt? Who asked you to go there anyway? And what exactly were you doing in Afghanistan? I want a full account of your trip when I return from the university this evening. And if I find out you have been in touch with your ugly girlfriend and ignored me, you are finished, my brother."

As usual, Fatima became protective of her son. "Now, now, Shahnaaz, let your poor brother recover from his tiredness, and he will share all the wonderful experiences of his trip to Afghanistan."

I interjected, "I have to leave now to go to the mosque's committee meeting. Let me propose that we discuss this during our weekly family meeting tomorrow morning, after prayer."

What a wonderful concept—the weekly family meeting. Over the years, I have come to appreciate even more the usefulness of the family meeting, which my mother started when we were young. There were six of us children, my parents, and my grandparents. Everybody was so busy—my father with his flourishing grocery store, my mother with her never-ending housework, my grandfather with his poetry club, and my grandmother organizing and volunteering with the new all-girls school in the village. Then the children, with our own schedule of learning the Quran, studying, taking music lessons, playing volleyball and football. It was impossible to get everybody together at the same time for anything, even eating. We were losing cohesion as a family.

I remember once when my seven-year-old cousin Zarina had the honor of singing the national anthem at the National Day celebrations. All our family decided to go to the celebrations to give Zarina moral support, except me because I was never informed, or I was not around when we were informed. I felt so bad that I was not there to hear my favorite cousin on the proudest day of her life at that time. Looking back, this was one of the small things in life that are actually big things.

The weekly family meeting provides an opportunity for everybody to joke, eat, inform, clarify vision, share our successes, our frustrations, make suggestions, brainstorm, clarify misunderstandings, learn from others, and teach others. Since everybody knows its regularly appointed day and time, it becomes an enjoyable ritual, and unless there is an emergency, everybody rearranges their schedule to attend the family meeting. It is like a Thanksgiving dinner held every week.

Shahnaaz and Nasib promised to be present for the family meeting at 10:00 a.m. sharp the next morning. Fatima and I rolled our eyes, resigning ourselves to the traditional half-hour-late start. *How can I get them to sleep early and get up half an hour early?* I thought.

THE BOMBSHELL

What a difference a day makes! The next morning, Nasib was up early. He looked refreshed and in good spirits and just in time for our morning prayer to the east. Fatima and I were doubly surprised when Shahnaaz announced her presence. "Surprise! I bet you thought I was going to come when the prayers were just about to finish."

I gave her a big hug. "I am very pleasantly surprised, no, actually shocked, to see you come in on time for our weekly prayer. Now let us get started."

I always wondered why some of the simplest requests seem to be so difficult for people to comply with. What is so difficult about coming on time once a week for the family prayer? After all, the children have willingly agreed to pray together and start on time. Why are we almost always on time to catch a train or plane? Is it because there is no immediate consequence of not being on time for the prayer? Missing a plane or train causes immediate disruption. It suddenly occurred to me that I had been thinking that both types of situations are the same. Coming to prayer on time requires self-discipline; whereas, catching a plane is the result of externally forced discipline. Sometimes it takes so long to recognize the difference. It takes even longer to recognize circumstances that we cannot control, like someone else's self-discipline. What freedom there is when we stop controlling the uncontrollable!

So I decided that I would continue to explain to others what is beneficial for them but will accept whatever they are able to deliver. The morning prayer was very peaceful and spiritually uplifting as usual.

Per family tradition, it became my duty to prepare the *halwa* before the prayer. How often it happens that the person who complains ends up having to fix the problem!

I had complained to Fatima that the *halwa* was never made consistently. Sometimes it was too dark, sometimes too light, sometimes too sweet, sometimes not sweet enough, sometimes too oily, sometimes too dry—mostly tasty but never consistent.

"Jee, why don't you make the *halwa* from now on?" challenged Fatima. "You seem to know exactly how to make it so that it looks, feels, and tastes right every time. You think following a recipe is all it takes. I will give you the recipe. I will do you another favor. I will even show you how to make it once."

It sounded so simple. I was absolutely convinced that I could always make it very tasty and very consistent. Here was my chance to refute any allegations from Fatima that I never cook! Just cook once a week!

The first time I cooked after the lesson from Fatima, the *halwa* tasted very good. "Hurray for Daddy," Shahnaaz and Nasib shouted together. They were so surprised that I could actually cook.

"Mom, Dad makes better *halwa* than you can. From now on, you don't make *halwa*. We want Dad to always make it," commanded Shahnaaz.

"But I am the one who taught your dad," protested Fatima. Children can be so cruel without realizing it.

"Now, now, Shahnaaz, how about being appreciative of your mother? She is the one whose cooking we have enjoyed all these years. She taught me how to make this *halwa*."

"Mom, I am really sorry. Didn't mean to hurt your feelings. I know your cooking is very tasty. I don't know what it is, but the way Dad has made it, it tastes better."

Shahnaaz's comment reminded me of many instances in life when something familiar but slightly different actually seems better.

The next week, despite my best effort, the *halwa* was a little darker.

Still tasted very good, but it was not consistent.

The week after that, it was lighter and oilier than the first time. It was not made consistently, but it tasted consistently good. This was despite following the recipe very closely.

Fatima teased me, "Sheikh Umeed Jee, what is going on? Why don't you make the *halwa* consistent? You know, like you said, the texture, the color, the sweetness, the stickiness, the taste? You always said it was possible."

Nasib came to my defence, "But, Mom, it tastes very good."

Shahnaaz teased Fatima, "Mom, it is so true. Dad does make the best *halwa*. And why do you never call Dad by his name *Zafar*?"

Fatima replied shyly, "Shahnaaz, this is the way we were brought up. *Jee* is considered a respectful way to address your husband. It is customarynot to call your husband by his fist name."

Shahnaaz stuck her chin out and announced, "Well, I am going to call my husband by his first name."

"So long as you are respectful, Shahnaaz," I added. "Only if he is respectful first," Shahnaaz protested.

I smiled and hugged her. "Shahnaaz, love is unconditional, and respect is mutual. Of course he will love you and respect you."

Nasib chipped in sarcastically, "Shahnaaz, with your attitude, his love will have to be particularly unconditional." Shahnaaz hugged me more tightly and stuck her tongue out at Nasib.

He ignored her and continued, "But, Dad, how come most people in the Afghan community address you as 'Sheikh Umeed'?"

"Children, I will be glad to explain. The word *sheikh* is an honorific title given to a respected elder or a learned Islamic scholar. *Umeed* is our family name, which I changed from *Khan* when I was twenty years old."

Shahnaaz widened her eyes and asked curiously, "I never knew that. Why did you change your family name?"

"When I was twenty years old, I was the captain of our cricket team in Kabul's cricket league, and there were some players in our team who came from Pakistan. Even when we were losing badly, I would always implore our team to be hopeful of victory. And we did win several matches this way. My name *Zafar* means victory, so the Pakistani players started to call me Captain Zafar Umeed.

"The word *umeed* in Urdu means hope. I really liked the word *umeed*, so I decided to change my name. But the continuation of the family name is extremely important in the Afghani culture, so out of respect, I asked my father if I could change my name. I was very relieved when he agreed.

"When people address me as Sheikh Umeed, it is a sign of respect, which I hope I have earned."

Then I looked at Fatima and commented cheekily, "When your mother refers to me as Sheikh Umeed Jee, she is annoyed with me.

"So, Fatima, I am sorry, but I realize that even with seemingly simple things, it is not possible to get the same results every time. Doing our best will usually bring good results but not exactly to the recipe we follow."

Shahnaaz summoned everybody, "OK, my familia, I have to leave in one hour, let us get started. It is family 'ladhi time.'"

I wondered how someone would understand the words that we coin—everyday words that we modify to make them warmer and loving or just invent them. So family becomes familia, and ladhi time becomes a time for light, fun conversation. Daddy becomes Haddy and Mummy becomes Hummy. Some new words are transitory, and some become permanent, at least in our family.

I overheard Shahnaaz's friend Jasmine asking her to get together for friends' 'ladhi time'. I thank God for these new words as a sign of our family closeness.

Shahnaaz continued to talk, "It is not fair that Nasib has visited Afghanistan and I have never been there. Mom and Dad, when will I be able to go to Afghanistan?"

Fatima sighed and replied, "Shahnaaz, as you know, because of political violence, our family had to flee Afghanistan in 1985 after our house was burnt down. Your Dad was thirty years old, I was twenty-seven years old, and Nasib was three years old. You were born in a refugee camp in Pakistan in 1986. It was the most fearful upheaval in our lives. Things are still risky, but I hope we will soon be able to go back, at least for a visit. We promise we will take you with us."

I elaborated on the tumultuous period that our family went through. "I was born in 1955 and Fatima was born in 1958, and we got married in 1980. Life was very comfortable until 1981. Then it became progressively more violent and in 1985 we had to flee with literally the clothes on our backs. In order to feed my family, I went to Germany and worked very hard to send back money. Shahnaaz, you were born while I was in Germany. But at least I was safe in Germany. Your mother had to bear the brunt of the terrible hardship in the refugee camp. I could not get the papers for all of you to join me in Germany.

"Meanwhile it took me nine years to get US immigration. Even that had to be done in a complicated way. In 1994, the three of you had to move from the refugee camp in Pakistan to Mumbai in India where it was easier to apply for US immigration. I joined you there where we stayed together for about six months.

"Things started to look up when we got the US immigration in 1994, and I left to establish a place for you to move there. Between 1985 when we had to flee Afghanistan and 1994 when we were together in India, your mother and I spent about two months together.

"Year 1995 was a very welcome break when we were all together in one place in the US. Nasib, you were thirteen, and, Shahnaaz, you were ten when you came to the US. So here we are, doing very well since then."

Shahnaaz hugged Fatima and me and said softly, "Thank you for your sacrifices."

Nasib showed his sincere appreciation, "Mom and Dad, we did not realize how much you had to go through. We are proud of you."

I prompted Nasib, "OK, Nasib, you must have a lot to update us about your visit to Afghanistan."

Suddenly he became very animated and angry. "Yes, Dad, will be glad to. This visit really opened my eyes. Islam is under attack from the decadent Western powers, and we are asleep. We have to wake up and attack back. We have to destroy them before they destroy us."

We were all taken aback by Nasib's outburst, the real anger in his defiant voice. While I was trying to digest what I just heard, Fatima held Nasib's hand and said, "Son, we have to be very calm-headed about our interpretations of how things are."

I composed myself and commented, "Nasib, I am surprised that you believe what you just said."

"You would believe me if you saw what I saw. But you are all asleep and oblivious of what is happening to Islam. Every single minute of every day, our women are being raped, our people are being tortured and killed, and we are asleep! Shame on us! It makes my blood boil to see such injustice and exploitation in the world. I tell you we have to take up arms and fight the infidels and destroy them in order to preserve glorious Islam and our values. To hell with the decadent Western values!"

Dead silence. We had never seen Nasib like this. He was seething with anger; his eyes almost popping out the sockets, his face blood red, fists clenched, breathing fast with exhaustion. What alarmed me the most was that this was not just a temporary outburst. It was the depth of his conviction, his righteousness that was most alarming.

"Why are you looking at me like that? You think I have become mad? But let me tell you I am not mad. I am enlightened and now have a clear purpose in life." This rationality disturbed me even more.

"Dad, do you remember the example you gave us once of the frog being boiled alive?" Nasib continued as we looked on in shocked silence. "We have been put in water which has been slowly heated by our Christian and Jewish enemies over the centuries. Like the frog, we have felt the heat, suffered, but adjusted. Then the water got hotter. We suffered even more but adjusted again. Over the last few decades, the water has become dangerously hot, and Muslims all over the world are suffering even more, but we continue to adjust to the heat. We will be boiled alive if we don't jump out. You just don't realize what is happening to us, do you?"

More silence. I now wished Nasib was just mad instead of the cold, rational-misguided person he seemed to have become.

Shahnaaz tried to make light of the situation, although still very confused. "Nasib, my brother, you are crazy. I think you have been brainwashed by the Taliban mullahs. But I still love you. I am sure I will be able to knock some sense into you."

I could sense the fear in Fatima's heart reflected in her nervous, quavering voice. "Nasib, my son, we must not think like that. There are many good ways to protect Islam. We have to take the wise route through tough times. Islam is a religion of peace."

"Mom, you just don't see it. Taking the peaceful route, we will die peacefully, but we will be dead! Our enemies will be so happy if they can kill us slowly and peacefully, without guilt. The way I see it, our only chance is to fight and defeat the enemies of Islam. I would prefer to die fighting than be killed peacefully."

I was even more saddened by the fundamentally flawed, fundamentalist thinking of Nasib. How can it happen that all my life I was teaching the true and peaceful path of Islam to my entire congregation at the mosque and my own son believes in a diametrically opposite direction? My sadness was transformed from deep gloom to horror at the result. I prayed that this was just a terrible but fleeting moment.

The terrible memories of the carnage of the 9/11 attack eleven years ago flashed across my mind—the planes crashing into the towers, doomed people jumping out of the burning buildings before they collapsed into a heap of utter destruction.

But then the terrorists had continued to multiply the carnage with the Bali bombings, the bombings in the Madrid trains, and in the London underground and buses.

It seemed to me that the terrorists were becoming emboldened with each dastardly deed.

Was my son being trained for another terrorist act? Only Allah knows where.

I composed myself just enough to speak hurriedly, "I think we are all much stressed. Let us end this family meeting and take time out. We will meet tomorrow evening. Fatima dear, we need to go to the bank to withdraw some money. Please be ready in fifteen minutes."

PREPARATION OR PROCRASTINATION?

This time Fatima got ready in five minutes. We really needed to talk about what had just transpired. We skipped going to the bank and bought some coffee and went to sit in the park on our favorite bench which fortunately was empty. We needed to clear our minds and try to digest what just happened.

"My dear, I am extremely worried about Nasib. I am trembling with fear. Nasib is in great danger!" Fatima started to weep as she held my hand tightly with both her hands. She pressed my hand so tightly that her knuckles turned white. Tears were rolling down her cheeks. It seemed as though the tears were overflowing from a deep lake of sadness. I had never seen her like that.

I was tempted to console her, to tell her not to worry, that everything will be all right. But I knew that this was a very different, very disturbing event in our lives.

"Fatima, I too am worried about Nasib. Indeed, he could be in danger. What I am even more worried about is that he could be a danger."

The park, like any natural setting, provides a calming environment. I asked her to close her eyes and take a few deep breaths. I did the same. When we opened our eyes, we felt calm, but the worries were still there. However, now we could progress from just worrying to taking action.

"Fatima, let us spend a bit more time processing our worries. After that let us promise to use our energies to find solutions and start implementing them."

Fatima continued in a low voice, still weeping but now trembling as well. "My dear, Nasib is a gentle, caring, and intelligent son. We have raised him to always do good in the world. What is happening to him? What have they done to him? Why is he thinking like that?"

I put my arm on her shoulder trying to console her. "Nobody has done anything to him. This is just a passing phase. I believe he is going through a phase of feeling gross injustice to Islam. Given time he will come out of it and again be the gentle, caring person he really is." My explanation was based more on hope than belief.

Fatima felt what I was feeling in my heart. No matter what we say, our heart always knows our true feelings. The heart is very good at showing the gap, indeed sometimes the chasm, between what we wish and what actually is. Yet I wanted to gain more time so that hope could exploit any break and convert it into a breakthrough. When we are facing difficult challenges and we do not yet know the answers, hopefulness will triumph over hopelessness. Hopefulness keeps our mind on the lookout for solutions when they appear. Hopelessness blinds us to solutions when they present themselves.

I tried again. "Fatima, I really believe Nasib is going through a phase. You remember the time when he was very upset seeing the disturbing images of emaciated children during the Ethiopian famine? He wanted to go there himself the next day and distribute food. Talk about naive sincerity! He wanted to change his courses to become an agricultural scientist so he could develop new seeds and new agricultural practices to eradicate famines. A few days after he forgot all that and life went back to normal, playing video games."

"Sheikh Jee, do you also remember that the next day he emptied out his bank account he had painstakingly built up with the money he earned distributing newspapers and donated it all to the Ethiopian relief fund. He may be naive, but he is very passionate about his beliefs. You talk about his naive sincerity. How about your naive complacency? You are ignoring something very serious."

"You are right, my dear. I am fooling myself not to worry when in fact deep down I am worried. I am hoping the problem will just go away. I have no explanation, no solution at the moment. Do you?"

"No, I don't. But why don't you have a heart-to-heart with Nasib and talk him out of thinking like that? He is such a good son, my Nasib." Fatima had suddenly become composed and confident.

"You think it is that simple? Something that you believe is so serious can be solved that simply?"

"Yes, Sheikh Jee, I believe a simple heart-to-heart is the solution. So when we go back home, talk to Nasib."

I was imagining the worst scenario of arguments with Nasib and our lives turned upside down, and here was Fatima imagining a short heart-to-heart and our world being normal again. It was much better than worrying. Action is the antidote to worry.

But how did I end up getting all the action?

"Fatima, my dear, you have given me all the responsibility," I complained. "What are you going to do?"

"Jee, I will make you a nice cup of tea!" she laughed, feeling very pleased with herself. "Now let us go home."

We walked home feeling refreshed by the walk in the park.

How am I going to start my talk with Nasib? I felt I needed time to prepare, to think things through. The implications were too grave if our conversation did not start well. My mind was flip-flopping between visualizing a very amicable resolution and hearing a shouting crescendo ending in parting silence.

Mercifully, Nasib was not at home, and it gave me time to reflect and prepare. Meanwhile, Fatima sighed with impatience because she could not see the happy conclusion. She felt that the dark cloud of uncertainty was still overhead, threatening us with a thunderbolt.

"Fatima, maybe it is good thing that Nasib is not here. I needed some time anyway to prepare myself."

"Sheikh Jee, you are always delaying things, putting things off. I believe you are procrastinating because you are afraid. Yes, you are afraid!"

I always know that when Fatima addresses me formally as Sheikh Jee, she is angry with me even if her tone of voice is polite.

"Fatima my dear, I admit that I am afraid. But this time I really need the time, the gap, to calm my mind so that I can think clearly. I need to silence my mind so I can listen to my heart. I need time to meditate and reflect on what this totally new and unexpected event in our lives means and what to do about it. If you don't mind, please do not pressure me with your need for an instant solution. There is a time for quick action, and there is a time for reflection before action. We have to learn to know the difference. I am sure you will agree that this event requires time for reflection before action."

"Jee, I apologize. I will remember that . . . reflection before action. I agree you need the time to process what has happened before proceeding. I can wait another day for the good news you are going to give us. Here is your cup of tea, reward in advance!"

I needed time to empty my mind. So after drinking tea, I excused myself and went to my personal retreat corner to meditate. I was taught by my father that we need to allocate time to pray collectively, like we do in a congregation, and then we need time to pray and meditate privately. He also taught me that we should remember Allah during times of happiness and when we are troubled. We always forget Allah when times are good and remember him only when we are troubled. When we were young, he told us that if we remember Allah when we are happy, we will never have troubles in our lives—we will always be happy. When I was older, I realized that our family kept on having major problems. So I questioned him on why he told us that if we remember Allah when we are happy, we will not have troubles in our lives. He patted me on my head, did not answer my question directly, but just smiled and said I had grown a little wiser. After that, he started saying that there is a major benefit in any misfortune. You just have to believe it and look for that benefit.

I had great difficulty meditating this time. Deep breathing did not help. It was paradoxical that to calm the mind, we need to meditate, and here I was not being able to meditate because my mind was troubled!

For some unknown reason, my thoughts went back to the time when my father's shop was burned down by the rival religious party's zealots.

He certainly had more than his share of extremely stressful episodes in his lifetime—a month after that he almost broke his neck after his car was hit from behind.

The physical pain was excruciating enough, but he was more hurt that his treatment meant that he had to pull us out of school for a year because he had no money to pay our fees. Yet he was always grateful to Allah during good times and bad. I remembered again his quote, "There is a major benefit in your misfortune. Believe it and find it."

So what were the benefits of his passage through misfortune? He explained that it was his faith in Allah that gave him the strength and resolve to rebuild his business after it was burned down and to recover quickly from his neck injury. He said he *knew* he would recover and rebound stronger than before. He explained that if he had not been remembering Allah when times were good, he may have been defeated by any of the troubles in his life.

Our grocery shop had grown very haphazardly as it expanded. It started to take increasingly longer time to serve the customers, and gradually we started losing customers and the business was teetering on closure. After the shop was burned down, he made sure the new building would be structured to serve customers much faster, and he made sure that there was room for two cash registers. Sure enough, when he reopened his business, customers flocked to our neat, clean, organized, friendly, and fast grocery shop. The customers commented on how clumsy, cluttered, and slow the other stores were. The two cash registers were just right to handle double the flow of customers we were now getting.

The one benefit that the children really enjoyed was no school for one whole year!

It wasn't as though we did not study. Our mother and grandmother stepped in to make sure we were still learning. Our mother taught us arithmetic and English. Our grandmother taught us Farsi, music, art, and poetry. She explained the meaning of any complicated words. She held us spellbound—reciting poetry of some very famous poets. It was very unusual because up to that time we thought poetry was an exclusive domain of men. In the process of teaching us, she started to write poetry herself. She had never done that before. Our interest in her oratory inspired her to start writing poetry.

I still do not know how they managed to teach the four of us all at the same time—two boys and two girls, with different ages and abilities. They made everything interesting and relevant. For once, we looked forward to learning in small, easily digestible doses. They did not have the time enough to bore us! How different from the rote teaching at school.

Our father requested the mullah from the local mosque to teach us the Koran. He was very different. He spent more time on how to practice the teachings of Koran rather than making us just recite and memorize the Koran. Before that, we would go to the mosque because we were told to, and we were expected to. Now we went because we wanted to, and we looked forward to it.

I began to recount the benefits—planned and unplanned, intended and unintended—that our family reaped in our journey which took us from ruins to rebuilding to recovery and onto riches.

Our mother and our grandmother grew by becoming excellent teachers and acquired skills they would have never otherwise learned. These skills were even more useful as they both spearheaded the project they proposed to the village elders of setting up schools for girls in several villages. Some of their students later on went on to become very accomplished professionals and became social activists to promote women's rights, and became very influential members of parliament.

As children, we had to grow up in a hurry. Being the eldest, I was required to make sure that the siblings did their chores and generally kept their noses clean. I started to flaunt my authority and enjoyed being a little dictator. This lasted for a short time until my brother and my sisters rebelled, and my father pulled me aside to help out. He showed me how to lead by example, show responsibility before showing authority, to earn respect instead of demanding respect. This was the most humbling but valuable lesson I learned in my life. Later on, I shared with my father that I was pleasantly surprised at the results—my brother and my sisters stepped up to the plate, and we became closer as a family. At this my father explained that I should not be surprised— all the lessons he had learned himself and taught me work because they are based on universal truths. Be thankful and not surprised when they work, and they always do. My attention again entered into the whirlpool of our current torment. What kind of trouble is our son in? Is he a member of a terrorist cell? Is he about to commit a terrorist act? The horror of the images of the airplanes smashing into the twin towers came to my mind. How can this be happening to us—a peaceful, pious family?

What possible benefit can there be in this terrible situation we find ourselves in?

I had no answers. The only thing that came to my mind was the hopelessness we felt when our shop was burned down. At that time, we did not know what benefits awaited us. We just saw the immediate destruction staring us in our faces.

Meanwhile, I still had the unexpected and unpleasant task of talking to Nasib. I began to feel uneasy and confused. Was I procrastinating under the guise of preparation?

The next morning I got up feeling physically refreshed but mentally exhausted by the prospect of opening up dialogue with Nasib.

There is a time for reflection, and then there is a time for action. Enough reflection, let me take action, otherwise I will stay in the whirlpool of procrastination, I urged myself.

I made my way into the kitchen expecting the worst but praying for a positive encounter.

"Hi, Haddy, what a beautiful day," beamed Nasib.

"Nasib, my son, it is a beautiful day indeed. I am very happy to see that you are well rested and—"

"Dad, I want to apologize for yesterday's outburst. I love and respect all of you. There is no excuse for exploding like I did yesterday. Will you forgive me?"

"Of course I forgive you," I rushed to reply, putting my arm around his shoulder, feeling immensely relieved.

Right away, Nasib responded to my embrace by declaring calmly, "I still believe in everything I said. Islam is under attack. Muslims are being suppressed and killed all over the world. We have to kill our enemies before we are killed.

"Dad, you have always told us to take action. Well, at the madrassa, I did. I gave my name to the mullah as a true Muslim who has sworn to die as a martyr in the cause of Islam!"

He continued very calmly as I listened incredulously. "I pray that Allah will grant my wish, and I get trained as a suicide bomber and destroy as many enemies of Islam as possible."

My heart sank! My own son, praying to be a suicide bomber! He was sorry only for his outburst. His thinking was still demented, according to me. However, he was very sincere about what he believed to be the newly revealed, absolute truth that others fail to see.

Why is this happening to me? Why can't life unfold in a simple straightforward line? I complained to myself. *Why does life have to be so convoluted and complicated? How do I make Nasib realize that he has been brainwashed?*

All I could see were more unanswerable questions on top of previous unanswered questions in our lives.

Suddenly I remembered something my father told me when I asked him how discussions were going on with the rival factions. He explained that they were in vehement disagreement but that he was very happy that there was still dialogue. In the absence of agreement, always do your best to maintain dialogue, was his simple advice. It keeps you in the game and gives you a chance to understand and be understood.

I found encouragement in the fact that Nasib and I still had dialogue, we were still communicating, but I had no idea how we would ever reach any understanding. I complained to myself again. *Why is it that supposedly sage advice never addresses any situation completely and never guarantees the results? It gives you hope but still leaves you to figure out the most challenging portion of the problem.*

So I reasoned that hopefulness is far better than hopelessness. And faith ensures that we keep on taking action in the belief that we will end up getting the results we desire. There could still be currently unknown factors, which only Allah knows that could lead to understanding and even reconciliation. Hope and faith is all I had, and now it struck me that this is all we need! Hope and faith will mobilize forces—internal and external, known and unknown—and work out all the details to get the best outcome in any situation! I had nothing to show but hope and faith, and that pumped me up!

Nasib was eager to continue, "Dad, did you read the terrible news in today's paper? The American drones dropped bombs onto a wedding party killing the bride and the groom and hundreds of guests. How terrible is that, killing innocent people on a joyous occasion?"

It felt very strange to be put on the defensive. After all, it is invariably the Taliban who target and kill innocent civilians. "This is indeed terrible, Nasib," I sympathized, resisting the temptation to explain away the horrible incident.

Nasib continued, sounding angry and calm at the same time. "This only made the news because in this case the truth could not be hidden. Every single day, thousands of innocent Muslims are being killed, individually or in very small groups, by the West which does its evil deeds through the traitors within Afghanistan. The only crime of these martyrs is to defend Islam."

I listened intently as Nasib spoke. "Let me tell you from firsthand experience what the consequences of this tragedy are likely to be. During my visit to Afghanistan, I passed through that very village. I do not know anyone personally, but I can tell you that the Americans have created ten times more martyrs than the innocent people they have killed. The villagers are ordinary people peacefully going about their lives, trying to make a living and raise their families under the most trying circumstances. On the one hand, their lives are threatened by the Americans and their allies directly, and on the other hand, they fear being killed by unknown traitors who have strayed from Islam and have betrayed Islam. These traitors spy on the villagers and kill anybody who they suspect of sympathizing with the Taliban."

I was tempted to respond that it is the Taliban who terrorize the villagers and operate on the principle that when it comes to the survival of Islam, neutrality is not an option, and that if you are not with us, you are the enemy. However, I wanted to hear fully what Nasib had to say.

"I can just imagine the bride's brother going to the Taliban and pleading with them to train him as a suicide bomber so he can take revenge on the Americans. Perhaps the Taliban are thanking the Americans for recruiting suicide bombers on their behalf. What do you think, Dad?"

I was still trying to digest the indigestible—my own son praying to become a suicide bomber! This was clearly not the script I had in mind. My vision was very clear—the extremists were terrorizing their own populations and the rest of the world to force their ideas of Islam. Their tactics were totally opposite to the principles of Islam. You do not harm innocent civilians. The terrorists were targeting not only the Western soldiers but also innocent fellow Muslims. Yet I could not but agree with Nasib in this case.

"Nasib, I agree that this time the Americans had made a terrible mistake, and yes, this would play into the hands of the Taliban."

Nasib felt very pleased that I agreed with him. He tried to extend my agreement. "You see, Dad, our freedom fighters are fighting a just fight."

"Nasib, I have been listening to you very carefully and trying to digest what you are saying. Please make sure that you do not confuse my listening to your views as my agreement with your views. And just because I agree with you on one thing does not mean that I agree with everything you believe."

"I have listened to you so far. Here is my view. The Americans do not target innocent civilians. They will launch an inquiry into this incident. And if indeed they have accidentally bombed innocent civilians, they will actually admit to their mistake and apologize. They may even compensate the villagers for their mistake. Meanwhile, the terrorists deliberately target innocent civilians, often fellow Muslims, with Sunni and Shiite terrorists blowing up each others' mosques. How can this be defended in the cause of Islam?"

Nasib started to answer almost before I finished my question. "Dad, there are sacrifices required—"

I interrupted, "My, son, I will listen to your response, but I would like you to think very carefully before you answer. This question requires a thought-out answer, not an automatic answer you may have been given."

This made him pause. "You are asking me very awkward questions, Dad. My head is hurting just thinking. Meanwhile, the world is carrying on. Let us lighten up and enjoy ourselves. Let us go out for coffee, you are paying, Hadster!"

I was relieved. He always calls me Haddy or Hadster when he is in a lighter mood. We were poles apart, but we were still talking.

"Nasib, please do just one thing for me. Do not tell anyone else about your wish to become a suicide bomber. Please do just this one thing for me," I implored to him, looking directly into his eyes until he nodded his head.

After Nasib and I came back from the café, Fatima smiled and greeted us. "You two seem to have had an enjoyable time. Why didn't you invite me to join you?"

We looked at each other, a little puzzled after Fatima had made us feel guilty. "Mom, Dad and I needed some bonding time. But you don't need to be jealous. This time the Hadster treated me, next time Hummy can treat me. Ha-ha!"

I could sense the impatience in Fatima's eyes. She wanted confirmation from me that everything was all right and normal with Nasib. Meanwhile, I tried to hide the deepest disappointment of my life, still wondering how our carefully nurtured plans for Nasib had gone totally wrong.

That evening, Fatima and I went out for a walk. "Jee, how did things go with Nasib? Is he all right? He seems to be. Tell me that everything is all right with him," Fatima squeezed my hand excitedly, expecting me to confirm her wish.

"Fatima, my dear, we are still talking, but things are not normal. In fact, they are very serious, deadly serious. He has sworn to become a suicide bomber!" I told her in a hushed voice, shaking my head.

Fatima let go of my hand. "I do not believe you! My Nasib is a good boy." She started to weep inconsolably and shook her head. "I do not believe you!"

I put my hand on her shoulder and sat her down at the nearest bench and started to console her. "I still do not believe this is happening to us. It is best if we accept the situation and start working out how we are going to overcome the biggest challenge of our lives. I have already told him not to tell anyone else about his wish to be trained as a suicide bomber, and he has agreed. This gives us time to figure out how to change his thinking."

She continued sobbing and asked, "Why is this happening to us? We have tried to do everything right. Allah, why is this happening to us?"

I waited until she quietened a little and continued softly, "Fatima, my dear, denial is dangerous. Let us both accept the situation and start asking questions which will take us in a positive direction. How can we make Nasib follow the peaceful path of Islam? Let us stop asking the *why* questions and start asking the *how* questions."

She finally stopped crying and straightened her shoulders and affirmed, "Jee, I agree. The *why* questions will keep us in an endless loop to nowhere, but the *how* questions will make us think of solutions."

I continued, "Fatima, do you want to know what we discussed when we went out for coffee? He put me on the defensive and raised questions which I never considered before."

"Oh, like what?"

"He believes it is the Western powers that are terrorizing the Afghans. He pointed to the newspaper headline today where the Americans bombed a wedding party and killed several people, including the bride and the groom."

"Yes, Jee, I read that this morning. This is terrible. Why did the Americans do that?"

"Fatima, I think they were probably targeting some top Taliban leaders who may have come as guests at the wedding. Perhaps they mistook the celebratory gun firing during the wedding. In any case, it was still a terrible, stupid mistake, playing right into the hands of the extremists.

"It raises questions even in my own mind, a very peace-loving Muslim. Why are the Western powers there in the first place? The people that the Western powers call terrorists believe they are justly defending their country against foreign invaders. They believe these invaders are simultaneously invading their territory, their values, and, worst of all, their religion. The Germans considered the French Resistance fighters as terrorists, committing terrorist acts against the occupying German forces as well as French civilians who were cooperating with the Germans. Today they are remembered as heroes. So what is the difference between the Taliban and the French Resistance fighters? Do you believe that the people who we brand as terrorists today will be regarded as freedom fighters by the world in the future, after peace prevails?"

"Sheikh Jee, you always bring up philosophical questions that I cannot answer. I am only interested in what is happening with my son, what is happening now!" Fatima retorted impatiently.

"Fatima, my dear, I understand your wish. My wish is the same—that Nasib becomes a gentle, peaceful citizen and not be involved with any extremist group. We just want to live our life in peace. But he has come under the influence of extremists. We are facing a very unpredictable and dangerous dilemma."

"Sheikh Jee, you are not getting through to him. I will talk to him. He is my son, he will listen to me, my poor baby," Fatima said angrily, almost accusing me for not succeeding.

"Go ahead, Fatima! He is my son just as much as he is your son. You believe I am not trying hard enough. I will be more relieved than you if you manage to change his mind. Go right ahead and tell me the good news tomorrow," I challenged her, feeling hurt.

"Jee, I am sorry. I know you are doing your best. This is the time for us to be working together, not to be fighting amongst ourselves. There is too much at stake here, deploying our family's mission statement of leaving a legacy of love, peace, and prosperity."

I was relieved that Fatima cooled things down and made me realize that if I sincerely tried my best, then I should feel good, not hurt, regardless of the outcome. My ego had clouded my thoughts and my vision. Our best efforts do produce the desired results, but not always. And it is not a given that we will succeed at the first attempt. We invariably need to try again. I remembered a wise saying, "The obstacles that we face in life are stepping-stones on the path to success."

"Fatima, I am sorry for reacting angrily. If you feel you can change his mind, please go ahead. There is a wide spectrum of outcomes—your emotional appeal could change his thinking instantly, or it might plant the seed for eventual change of mind, or it may have no impact on him, or it may harden his position. As usual, there are so many possibilities but only one which matches our wishes. Since we do not know the outcome, we may as well expect the most favourable result, but be prepared to persevere if we do not succeed."

"Jee, what if instead of me, we asked Shahnaaz to talk to him. They are very close, and she can relate better to him."

"Fatima, this scenario did not occur to me. I am glad you brought it up. Mind you, this raises another question. How do we tell her that Nasib is involved with terrorists? Should we tell her that he is involved with terrorists? Just because he volunteered his name as a suicide bomber does not make him a terrorist."

"Maybe he is not involved with terrorists," Fatima reasoned wishfully. "My dear, let us not mince words here . . . Nasib *is* involved with terrorists," I reiterated.

"Sheikh Jee, what you are implying is that Nasib is a terrorist. There are a lot of very angry Muslims and would-be suicide bombers, but they never act out their anger. What makes you assume that just because he is so angry, he is a terrorist? Maybe you are paranoid," Fatima said, clinging to denial.

"Fatima, I will be so happy and relieved to find out that I am paranoid, but as the saying goes, paranoids have real fears too," I said, trying to lighten the mood.

"If we were in a court of law, maybe I could not provide enough convincing evidence to deem Nasib a terrorist. However, from all the evidence and Nasib's behavior, we will have to assume the worst and take preventive action. We could not forgive ourselves if through inaction we allowed something catastrophic to happen. My love for Islam will not allow me to take that chance."

"So, Jee, you think it is not advisable to ask Shahnaaz to talk to him?"

"Fatima, now I am sure we should not get her involved. This is extremely serious. Under Western law, anybody who withholds information on terrorist activities can be prosecuted. I believe in the Western justice system, but their ever-widening dragnet has caught many innocent people and ruined their lives before they were found not guilty, Fatima. We will never do anything which remotely puts our bright and lovely Shahnaaz to any risk." My eyes filled with tears as an image of Shahnaaz flashed in my mind, defending herself bravely and eloquently in the court, charged with aiding and abetting a terrorist.

Fatima and I held our hands and vowed in our hearts to protect Shahnaaz from any harm.

"But what about us, Sheikh Jee? Should we report our suspicions to the authorities?"

"The actions and directions we need to take should be governed by our moral compass, not the legal system. Mostly they will coincide but not always. At this stage I suggest we report nothing," I replied, having composed myself after imagining a fearful court scene.

"We also need to be fearless. We need to have the faith that our moral compass will always guide our actions in the right direction."

"Sheikh Jee, I never thought we would ever be discussing these issues. I just wish we were never in this situation," Fatima sighed painfully.

"I too wish we were discussing pleasant things, like our vacation plans, hiking in the mountains, relaxing on the beach. But life sometimes takes us on totally unexpected, unknown, and frightful detours. And it does not ask for our permission when life changes course."

"Jee, does life also take us on totally unexpected, unknown, and joyful detours?"

"Yes, it does! Sometimes we truly appreciate and enjoy them and thank Allah, but mostly we take them for granted, believing we have earned them and forget to be grateful and thank Allah."

"I agree that we do not want to involve Shahnaaz. As far as I am concerned, I do not feel comfortable talking to Nasib. So who will take up the challenge, Sheikh Jee?" Fatima asked mischievously.

It felt bizarre. Here we were discussing issues of such gravity, and we still found humor in the midst of seriousness.

"Foiled again, Fatima! But I am no chicken. I will be brave and figure out how to continue the dialogue with our son. I deserve a hot cup of tea, made lovingly by you."

When I was alone afterward, the weight of responsibility weighed me down. I held my lowered head in both my hands, breathing deeply, wondering how I was going to ask, indeed whether I was going to ask Nasib if he is involved with terrorists, correction, if he is a terrorist.

When the situation arises, we agree quite readily to take action without realizing the scope of our undertaking. Then we doubt our abilities to follow through.

As what happens during so many times of difficulty and doubt in my mind, the wisdom of my elders lit up the path I needed to follow.

I remembered my grandmother telling the children one night before we were going to bed, urging us to volunteer our time for rebuilding our mosque after it had been bombed by the rival faction. They were threatening to kill anyone who tried to rebuild the mosque. "Whenever you have an opportunity to do good in life, stick your neck out. You will fear people will chop off your neck, but Allah will protect you and put a garland of flowers around it."

Not only us children but also the whole neighborhood volunteered, and within a month, the bombed section was rebuilt. Nobody could tell that the catastrophic event ever happened.

I went downstairs to the living room, expecting to find Nasib and talk to him. He was not there, but instead I found Shahnaaz and Fatima talking and laughing with each other.

Shahnaaz was bubbly as usual. "Hello there, Haddy, come sit down with us. We have something to discuss with you."

I really needed to talk with Nasib at that time, but this was a welcome, ready-made excuse for me to postpone another apprehensive task.

"You know your birthday is coming up, and Mommy and I were guessing what you would like for your birthday. Whoever is closest to what you want wins $100. So tell us what you would like."

I looked at both of them trying to guess what the bet was and trying to guess what I should say. Just the day before I had told Fatima that I wanted a sweater. Then I told her that maybe it would be better if I just got a gift certificate so that I could buy whatever I needed afterward. This way I would not end up with a sweater I did not really like and have to return it.

"Jee, it is a bit impersonal to get a gift card. Shahnaaz and I will buy a very stylish sweater I just know you will really like," Fatima had explained.

"Well, ladies, I don't know what you two have schemed, but I hope I will not get into trouble with either of you."

"Don't worry, my Hadster, I am sure you will not get into any trouble. I am sure Mom will lose the bet, and she will have to give me a hundred bucks. Go on, tell us what you really want," Shahnaaz smiled as she squeezed my cheeks.

Breathing in deeply I replied, "I would like to have a gift certificate so I can buy something of my choice that I really need."

"Hurray for me!" Shahnaaz jumped up, laughing gleefully. "Mommy dear, you owe me a hundred bucks. I will give you my share of fifty dollars for the gift card for Dad."

"Shahnaaz, you are so sneaky. Jee, do you know what her bet was? Why don't you tell your dad?"

Shahnaaz started to explain, grinning sheepishly. "I know Dad too well. He always wants to try on the clothes he wants. Besides, he has so many clothes, he would rather buy something else. A gift card, perhaps a little impersonal would be so convenient for him. I was right, wasn't I? Right on, Mommy!"

Fatima laughed at Shahnaaz's antics. "Do continue, tell your dad what would happen if you had lost the bet."

Blinking her eyes and smiling, Shahnaaz replied, "Well, if I had lost, *Daddy* would give Mommy a hundred dollars."

Fatima and I hugged Shahnaaz tightly. "Shahnaaz, we have spoiled you too much, but we just 'loveded' you!"

Meanwhile, my task at hand was still pending. How do I ask Nasib if he is a terrorist?

I had imagined that our life would be permanently turned upside down. I was surprised that it was carrying on mostly as usual but punctuated with dark omens lurking beneath the happy family atmosphere.

"Where is Nasib?" I asked, hoping the answer would be that he has gone out.

"I think he is upstairs, phoning his girlfriend," Shahnaaz replied, rolling her eyes. "He doesn't have time for his family since he came back from Afghanistan."

I went upstairs to Nasib's room. The door was open. He had his cell phone in one hand, and the other hand was tightly squeezing his furrowed forehead. "I don't know, Salma, I will have to call you later." Nasib hurriedly ended the conversation upon seeing me.

"Son, is everything OK?" I asked sympathetically.

"No, Dad, I need to work out some things. But do not worry, everything will be alright," Nasib replied quite calmly.

I was assessing whether it was a good time to ask Nasib more about the nature of his activities in Afghanistan. Had he received any training, or was he just on the list of volunteer suicide bombers? I was pleased and relieved to be able to overcome my hesitation.

But just as I was formulating the opening in my mind, he spoke, "Dad, I have thought about the question you raised about Islam's position on suicide bombings. Of course, it is wrong to kill innocent civilians. The Americans have closed other means for Muslims to protest. They kill us at will with their sophisticated and powerful weapons. The

American soldiers are too well armed and too well protected. So suicide bombing is a legitimate means of protecting Islam from our enemies. We are at a very critical stage of defending Islam, and our *shaheeds* are gladly willing to sacrifice their lives. They are brave and fearless freedom fighters."

"Targeting soldiers is one thing, but targeting innocent civilians is what I would like you to address," I asserted.

"Look, our *shaheeds* actually target soldiers, but innocent civilians are accidental casualties. Just like what the Americans do. They say they target terrorists, but along with those who they brand as terrorists, they end up murdering our innocent people who are going about their everyday lives. And sometimes there are no terrorists at all, just innocent civilians."

Nasib's response made me think again. Other than the strong and partisan descriptions he used, "they end up murdering our innocent civilians . . . fearless freedom fighters instead of suicide bombers," what he was saying was actually correct. And at the same time, I knew there is a foundational difference between the tactics and intentions of suicide bombers and the American soldiers. Intuitively I knew that what the suicide bombers are doing is wrong, but I found myself reexamining my firmly held beliefs, things being just right and wrong, black and white. There must be shades of gray, and the shades turn to black or white depending on our preconceived beliefs. I realized how convenient it would be for the extremists to use this kind of segmented truth to convert susceptible Muslims to become suicide bombers.

I continued, trying very hard to differentiate between the suicide bombers and the American soldiers. "Nasib, I agree with you that both the suicide bombers and the American soldiers end up killing innocent civilians. Tell me what the justification is for suicide bombers to target mosques. There are no American soldiers in there, only innocent, unarmed Muslim worshippers."

For once Nasib was pensive, not so sure of his stand. Scratching his head and with a pained look on his face, he responded, "In any struggle, there is rough justice, sometimes very rough justice. These

Muslims die for a greater cause, the preservation of Islam. They go straight to heaven, along with the martyrs."

I was deeply dismayed as to the extent of brainwashing he had undergone. What had happened to my clear-thinking, peace-loving son? He had become a completely different person since his visit to Afghanistan. If the extremists can influence my son so easily and so terribly, what are they doing to other people who are unaware? I do not doubt the sincerity of these extremists, but they are not restoring Islam— they are unwittingly destroying Islam.

I could see that the extremists are doing their job very effectively indeed. It is the peaceful Muslim majority who need to shift gears from being passively peaceful to being actively peaceful. They need to take charge for the preservation and promotion of Islam and restore the long-lost glory to Islam, the religion of peace and prosperity. I closed my eyes, and there and then I solemnly vowed to become active and peaceful instead of being passive and peaceful. I did not know how I would do that, but I felt energized by Allah, and I visualized my vow becoming a wow.

I felt disgust at the tactics of the extremists who use gullible people to carry out their dastardly acts. "Nasib, I believe that the suicide bombers who target mosques are not brave—they are cowards. They kill innocent people, and to escape personal accountability, they commit suicide."

"Dad, you call our brave *shaheeds* cowards! I will tell you who the real cowards are! They are the American soldiers who, in the comfort of their air-conditioned bunkers in Arizona, while sipping cold coffee lattes, guide the unmanned drones to drop bombs on poor, unaware civilians. They celebrate their hits as though it is a video game. In an instant, the lives of innocent Muslims are destroyed. Even more cowardly are the generals who instruct their soldiers to drop these bombs," Nasib retorted very angrily and defiantly and continued. "The *shaheeds* trip over themselves to offer their lives in a cause they believe in sincerely and passionately. They are extremely disappointed if they are not chosen to physically die for their cause. They leave their professions, their jobs, and their businesses voluntarily. They give up material comforts and suffer the insufferable discomforts voluntarily. They risk being captured and tortured, a fate worse than death, by the Americans and their puppets, who have strayed and betrayed Islam. Compare that to the American soldiers. They are there unwillingly and only waiting impatiently to finish their tour and go back to their home comforts. Who are the real cowards, the *shaheeds* or the American soldiers and generals?"

I wanted to respond that he did not answer my question of the bravery or cowardice of suicide bombers blowing themselves up in mosques and that perhaps the suicide bombers have been brainwashed to commit these terrible deeds. And if he was to go outside the segmented truth that has been defined for him and look with a wider perspective, he may change his mind. However, I felt that now is not the time to prolong the discussion.

"Nasib, I hear what you have to say. I think we both need to calm down and talk tomorrow."

Nasib closed his eyes and nodded his head without saying anything. We were both tired and exhausted by each other's uncomfortable questions. The good news was that we were still talking. We were in an impasse, but I felt there was still hope. A faint smile forced itself on my face. I slept soundly that night, both due to mental exhaustion and still having hope for the future.

Getting up in the morning was very difficult. I had great difficulty concentrating during the morning prayer. The real task at hand was still pending, making me feel more uncomfortable. I was beginning to change my mind about actually asking, perhaps confronting Nasib about whether he is a terrorist.

I began to question myself. Is it appropriate to ask him? Will he deny it even if he is a terrorist? Who is a terrorist anyway? Clearly, someone who plants a bomb and physically kills people is a terrorist. But what about a person who is sympathetic to the terrorists and believes terrorism is a valid strategy? What about a person who provides financial support to charities who may be supporting terrorism? What about a person who provides moral support to terrorism? I had never thought about it before, but now I realized that other than the obvious terrorists, there are many other people who we should not paint with the bloody brush of terrorism. It occurred to me that the legal definition of a terrorist may be narrow, but the rest of the world has become so fearful and suspicious that even a potential terrorist is a real terrorist.

Coming back to the situation at hand, what if Nasib was merely just very sympathetic to the terrorists? If he was merely susceptible to becoming an active terrorist, does our family still need to take preventive action? I sighed to myself. There were so many questions but still no answers or action. Was I procrastinating, or were these valid questions to be considered before taking action? Damn, another question!

"Jee, your breakfast is ready, come down before it gets cold," Fatima called from the kitchen. I knew what question Fatima would ask me. Even if I wanted to, she would not let me procrastinate! *Maybe it is better like that*, I thought. After all, it is only the pleasurable things we do without being prompted. The rest of the awkward, difficult actions require us to be encouraged but mostly forced to do.

"I have not had the opportunity to ask Nasib about his involvement in terrorism, Fatima," I started before she could ask me the question.

"And what makes you believe I was going to ask you about that? Honestly, some people are so presumptuous," she said teasingly. "What I really wanted to ask you was where we should go for our long-delayed personal retreat. But since you brought up the subject, when are you going to ask Nasib?"

Once again, I was surprised that our life seemed to be carrying on as usual. It seemed that humans have the ability to block out and even deny ominous possibilities they have no control over. I seemed to be the only one left believing that something bad was about to happen imminently.

Before I could answer Fatima's question, she started again, "Jee, what if Nasib was merely sympathetic to the terrorists' cause and not directly involved? After all, there have been many martyrs or *shaheeds* in the history of Islam. Today we all sing praises of their glorious sacrifices to protect Islam. They sacrificed their lives to preserve the Muslims' right of practicing their religion. I wonder whether their enemies considered them as terrorists at the time they were alive. There are millions of Muslims today who sympathize with the extremists even though they do not agree with their tactics. Who is a terrorist anyway?"

Here was Fatima, an avowed pacifist, raising very similar questions as I was after going a bit deeper than the superficial definition of a terrorist, the Western definition of a terrorist.

She continued again, "I believe we should not pressure Nasib. I suggest we just monitor things very carefully before any active intervention. Let us just trust that Allah will alert us about anything serious about to happen. We cannot let fear rule our lives."

"Fatima, this is a big relief to me. I thought that I was procrastinating because I feared questioning Nasib. Now I understand that this situation requires more time. I have been preparing, not procrastinating! I can justify in my heart of hearts that in case something calamitous happens, it will not be out of negligence on my part. And I do have faith that Allah will alert us to take preventive action before that calamity. This situation requires us to be consciously inactive for the time being."

"What do you mean by being consciously inactive?"

"Up to now we were actively pursuing how to question and find out what Nasib is up to and what to do to change his way of thinking. We have never been in this situation before, and we do not presently know how to navigate our way. It is also possible that our active intervention may make things worse. So we are consciously deciding to let things take their own course for now. Remember, this is very different from ignoring the situation. As things change dynamically, we will be ready to intervene actively. And you are right, we will not be fearful that something calamitous will happen. We will have faith that we will be alerted beforehand."

"Jee, thank you for the explanation. Now, please tell me where are you taking me for our long-awaited personal retreat? You are so serious.

Lighten up! Let me remind you that you are the one who says seriousness and romance don't mix," Fatima said with a naughty smile.

"Fatima, allow me to be seriously romantic," I smiled back, hugging her, very relieved to be off the hook. "I have been thinking of flying to Calgary to see the Canadian Rockies. We have never been there, and I have been told by my friend Bruce that the Banff National Park is a spectacularly beautiful place. This will be a very romantic getaway for us. What do you think?"

"Hmm, sounds very exciting! I am very happy wherever you take me, so long as you romance me. Just promise me that you will not bring up any serious subject."

"My dear Fatima, you just reminded me that seriousness and romance don't mix. I would not dream of bringing up anything serious if you don't. However, I do not understand one thing. Why is it that I am always the one who has to romance you?"

"Because you need the practice, Sheikh Jee," she grinned.

PERSONAL RETREAT

"Jee, this is absolutely fantastic. Lake Louise looks so tranquil, and the mountains surrounding the lake are so majestic. It feels so peaceful. Thank you for bringing us here. You are such a romantic!" Fatima cooed, looking into my eyes.

"My dear, I am truly happy that you like it here. The last few weeks have been very stressful for us. We will be able to relax, clear our minds, and go forward again. I am always thankful to our friends Shabnam and Rafiq for introducing the practice of taking time out for personal retreats. They explained that it clears their mind and relaxes them. They get an opportunity to make sure their lives are headed in the right direction and make adjustments if need be. And they make sure that they are aligned as husband and wife. They discuss some awkward situations in an atmosphere that is conducive to reaching honorable agreements and reaching respectable understanding where they cannot agree. They call it preventive nourishment of their relationship. They always enjoy themselves and return fully rejuvenated.

"Every time we have gone on a personal retreat, we have always made breakthroughs in our lives, both individually and collectively. Remember the last time we were on a personal retreat in the Grand Canyon? That resulted in a big breakthrough for me. Jee, do you remember what it was?" Fatima asked excitedly.

"No, I don't remember, my dear, why don't you tell me again?" I replied with a smile, pretending I did not remember.

"Sheikh Jee, I will tell you again because I was very proud of my accomplishment, and you seem to trivialize it," Fatima replied while pouting.

"Well, since you have forgotten, I will tell you once again. I had tried so many times to lose weight before but every time I did, I seemed to be successful for a short time and then I would go back to my old junky habits. When we were at the Grand Canyon, we were reading together this book, *Ageless Body, Timeless Mind* by Deepak Chopra, at a picnic table. I remember very clearly, the blazing sunshine at the top of the canyon, the cool wind blowing, and the spectacular scenery of the Grand Canyon from the edge of the rim.

"The major breakthrough I made was that instead of focusing on losing weight, I learned that I should eat healthy food. I made a silent, solemn, and sincere vow there and then. That was a eureka moment for me! Since then I have been eating healthy instead of dieting. I have lost the weight I wanted to lose once and have not gained it back. I feel so good!" Fatima said while raising her fist in the air, proclaiming a lasting victory after losing many battles with the bulge.

I realized the significance of her accomplishment, lowered her hand, and looked gently into her sparkling eyes. "Fatima, I am truly proud of you."

While our eyes were transfixed for a moment, which seemed like an eternity, I came to another stunningly stupendous realization. Without being consciously aware, I had also started to eat healthy and started to do regular exercise. It is indeed true that when we change for the better, everything around us benefits positively.

"My dear, let me share something even more far-reaching, which I did not realize up to now. At about the same time, I started to improve my eating habits. Even better, I started exercising at the gym subsidized by our company. And that helped me further to become aware of how we unwittingly end up eating very rich food. It takes me about half an hour to burn five hundred calories. One day, I casually read the label on the muffin I used to eat every afternoon with coffee. That muffin had five hundred fifty calories! There was no way I was going to undo all the effort I was spending at the gym. I now eat muffins or other junk food as a treat. Before, I ate junk food without thinking. Now whenever I eat junk food, it is a treat that I enjoy without guilt. Actually, even the junk food that I eat now is haute cuisine junk! I eat expensive chocolate instead of cheap chocolate bars. I want to thank you for the unintended benefit I received in my life."

"Jee, you are most welcome! So glad to be of service. Do you think we will have breakthroughs this time as well?" Fatima asked eagerly.

"I do not know. Let us just expect them. I believe there are two mechanisms of life changes. There are what we call instant awakenings or eureka moments. Then there are the slow, imperceptible changes, which, over a period of time, shape our lives. Both of these are very powerful forces. Osmosis is an example of a slow change. Trees absorb water through osmosis—a slow but a very powerful force. Remember, some instant awakenings occur long after osmosis has been patiently and silently exerting its influence."

"Wow! I never thought of it that way. I guess it is possible that the final decision to eat healthy came as a result of slow changes that were happening, which led to my instant awakening. If I had not been trying and failing and trying again, that instant awakening opportunity would have been stillborn. Come to think of it, how many instant awakening opportunities have I missed so far in life?" Fatima questioned, feeling puzzled and exhausted.

I could predict what she was going to say now. "Sheikh Umeed Jee, you and your complicated analysis of life! I am just happy and grateful to Allah for showing me the way, however He showed it." The triple formality—Sheikh, Umeed, and Jee—added the extra sting to her annoyance.

"Fatima, I am sorry that my analysis of everything annoys you. It is a way for me to learn what works in life and what does not, especially what does not work. That is a golden opportunity to learn. Please bear with me sometimes."

"Jee, I apologize for my impatience. You are right, and you are right annoying," Fatima said laughingly.

I was confused. Was that a compliment or a complaint?

"So what breakthrough can we expect this time?" Fatima continued. "I have a wish. Do you know what it is?"

We both knew what it was, but I wanted Fatima to say it.

"I wish we would get a breakthrough on how to change Nasib from being a terrorist sympathizer to becoming a peaceful Muslim again," Fatima stated calmly and in a hushed voice.

"Fatima, that is my wish as well. I do not want this very serious topic to rob us of the pleasure of our personal retreat. I do not want to trivialize our past breakthroughs, but this is a very complex problem."

Fatima responded quickly, "Jee, but you said yourself that some breakthroughs happen as a result of slow and patient progress. If we do not start, how will we ever reach there? And who knows, we may indeed get a breakthrough since we are expecting it."

"My dear, Fatima, thank you. That makes perfect sense. However, we need to brainstorm this very privately."

"Jee, don't look now, but I believe that the couple at the table across the room have been staring at us ever since they sat down," Fatima interrupted our conversation in a hushed voice. "It makes me feel very uncomfortable."

"Oh, how I wish people saw us as just fellow human beings! Fatima, we have to get used to this in America. Mind you, I often wonder if this is something we could ever get used to. For you it must be even more difficult with your hijab making you look outstandingly different to put it politely, or weird to put it bluntly," I said, trying to be empathetic.

"Jee, please excuse me while I go and talk to the curious couple," Fatima said as she promptly and confidently walked to their table, before I could say anything to her.

My apprehension gave way to relief as I could see the couple and Fatima exchange a few words and break out into smiles.

"What did you say to them, Fatima?" I asked, very impressed by her boldness and calmness.

"Let us go to our room and talk about it," Fatima replied, feeling very pleased with herself.

When we entered our room, Fatima was very excited to share the actions she took. "This formula invariably works in all kinds of situations. I smile and visualize a happy outcome. In this case, I smiled and walked up confidently toward them. 'Good evening, folks! I am from Afghanistan, currently living in New York. Where are you folks from?' I don't know what they were thinking before, but they told me that they were from Dallas and enjoying themselves in Canada. I think it completely disrupted their train of thought, and they felt a little embarrassed that they had been staring at me."

"Now, you folks, have a good time in Canada," the man said to me after exchanging some more pleasantries.

"Fatima, that was a pretty good Texan accent you spoke with—wearing the hijab, speaking with a Texas accent. How humorous and incongruent!"

"You think so? I am still getting used to being so different. To continue to wear the hijab in America is a choice I made, and I have to live with it. Other people are free to think and feel whatever they want to," Fatima replied defiantly.

"I used to wear the hijab in our country and wherever else we sought sanctuary after our house was burned down. In Pakistan and India, I had no problem, but in America, it is a very different situation. I must admit I was tempted to remove the hijab when we first moved to America. After all, a lot of other women from our country were wearing Western dress. They strongly recommended that I do the same. It would be easier for you to get a job, feel more at home in a foreign country, they explained.

"I must admit that I was tempted and it would certainly have made my life easier, but I would still be a foreigner."

"Oh, what makes you say that, Fatima?" I asked curiously.

"Well, with my almond-brown complexion, I would still be different. Even if I had white complexion and looked visibly indistinguishable, as soon as I opened my mouth, my accent would be different. However, I am so glad that I made my decision to wear the hijab because I wanted to preserve my original identity, not because I could never blend in. In any case, where would it stop? The differences would never end—shape of one's eyes, nose, hair, to name just a few. I honestly believe that my decision to preserve my own identity has made me a stronger person because I overcame prejudices of others. I am who I am. Nobody has the right to directly or implicitly force me to comply with their image of what I should be!"

"Fatima, you have done exactly what I preach others to do. Be yourself. Be proud of your heritage. Above all, be proud of your religion! We have a beautiful language, music, art, poetry, rich traditions, and a glorious history. But what binds us all Muslims is the religion! Let us be proud to be Muslims!" I proclaimed passionately.

"Jee, what were your experiences when you first went to Germany?" Fatima asked.

"My dear, I believe I had a much easier time to blend in. To be honest, I did succumb to pressure. Remember the long beard I used to have in Afghanistan? Well, I shaved it. All my friends had done the same. It is true that people stared at my long beard and the shaved moustache. Yes, I definitely looked weird to the Germans.

"Since I did not speak German at the time, I could only look for menial jobs. I had the bitter experience of being rejected for jobs I could very easily do. This continued for a couple of months. I was getting desperate not having a job and not able to send any money to you to feed our family. So I shaved my beard.

"I got a job the next day. Coincidence? Most probably, but I was not sure. Later on I met other people from Afghanistan who never shaved their beards and had decent jobs and were doing very well indeed. Why, some of them were running their own businesses and shops and spoke broken German at best. I bet if you were with me, you would have talked to me and persuaded me to persevere."

"Sheikh Jee, with respect I would indeed have asked you to persevere and succeed anyway," Fatima said smugly.

"Why, thank you, Fatima. What would I do without you?" I said cheekily.

"Do continue, dear. Tell me about your experiences after you shaved your beard."

"Well, the factory job provided the financial springboard for my future progress. The assembly job was very boring, stamping parts for a company which supplied parts to BMW. I worked very hard and put in as much overtime as I was asked to do. Some weeks I had to work seventy hours. But the pay was very good with the overtime I was putting in. The first year was very difficult indeed. Fatima, I am deeply indebted to my foreman, Gunther, who saw the situation I was in and provided moral support and guidance to me.

"By now, I could speak enough German to get by. During the second year, Gunther suggested that I become proficient in German. I cut back on overtime and took night classes to learn German, and by paying close attention, I ended up speaking German with a German accent!

"Since Gunther knew that I had an accounting degree from Kabul University, he suggested I take some accounting courses in German to get German recognition as an accountant. Another tough year! Full-time work and part-time study consumed all my hours. Weekends were spent doing all the homework. How can I thank Gunther enough? His wife, Gertrude, found out about me and would invite me home for dinner during weekends so I could get a break from work and study. As soon as she found out that I ate only halal meat, she started preparing some very nourishing vegetarian dishes and sumptuous desserts for me. My mouth still waters thinking about the soft, chewy, and delicious fruitcake smothered in custard. Yes, indeed I owe them a lot."

It was the first time that I had explained in detail my experience in Germany when our family had to flee from Afghanistan and got scattered after our house was set on fire.

"Jee, you always wrote to me saying that you were doing fine in Germany. The first year when you visited us in Pakistan, you seemed pretty relaxed. You never let on how much you were struggling to provide for us," Fatima said with wrinkles on her forehead.

"Fatima, my dear, you may have forgotten now, but you were fighting your own battles to keep our family *safe*. You gave birth to Shahnaaz in the refugee camp in Pakistan!

"My life was not in danger when I was in Germany. To send you money from Germany was a much easier task than what you went through. Fatima, I do not say it often enough, but I really appreciate and cherish you," I said, holding her hands and looking into her eyes.

"Thank you," Fatima said softly. "Please tell me how you ended up becoming a manager in BMW's accounting department."

"Well, Gunther's company used to supply parts to BMW. One of Gunther's school friends was the director of accounting in BMW. He talked to her about me. One Sunday when Gertrude invited me for dinner, she invited the director as well. We started talking, and she seemed very impressed with my qualifications and my proficiency in German.

"By now I could write German very well. She asked me to send my resume once I got my German accreditation. Her departmental manager interviewed me, and I got a job as a junior accountant. Of course I worked extremely hard, and the rest as they say is history. I was the first Afghani promoted to an accounting manager's position in BMW!

"Gunther and Gertrude were even happier than me. I learned so much from them. One thing that I particularly benefitted from was when they celebrated each small success that I made. I think I was too hard on myself. Normally I would only allow myself the pleasure of celebration once everything was completed. But what I discovered was that celebrating each small success motivates us to accomplish the next step even faster. One other expression Gunther was very fond of saying was that when we start climbing a mountain, the first steps are just as important as the last steps."

"Jee, I am so proud of your accomplishments," Fatima said gleefully and then added sarcastically, "I guess you were not paying attention when I used to tell you that you were too hard on yourself. I am happy that Gertrude and Gunther knocked some sense into you. I would love to meet them one day."

"Yes, Fatima, *Inshallah*, we will," I said wistfully. "I can never repay them for helping me when I was really down. Whenever I used to tell them that, Gunther would reply that I should help someone else who may never be in a position to repay me directly. Amazingly, he used the exact words my father used to say to us!"

"Jee, I thank Allah that we have indeed been able to help many people in our lives. I don't know about you, but it gives me a deep satisfaction and a peaceful feeling whenever I am able to help someone, without expecting anything in return," Fatima added.

"You said the key words, Fatima . . . without expecting anything in return."

"Thank you. But you did not tell me about how your life changed when you shaved your beard and tried to blend in."

"Ah, yes. I digress a lot, I guess because I was not happy about having to compromise my beliefs. However, once I shaved my beard, I found that people did not stare at me anymore. Having a very fair skin and with my light green eyes, I could easily pass off as a German, until I opened my mouth, that is. But the overall day-to-day life became easier, without the added burden of constantly overcoming initial apprehension and negative impression of many people. Mind you, before I shaved my distinct beard, sometimes I would be treated especially well because I looked different. Those rare experiences made me feel good and reestablished my faith in human decency."

"What was the reaction of the Germans when they heard your foreign accent?"

"Sometimes they reacted with hostility and used phrases like 'Damn immigrants!' But mostly it was a disinterested, neutral reaction."

"Jee, how did their hostility affect you?"

"Fatima, initially I felt extremely hurt. I consider myself to be very competent and a dignified person. Up to that point in my life, nobody had ever openly shown their hatred and disdain for me! I normally don't judge people, but mostly these people who showed that hatred were far less accomplished than me. Oh, how painfully that stung me.

"As time went on, anger made a home in my heart and mind. Deep sadness followed and led me to dark and gloomy depths I never knew existed. How can people be so arrogant and cruel? How did I overcome my anger, you may ask?

"Well, I would be lifted from my gloom by a simple act of kindness, a simple friendly gesture. One time it was raining very hard, and I had forgotten my umbrella. As I crossed the road, an old man with an umbrella was waiting and asked me where I was going. Then he walked me to my bus stop, which was a quarter of a mile away. He did not even know me and went out of his way for a total stranger! That gesture reestablished my faith in humanity. Not all Germans are decent folks, and some of them are arrogant jerks. But most of them are considerate, and some are very kind. They are just like us!

"But that simple gesture on that rainy day taught me one very important and lasting lesson—it is much better to be uplifted by kindness than be dragged down by cruelty.

"So after that, I would be encouraged by the positive experiences and use the negative experiences to make me even more determined to succeed. It may sound counterintuitive, but I started to silently thank people who discriminated against me. Thank you for boosting my efforts to succeed, you jerk!"

"Jee, look we have a phone message. I bet you it is our children phoning to find out how we are doing," Fatima said excitedly. "Can't wait to hear their voices! Let me check the message."

The message was from Nasib. "Hi Mom and Dad. Hope you are having fun. Dad, can you phone me as soon as you get this message. It is very important."

"I don't like the sound of this message. Please phone Nasib and find out. I hope he is not in some sort of trouble," Fatima said with a worried look.

"I do not like the sound of it either, Fatima. Please dial home."

It was a strange and a worrying request. Nasib had to go back to Afghanistan for a month. His friend from the madrassa he visited was in danger, and he needed Nasib's help. Nasib wanted me to lend him five thousand dollars so he could go there.

"Jee, this request is very worrying. I think we should refuse to lend him the money. Then he won't be able to go."

"Fatima, my dear, this is indeed very worrying. Nasib has always been very careful with saving money. I am sure he has spent all his money while he was in Afghanistan, on what I do not know. But some madrassas are fronts for funding terrorist activities. And under the guise of helping the cause of Islam, they put you in a position that either willingly or unwillingly you end up giving them money.

"As far as refusing to lend him the money, that will put us in an even more awkward and uncertain position. I just know that there are many people who mistakenly give money for what they believe is helping the cause of Islam. Nasib is just pressed for time to get the money. If we refuse, I bet you his friend will be able to give names of some people who will promptly and without question give him the money, and not merely lend him the money. These people consider themselves lucky that they are in a position to help people who they believe are fighting for the cause of Islam."

"Jee, how do you know all these things?"

"In the same way that we know that there are gangs in this country. Just because we do not know any gangster does not mean they do not exist.

"So what I told Nasib is that when we return home, I will buy his ticket for him, and he can repay us when he comes back. At least we will know when he leaves for Kabul and when he is going to fly back.

And I will buy his ticket on my credit card. This way he cannot sell the ticket and pocket the cash.

"This will give us the opportunity to ask him some details of his trip. Any reliance on us can only be helpful. I always believe in keeping any channel open and not shut the door."

"Jee, why can't we just have a normal, peaceful existence?" Fatima complained with a pained look.

"Fatima, sometimes life makes us face totally unexpected difficulties, not of our own making. We complain about them and feel like victims who have been treated most unfairly. Facing difficulties often feels like facing impossibilities. But in the midst of difficulty lies opportunity," I said, trying very hard to believe what I was saying.

"You and your philosophies! I hate these vague and hopeful platitudes! I don't want to dig through difficulties to find opportunities," Fatima retorted indignantly.

"I have no concrete answers or plans at the moment. If you have any solution I would love to hear it," I responded, trying very hard to remain calm.

"No, I have no answers or solutions. We came here to relax and have a good time, and I intend to do just that. We have worked too hard to let anything rob us of our hard-earned pleasures. Now let us sleep early so that we can get up early and go for a long hike and admire the view of Lake Louise from the top of the mountain. We have to learn to enjoy the good things in life in spite of turmoil in our lives," Fatima replied smugly.

I prayed that we learn this one unintended life lesson during our personal retreat.

GRADUATION IN TERRORISM

"So when did you two lovebirds sneak in last night?" Shahnaaz asked mischievously as Fatima and I came down late for breakfast.

"Yea, Mom and Dad, Shahnaaz and I made your favorite breakfast foods, French toast with maple syrup and fruit medley with vanilla yogurt," Nasib added in quickly.

Shahnaaz added hastily, "Yea right, Nasib! Guys, I made the breakfast, and he watched me make the breakfast. All he did was boil the water! You are such a liar!"

Yes, our household seemed like it was back to normal while Fatima and I continued to feel uneasy about the one ominously changed aspect of our lives.

After we had finished breakfast, Nasib and I went to my study room to talk.

"Dad, I appreciate your offer to help me in an emergency," Nasib started in a casual way. "I can't tell you much, but I need to borrow two thousand dollars to go to Afghanistan."

He had forgotten that initially he had asked for five thousand dollars. "Nasib, I am most concerned about your safety. I need to know why you have to go to Afghanistan in such a hurry, and I need to know the honest truth. So why do you need to go to Afghanistan? What is the emergency?" I asked firmly but politely.

"The less you know, the better for you, Dad. I am just as interested in your and the family's safety as you are in mine" Nasib replied quite calmly. "And don't worry about me. I have plenty of friends who will ensure my personal safety."

I became very angry with Nasib's evasiveness. "Let us not be naive. We are living in the United States of America. We are citizens of this country which is at war with terrorist groups in Afghanistan. I need to know if you are receiving terrorist training. You say you have our family's safety in mind. Your misguided beliefs and recklessness are making our family the target of prosecution by the US government and our extended family in Afghanistan the targets of assassination by other terrorist groups. You just do not realize the consequences of your actions, do you, Nasib?"

"Damn the consequences! The Americans and their allies have invaded our country. They are attacking our religion and destroying our country. They have turned Muslim against Muslim and put their Afghani puppets in charge of running our country.

"If you must know, the same terrorist group that you told us burned our shop and then our house and drove us out of Afghanistan have bombed the house of my friend Aziz. And as you well know, this terrorist group has no religious agenda. They are just gangsters using Islam as a shield for amassing wealth by terrorizing the population. His father, mother, and sister who was getting married in two weeks all died in the explosion. They were targeting Aziz, but he was out that night. Aziz was the most devout and dedicated Muslim at the madrassa where I learned about the threats to Islam. He is my religious guide, my mentor. He needs my help to avenge the death of his family, and I gave him my word that I would help him whenever he needs it."

I shook my head with sad disbelief and horror. What a perfect, innocently unaware target Nasib must have been for the misguided mullahs in the madrassa! And now he was being used for what purpose? How many more people have they brainwashed? But I realized that the more I tried to convince Nasib, the more firm he would become in his newfound enlightenment.

I visualized the carnage of the terrorist bombing in Bali, the Madrid train bombings, and the recent bombings of the London underground and the buses.

I could not help thinking that Nasib could easily be inducted to commit some terrible incident like that. I shuddered and shook my head.

However, I calmed myself and focused my mind to the problem at hand.

"So what kind of help is Aziz asking for?"

"I don't exactly know. Probably logistics and planning. I am ready to do whatever I am asked to do," Nasib replied, without waiting to think if he should be telling me all this. How anger makes us impatient and clouds our judgment!

"Look, Dad, you should understand. Aziz is willing to die for Islam, and these thugs are willing to kill for money and power. They are opportunistic vultures who are undermining Islam just as much as the Americans. Besides, this group burned our shop and then our house and caused us to flee from Afghanistan. I want to avenge that injustice as well."

How revenge makes us rationalize the irrational!

He continued without letting me respond. "But do not worry, Dad. This operation is not against the Americans. It is a very specific operation against non-American enemies of Islam. Without meaning to I may be helping the Americans because these people have also killed Americans to gain credibility as defenders of Islam."

I could not believe his twisted logic and his desperate commitment. How easily he could be molded to do whatever his masterful mullahs wanted him to do! Whenever they wanted to, he could be just as easily enlisted in an operation against the Americans, most likely in America.

I did not know how to respond, so I tried to put into practice a lesson my father had taught me: keep the dialogue open and buy some more time.

"Nasib, my son, I really believe that for your own protection I should refuse to lend you money and you should not go. However, I will rethink my position, and we can continue tomorrow. In the meantime, you may want to think how best you can serve the cause of Islam."

"Dad, my mind is already made-up. If you do not lend me the money, I will ask one of Aziz's friends. It may take me a few days longer, but I will get it, and I will go to Afghanistan. Tomorrow I need your answer," Nasib replied in the form of an ultimatum.

I was not surprised by his answer, but I had bought some time, and we were still talking. Some consolation!

As usual, Fatima was anxious to hear what had transpired with Nasib. She peppered me with questions. "What did he say? Is he in danger? Have you talked him out of going there?"

"Fatima, my dear, his mind is made-up. We don't have much of a choice. He gave us an ultimatum. Either we lend him the money, or he will get the money from one of Aziz's friends. Before you ask me who Aziz is, I will tell you—he is Nasib's religious mentor who he met at the madrassa during his last visit to Afghanistan. What is extremely worrying is that both Nasib and Aziz have been brainwashed by the mullahs at the madrassa.

"They are prepared to do anything they are commanded to do. I would never have imagined that once sane and rational people could be transformed into doing deeds they would never have done before. They become eager and willing accomplices, believing they are doing the right thing for a greater purpose.

"Unfortunately, this is not the first or last time this has happened. Look at the German citizens who committed the most horrific crimes of humanity against the Jews and other minorities. They were willing accomplices in an institutionalized slaughter machine. Unimaginable but true, millions of Jews and minorities were herded and systematically put to death."

"But why don't you explain to him that what he is doing is not good?" Fatima questioned as though I had not done that already.

I sighed with frustration, "Everything seemed to be going well. For the last two years, he has been doing extremely well in his job with the aerospace company. He seemed reasonably happy with life. I don't know what has gone wrong.

"Fatima, he has everything figured out and rationalized. He is going to help his friend Aziz avenge the death of Aziz's father, mother, and sister who died when their house was blown up. Aziz's sister was going to get married in two weeks' time. It is very sad and gut-wrenching. Can you imagine if this happened to our Shahnaaz? And this is the same group that first burned our shop in Kabul and then our house."

"Jee, no wonder why Nasib wants to help Aziz avenge his sister's death. I know it is easy for us to preach that revenge is not the answer because we have not suffered like Aziz. The authorities in Afghanistan are in no position to stop lawlessness. In situations like that, people administer their own crude justice. But there is no way I would want Nasib to put his life at risk. I am his mother, I will talk to him. You think too logically and explain things rationally. These have to be put in an emotional context to connect with peoples' hearts," Fatima said adamantly.

"My dear, please talk to him. I will be very happy if you are able to convince him not to go," I replied, sincerely acknowledging my left-brain tendency. "I appreciate that you are able to compensate for my limitations, Fatima.

"In the meantime, I just hope Nasib is only discussing these things with us. He is so consumed with anger and revenge that he is not thinking clearly at all. Initially he wanted five thousand dollars, today he asked for two thousand dollars. Now he has settled for me paying just for his ticket. He cannot get cash refund for it. We know that he is going tomorrow and that his return flight is one month from today. He is very clever and calculating on one hand and very stupid and naive on the other hand. This is very typical of all the people with extremist views. Fortunately, they mostly fail through carelessness. They leave behind many clues and tracks. He will soon realize that he has told us much more than he really wanted to. I am sure he has told his extremist friends that he has not told us anything."

"Jee, I am very surprised that you are not more worried about Nasib's life. Do you know something that I don't?" Fatima asked, looking concerned and puzzled.

"Fatima, of course I don't want him to go there at all. But I think he will come back safely because he will be protected by the mullahs," I replied, more with hope than certainty.

"Besides, we cannot force him to not go. It is very humbling to realize that we have to let go after trying our best. We will pray for his safety."

"But, Jee, why do you say that he will be protected by the mullahs?" "Look, the vast majority of the madrassas are peaceful proponents of Islam. A tiny minority has been infiltrated by the terrorists. They recruit people to carry out terrorist activities, like suicide bombings. These terrorists are very efficient and very good at strategic planning. They have enough local recruits for what they want to do in Afghanistan. Nasib, having been brought up in America and being an American citizen, is much more useful to them in America. I believe they just want to keep him involved while they find a much bigger role for him, in America."

"Jee, but how do you know this? Are you sure Nasib will be safe?" Fatima asked, hoping what I said was true.

"Real life is lived on probabilities, not guarantees. It is very much in the interest of the terrorists to protect Nasib. Mostly they are successful in what they plan, but there is no guarantee. That is why I believe Nasib will come back safely. If you want to guarantee his safety, convince him not to go there in the first place!" I replied tersely.

"Yes, I will convince him not to go," Fatima replied with quite determination while looking into my eyes.

At night, I tried several times to breathe deeply, meditate, and still my mind to relax. It worked most of the time. But this night was very restless. True indeed, real life is lived on probabilities, not guarantees.

"Fatima, it has been two weeks since Nasib arrived safely in Kabul, and he is supposed to return in two weeks. Have you heard anything from him?"

"No, but he has contacted Salma. I would have thought he would call me first, his mother. I gave birth to him and cleaned his shit. How ungrateful! He contacted his girlfriend first!"

"Fatima, do I sense a hint of jealousy? Let us be grateful that we heard from him," I said teasingly.

"Jee, it really bothers me that he did not call me first. I know I should not feel this way, but I can't help it. I should feel relieved that he called to say that he is safe, but instead I feel jealous," Fatima continued painfully.

"Fatima, I must admit I have similar challenges which I wrestle with privately. At least you admit it openly. A very good start toward overcoming our shortcomings," I responded encouragingly.

"And there is one other thing that really hurt me. I was not able to convince my own son to not go to Afghanistan. I was so sure I would be able to, but I failed," she blurted out, tears rolling down her cheeks.

I held her consolingly. "You did your best. There are factors which are completely outside your control, outside my control. I wasn't able to convince him either.

"To look at things positively, you did get Nasib to think about getting married and settling down. You oriented him in a very positive direction. I know it seems we are directing Nasib's life, but I would much rather that we direct his life than the terrorists who take away his freedom of choice and, worse, use him to further their aims. You have done well to at least keep him under our guidance. Focus on what you have succeeded at, even partially, not on what you failed at. I am very proud of you, Fatima."

"Thank you for your encouragement," Fatima said, wiping her tears. "And one other thing. I managed to do what Salma has not been able to do for years," Fatima said smugly. "It is I who made Nasib think seriously about settling down."

"But are you sure he will actually settle down after he returns?" I asked the type of question Fatima usually asks me.

"No, I am not sure, but there is a high probability that he will. Sheikh Jee, remember, you are the one who always says that real life is lived on probabilities, not guarantees," she replied, feeling very pleased with herself.

"Fatima, my dear, but then he will end up marrying Salma, and you will lose control over Nasib again," I said teasingly.

"Sheikh Jee, you can be so sweet and cruel. Tonight you will have to cuddle up alone in the closet," Fatima said as she stuck out her tongue at me.

Life seemed to be carrying on as usual amidst the uncertainty and turmoil.

The following day, Fatima asked me a very curious question, "Jee, do you think I am still controlling Nasib's life? He is still our child, but he is twenty-six years old."

"Fatima, you ask a very general question, so I will give you a very general answer. Concern does not have to mean control. I used to question myself a lot if we should give our children the independence to make their own life decisions when they were young. I got very good direction from my friend George when Nasib was struggling to decide what college to attend and what courses to select. George's daughter was struggling with the same decisions.

"As parents who have invested blood, sweat, and tears in raising our children, we have the responsibility to be full participants in decisions affecting their lives. Let us not be fooled into inaction under the guise of the modern independence to make our own decisions. What invariably happens is that while we are innocently giving them freedom to make their own decisions, other people, for example their teachers and their friends, are influencing them to make the choices they think are best for our children. Of course they are doing this unknowingly, but it can easily happen that our children chose the college based on what their friends think and chose their courses based on what their teachers think.

"Unless we are confident that our children are confident in the direction they are taking, we must guide them. Otherwise, we are the ones who will end up paying for our children's mistakes.

"While we are giving our children the independence, other people are making their decisions for them. And just because they reach an arbitrary age of adulthood does not mean they are able to make mature decisions in all situations. Look at us, supposed adults but still with limitations and blind spots. George's bottom line was that we have to be proactively engaged in decisions affecting close family members and friends. He said to just trust your intuition, and you will realize when proactive intervention is required and when you should just let things take their course. There will be some, albeit very few situations when you will know you have to intervene. Just trust your intuition. He summed it up very succinctly—exercise concern, not control."

This seemed a little contradictory to Fatima because we had always told the children to exercise their freedom of choice and make their own decisions, good or bad.

"Jee, I understand that in this situation we absolutely have to intervene because Nasib may end up doing something unimaginably terrible. He has not done that yet and may never do it, but we cannot take the chance. What other mundane example can you give?"

"Fatima, my dear, if you found out that either Nasib or Shahnaaz were to start drinking too much, would you want to intervene proactively or watch passively and just let them be adults and suffer the consequences?" I asked, already knowing the answer she would give.

"Well, of course, I will do my best to make them realize the dangers of alcoholism. But after that, it will be up to them. They will have an independent choice to make. I think it will be much easier for me to do that than to watch them suffer afterward," she replied, nodding her head.

She continued, "It is much clearer now for which types of situations it will be better for me to intervene. But if they do not understand, how will I know when to stop telling them?"

"Fatima, like my friend George said, trust yourself and you will know when you have done enough," I replied.

"Sheikh Jee, I wish life was simple and straightforward," Fatima sighed. "Although looking back I must say that whenever I made determined effort, mostly I got the desired results. Invariably it took longer and required more effort and tries than I thought, but mostly things worked out."

"You are absolutely right, Fatima. We need to pray to Allah to give us the wisdom and patience to accept His will when things do not work out. My father used to say that there is some hidden reason and benefit when things do not work out."

"Jee, now you are giving me a headache with all these hidden reasons and benefits. Why didn't you just let me savor the realization that whenever I put in the effort, I mostly succeeded? Instead, you piled on another lesson I need to learn. To compensate for that, you have to make a nice cup of tea while I relax and feel good about what I have accomplished," Fatima commanded.

"Yes, my dear, it is good for me to know when to stop. One lump or two?"

On the morning of Nasib's scheduled arrival, Fatima was very happy when she greeted Shahnaaz and me at the breakfast table. "Guess what, guys! Nasib phoned last night, and while you two were snoring away, I talked to him. He didn't talk for long but asked to be picked up from JFK airport at 9:00 p.m. tonight. And listen to this, he asked me to tell Salma that he is safe. For once he called me instead of her."

"Hummy, you are so competitive! Poor Nasib, he is destined to be Mama's boy forever, thanks to you!" Shahnaaz said, rolling her eyes.

"Listen, you two, let us just be thankful Nasib is coming back safe and sound. I am going to the mosque tonight. Fatima, would you be able to pick him up from the airport?" I said, trying to disrupt their friendly squabbling.

"Sure, I will be there. And I will ask Salma if she wants to come with me," Fatima replied, feeling very accommodating.

When I returned from the mosque that night, Fatima was subdued instead of being ebullient. After all Nasib had arrived safe and sound!

"What is the matter, dear? Is everything OK with Nasib?" I asked, a little worried myself.

"He was very distant and aloof. He hardly said a word to Salma or me. He looked very tired, so we told him to sleep and we would talk in the morning. Something very bad happened during his stay in Afghanistan. I am extremely worried about him," she said very sombrely. "I am extremely exhausted. We will talk in the morning, after our weekly family prayer."

It seemed as if we had to brace ourselves for more turmoil and turbulence in life.

"Yes, dear, let us get well rested. Tomorrow will be a bright new day," I said hopefully, trying to cheer us up.

This time I was able to meditate easily and woke up refreshed.

Nasib looked rested and very neat and tidy as usual. He smiled faintly and was quiet but polite. As usual, family prayer was very serene and peaceful. Fatima looked at the figurine which she always placed on the dining table, saying, "A family that prays together stays together" and then turned toward me and looked directly into my eyes. She said a lot by saying nothing!

I had made the traditional parshaad, which everybody ate quietly. The family meeting was very brief although we all knew there was a lot to tell and discuss after Nasib's second visit to Afghanistan. But this was not a topic we had ever envisaged we would come across so directly. Even Shahnaaz was unusually quiet.

It was Nasib who broke the awkward silence. "Dad, can I speak to you alone, upstairs?"

As Fatima had told me before, Nasib was distant and aloof. "I want to thank you for buying me the ticket to go to Afghanistan. I promise to pay you back the money as soon as possible. But don't worry if I am late. Just tell me how much extra interest I owe you."

I tried to make light of his laconic style. "Son, I am very happy to see you back home, safe and sound. I know you have plenty on your mind right now. Take your time to tell me anything whenever you feel ready, and I will understand if you do not want to say anything. Your mother and I are only concerned about your safety and well-being. We wish you well whatever you decide to do in your life. We just want you to know that you will always be our son, and we love you!" I said as I put my arm around his shoulder.

Initially he was passive and unmoved but then excused himself to go to his room and bring a Farsi newspaper from Afghanistan. He showed me the headline on the first page. "Jahanbaksh and Seven Bandits Killed in Bomb Blast by an Unknown Group."

"Dad, you will soon know about this anyway, but I might as well tell you myself. I helped make this possible. I am not exactly proud of this, but this had to be done," he said coldly.

My jaw dropped! It was a remarkable feat that Aziz and his allies had been successful at their operation. It must have been very well planned. Jahanbaksh was the bandit turned mujahedeen, one of the fiercest foes of the Russians! To his enemies, he was a ruthless robber, but to his supporters, he was a fearless freedom fighter. He was well-known for extorting money from wealthy Afghani businessmen. This is why our shop was burned down because our family refused to pay any ransom. Other than to his loyal supporters who he rewarded with looted money, he was just a bandit taking advantage of the confusion in the country. In a clever move to gain respectability, he had allied himself with the mujahedeen who were targeting American soldiers. But he had made too many enemies and was always in danger of being killed. If Aziz and his allies had not killed him, some other group would have. It was just a matter of time.

Although in my mind Jahanbaksh got what he deserved, I was not happy that he had been killed. This could easily escalate into an uncontrollable spiral of revenge killings. When you fight fire with fire, you end up with ashes. And Nasib could get sucked in the inferno.

"Nasib, I don't know what to say. All I know is that this is not the right path. I just wish you were not involved. What was your role in the operation?" I asked, expecting that he would refuse to divulge anything.

I was very surprised that he was eager to talk. Again, I prayed that he was not talking to anyone else about his activities. "Dad, Aziz had planned everything, all the logistics of obtaining the explosives, making the bomb, and planting the bomb. He has very trained people to do all that. He just did not know how to locate Jahanbaksh. All he knew was the e-mail address belonging to one of his trusted nephews that Jahanbaksh was using to communicate with his people."

He continued, "My job was to hack into his nephew's e-mail and try to find where he could be from his e-mail communications. Dad, I tell you I was both impressed by how technically sophisticated these people are and how stupid and careless they can be. To hack into the account was very challenging. There were many layers of security. I had almost given up but had a stroke of luck and finally succeeded after one week. Of course I can't tell you more, but after that, it was like stealing candy from a kid. The e-mails were in Farsi but were not encrypted at all. Anyone could read them! In one e-mail he sent to his followers, he told them where and what day they would meet at one of his friends' safe house in Waziristan. How stupid and careless can you get?"

By this time, Nasib was feeling quite proud of his role in the operation.

The gravity of what Nasib had done suddenly sunk in. I did not want to believe that Nasib had committed a terrorist act. But there it was, justified or not, it was a terrorist act!

I held my head in my hands, and seething with anger, I cried out, "Nasib, I hope you realize that you are no longer a terrorist sympathizer—you are a terrorist. Even though you did not explode the bomb, you are just as implicated in the killing of eight people, whether they were bandits or freedom fighters. I never imagined that my own son would become a terrorist!

"All my life I have preached to all Muslims to follow the path of peace, and here you are, my own son, returning home after graduation in terrorism!"

Nasib remained surprisingly calm. "Look, Dad, I really don't care what you brand me as. I am a freedom fighter, not a terrorist. I am defending Islam. I am liberating my homeland. The only difference is that I am not enlisted in an army. If you believe I am a terrorist, please go ahead and report me to the authorities."

He continued, "I am prepared to suffer and die for my cause. I respect your beliefs, but it is just too bad that my actions do not fit your belief system. They cause you great inconvenience, and for that, I apologize. In fact, I am going to move out so that you can live your life the way you want to and let me live my life the way I choose. I believe in fighting for the survival of Islam. You believe in peaceful engagement with the Western world. We have completely different worldviews. I do not see any convergence. It is better that we follow our own paths."

I was about to respond, but he continued, "My life has taken a new direction. I am going to break off with Salma. This is one of the hardest decisions I have made because I love her very deeply. I do not want to deceive her. I cannot give her the life she is expecting. I know she will be very hurt, but she will get over it."

I had never felt so helpless in my life. Here I was, being peppered with one blow after another with no defense or answers. It was extremely difficult to give in to reflex action and tell him to get out of my house and go to hell and that I would report him to the authorities. But fortunately, Allah gave me the courage to compose myself so that I could keep the dialogue going, however hopeless it seemed.

I told him very calmly and very sternly, "Nasib, you are so fortunate to live in a free country where there is rule of law and justice. I will decide when and if I will report you to the police. You seem to have everything figured out in life. So go ahead and leave right now. You are on your own."

And he left without saying another word or making eye contact with me.

Navigation through Unchartered Territory

The atmosphere in the house was dark and sombre, to say the least. The whole fabric of our family had become unravelled in an instant.

"Sheikh Jee, I want you to know that I support you in how you handled the situation. Nasib is our son, but there is no excuse for his behavior," Fatima said softly, rubbing my hand gently, trying to comfort me.

I closed my eyes and shook my head slowly. "Fatima, my dear, never did I imagine that after painstaking nurturing and trying to do everything right for our children, things would turn out so diametrically opposite to what we envisioned.

"I really do appreciate your support. Now is the most important time for us to work together. We may not know the how right now, but let us vow that we are going to get through this situation. Let us go to the park and sit on our favorite bench. We need to have a long talk."

Fatima started to talk after we had sat silently for what seemed an eternity. "Jee, I feel the same way. I mean we know many families we think are dysfunctional, and they seem to end up doing not so bad. At least they do not suffer such catastrophes. I am not complaining to Allah, but we really do not deserve this outcome for our sincere efforts."

I was too exhausted by the traumatic experience to respond.

Fatima suddenly straightened up and said, "Let us not blame ourselves and certainly not Allah. This is a violent thunderstorm we are going through in our lives. It will pass, and the sun will come out. We have overcome many adversities in life although never like this one.

Now is the time to have faith in Allah. He will give us the wisdom and courage to face this challenge as well. We will not only survive, but we will thrive!"

She shook me out of my gloomy daze. "Fatima, this is another reason I love you very much. When I am down, you are there to encourage me to get up. You do not let me stay down. No wonder we always end up succeeding! As Shahnaaz says, I just 'loveded' you!"

For the first time in a long time we smiled. We did not have any idea how things would work out, but we just *decided* that they would work out.

When we reached home, Shahnaaz was eager to share a development. "Mom and Dad, Nasib just phoned me and wants me to meet him at the café tonight."

I was happy that he was communicating with one of us. "By all means, Shahnaaz, he is your brother. I would like you to be as sisterly with him as you have been up to now. Just because there are differences between us does not mean you two should not get along together."

Shahnaaz as usual was always ready for action to bring the family together. "Haddy, I want you to know that I really do respect you and love you. Nasib is not his usual self. He has never disrespected you before. Don't know why he would do that, but I will talk to him. You know I can get him to do anything for his little sister," she offered her help innocently.

She obviously had no idea what had transpired with Nasib in Afghanistan and between Nasib and me. "Shahnaaz, I have the full confidence that you will do your best to bring about peace in our family," I told her, giving her a big hug.

"Fatima, aren't you proud of our daughter?" I asked, beaming with pride as she left to go to the movies with her friends.

"Jee, who else do you think knows about Nasib?" Fatima asked in a hushed voice. "I hope with all my heart that we are the only ones who know. He hasn't told me anything. All I know is what you have told me.

"I cannot bring myself to believe that my own son is a terrorist. We raised him so well. I am very worried about him. What do we do now?"

I felt very despondent again. "Fatima, I have no idea how things turned out this way. I never used to question myself, but now I am really questioning myself. Were we too lenient with our children? Gave them too much freedom? Were we too religious? Are we to blame? There are so many doubts that have suddenly appeared on how we raised our children. I even question myself on how I have lived my life."

Fatima put her arm around my shoulder. "Sheikh Jee, I understand your disappointment. I am bitterly disappointed as well. But if I may say so, we should not blame ourselves. We should not doubt ourselves. Allah knows we did the right things with the abilities we had. We taught our children good from bad, helped develop their decision-making abilities, and then gave them the freedom to make their own decisions. As you have always said, life is based on probabilities, not certainties. Despite our best efforts, we cannot guarantee the results. There are other factors outside our control which can override our best efforts. Please don't blame yourself."

"Fatima, I know what you are saying is correct. That is the same advice I would give to someone else if it happened to them. It is much easier to give advice than to receive advice. When we give advice, someone else is suffering. When we receive advice, it is because we are suffering."

"But, Sheikh Jee, in this case we are both suffering. So let us both take the same advice and stop blaming ourselves. This advice is bitter medicine, but it will end our suffering. It is good for us. Open wide . . ."

She made me laugh. "That was a very funny way to put it! Fatima, I thank you for lifting me out of gloom. You disrupted my negative thinking."

Feeling energized, she continued, "Let us see what actions we can take. Again, this is the advice I have heard you give to others—don't worry, take action."

So I found out right away that as my mind got switched to active mode, I could not worry. "Well, the first thing we have to decide is whether we should tell the police."

"I don't know, what do you suggest?" Fatima asked, maintaining momentum.

"Fatima, I do not believe we need to." "Jee, why do you believe that?"

"Fatima, because I do not want the police to question us like you are questioning me now!" I replied humorously.

"But seriously, Fatima, I am not sure if we should tell or not. We need to consider our moral obligation and our legal obligations. I hope both lead us to the same decision. I think we should consider consulting a lawyer. Nothing imminent is going to happen with Nasib."

"Jee, I am not sure we should consult a lawyer. What if the lawyer reports Nasib to the police anyway?" Fatima asked, feeling paranoid.

"Fatima, you are thinking too far ahead. We are going to ask a what-if question first. Besides, the western legal system is enshrined in lawyer-and-client privacy. All this is very new to me. You know I completely trust the American legal system. If anything, it is excessively protective of the defendant. But come to think of it, I am not sure if a lawyer would be obliged to report to the police if state security is threatened. Look what we are trying to figure out, no thanks to Nasib," I replied, feeling frustrated, faltering at the first step toward action.

"Jee, let us continue. What is the next scenario we should consider? I know, do you think that Nasib will contact us or just use Shahnaaz as the intermediary?"

I had a ready answer for this one. "Fatima, either way will be very good. If he did not communicate, that would be very bad sign. At the moment, he probably does not know what to do. He is too angry and consumed in his own world to think clearly. If he was not forced to, he would have nothing to do with us right now. But necessity will force him to keep in contact with us, at least initially."

"Hmm, Jee, I see what you mean. All his stuff is still in his room. How can he function without his clothes and especially without his laptop? I suppose he could ask Shahnaaz to bring his clothes and laptop," Fatima tried to answer her own question.

I gave her my assessment of the likely scenario. "Fatima, I am sure Shahnaaz would not do that for him. She will ask Nasib to do his own tough stuff. I can just imagine her asking him if he is a man or a mouse and laughing about it. I think that Nasib is using Shahnaaz to figure out how to get in touch with us without losing face. When he does that, it will be our responsibility to let him save face without condoning his actions. This will be mutually beneficial."

Fatima gave her own forecast of how things would unfold. "Jee, I could not agree more. Now I predict that Nasib will want to come back to stay with us for another month or two."

"Oh, Fatima, I wish I had access to your crystal ball!" I said, trying to lighten the conversation.

"Well, since you made fun of me, I won't share my prediction," she said as she pouted.

"Fatima, I am sorry I made fun of your crystal ball. I know you can make the same prediction just with your own abilities," I continued, mocking her.

"Sheikh Jee, you are mean, and you are pushing your luck. I will forgive you because this is too important. I predict that Nasib will ask you if he could move back for a couple of months because he is broke! Remember he borrowed money from you. He had no income for the unpaid weeks when he was in Afghanistan. He does not want to explain to anyone why he moved out, and you know why he wouldn't want to. He will stay in a hotel for a week or so and will max out his credit card. He will not ask for money from anyone else because he is too proud. He will be forced to come back to gain time to set himself up sustainably. There!" Fatima finished with a thump on the table.

"Wow, Fatima, you are absolutely right! That scenario never occurred to me. You are pretty smart. I mean pretty and smart," I said, genuinely impressed.

"Good comeback. You are like a cat with nine lives. Jee, be careful in the future, you have just one more left!" she said very smugly.

Later on that night, Shahnaaz told us that Nasib wanted to know if he could come for breakfast the next morning. Of course, we were relieved that we were still talking. I remembered my father telling us that when life seems the gloomiest and the darkest, Allah always shows us tiny breaks in the clouds. That light gives us the hope and encouragement that life will become brighter once again.

"Jee, I am so happy that my son is coming back. I am going to make his favorite breakfast dish—cinnamon waffles with cream and English breakfast tea," Fatima said excitedly.

"Fatima, you may want to reconsider that. Remember why and how he left. What I suggest is that both of us treat him with courtesy and no more than that. After that, we will decide how friendly we want to be depending on his conduct. It is very important that he does not exploit the difference between your motherly affection and my hard-line attitude."

Fatima was very understanding. "Yes, of course! It will be a simple breakfast, and I will curb my motherly instincts for the greater benefit we can get. I agree that we will show complete unity among us."

I sensed that this is the little light that would give us hope to carry on. I started in a very solemn tone. "Fatima, this is a very good opportunity for us to influence Nasib so that he starts to deploy the true message of Islam—peace toward all mankind.

"If Nasib does not communicate with us, we can no longer influence him. He will be under complete and continuous control of the terrorists. You can rest assured that they are very forceful and persistent on making others believe their point of view. We need to be even more vigilant and proactive to make our message of peace be believed by all Muslims and non-Muslims."

By now, I had become very passionate. "Nasib's mind has been made-up by the terrorists. They glorify terrorism as the path to personal salvation and the salvation of Islam. They convince others to become martyrs so that their name lives forever. What an insult to the true martyrs of Islam! We need to restore Islam back to its true glory!"

Fatima listened very intently and kept looking into my eyes all this time. "Jee, I sense your passion and sincerity. How are we going to achieve all that?"

I continued even more passionately, "Fatima, I have no idea how we are going to do that. But the real question is *why* we need to restore the glory of Islam?"

"So why do we need to restore the glory of Islam?" she asked. "Because a glorious and powerful Islam will bring peace to the whole world. The whole world will benefit," I replied, raising both fists in the air in a triumphant gesture.

"Wow, you really mean that," Fatima nodded convincingly.

"Yes, Fatima. The *hows* will show up by themselves. But in the meantime, we need to take massive action for the glory to manifest. We will need to start with ourselves first."

I was pleasantly surprised with Fatima's response. "Jee, I am convinced and will start taking massive action. I already have some ideas I had already been thinking about, but I will put them into action this time. I will share them with you tonight. In the meantime, let me prepare breakfast for us. Nasib will be here shortly."

Nasib arrived, smiling as though nothing had happened. "Hi, Mom and Dad, how are you?"

"Fine," I replied laconically. "Have a seat. How was your night?"

He got the message by my brief response but ended up saying a bit more than he intended. "Oh, my night was restful. I really missed sleeping in my own bed. Can I stay here tonight? Actually, I would like to stay here for a couple of months while I sort out things. Looking for a new apartment or condominium, you know. But, Dad, let us eat mummy's yummy breakfast first. Then you and I can talk."

Fatima resisted smiling after hearing that Nasib wanted to stay for a couple of months. I maintained my terse but polite tone. "Son, you left on your own accord. Also, we will talk while we are having our breakfast, while your mother is here. As far as moving back for a couple of months, that will depend on your conduct. That is a decision your mother and I will make together."

He was a little taken aback with my response. Fatima tried to soften things. "Nasib, my dear, you are our son. We will listen to whatever you have to say. We have always been reasonable. We will do whatever we feel is mutually beneficial for both you and the rest of our family."

Fatima and I exchanged a quick glance to indicate that we were both giving the same message. I continued, "Nasib, we are not going to do anything irrational. I am not going to ask about any of your activities with your militant friends, and I do not want you to tell me anything either.

"However, there is one piece of information I need to know from you. This will determine many decisions we make about you. Other than what you have told me and I have told your mother, who else knows about your militant activities?" I asked, not knowing if Nasib would answer.

There was a very long and uncomfortable pause. "Dad, I have not told about this to anybody else, and that is the truth. Of course, Aziz knows. But nobody else who was part of the operation knows about me. I realize now that I should not have told you either. I may have put you and Mom in a very awkward and potentially dangerous situation. For that, I apologize.

"I honestly feel it was both just and justified that we finished off Jahanbaksh and his gang because they killed Aziz's family. Additionally, they firebombed our shop and later our house. You and Mom could have been killed. The only reason I told you was because his gang could easily have killed us, and I thought you would be proud of me."

I shook my head in disagreement and disappointment. "First of all, I believe that you have told me the truth and that you have not told anyone else. From the successful operation he executed, I can see that Aziz would make sure that none of his people knows each other. But, Nasib, killing is wrong. Murder is murder. Why do you think we decided not to kill Jahanbaksh? He probably had similar sad stories in his life to justify his actions."

"Dad, that was your choice. Maybe you were afraid. You decided to flee instead of fighting for justice. I firmly believe in fighting for justice."

It pained me to realize Nasib's limited understanding of choices we are sometimes forced to make in life. I continued, "Nasib, I believe you may be confusing revenge and justice. However, there is one thing we agree on, and that is our love and devotion to Islam. We both want Islam to flourish. Would you agree with that?"

Nasib was very quick to agree. "Yes, my love for Islam is so strong that I will sacrifice my life for it," he replied proudly.

"Would it be OK if I were to show you better ways of benefitting Islam? And you will be free to show me how your ways are better?" I asked him pointedly.

"Look, there is no way you are going to convince me that we don't need to fight to preserve Islam. Otherwise, we will be strangled by the West," he replied.

"Nasib, are you afraid that your tactics may actually be detrimental to Islam? Remember, we are talking about benefitting Islam, not whether you are right or I am right. So are you afraid that your tactics may actually be detrimental to Islam?" I asked, pressing my point.

"No, I am not afraid that militant tactics are detrimental to Islam.

You are free to point out better ways, if they even exist, that is."

Then Fatima intervened to stabilize the atmosphere. "You two, the breakfast is getting cold. Be civil to each other. We are talking about finding the best ways to make Islam flourish, whosoever's way it turns out to be. That is an order, not a request."

"Yes, ma'am," Nasib and I said, smirking in unison, as we started eating breakfast.

As we had guessed, Nasib had his own immediate agenda. "So, Mom and Dad, is it OK if I stayed with you for a couple of months? It will take time for me to find suitable accommodation near my job. I have to buy new furniture and new appliances. I am quite looking forward to be on my own. As you guys pointed out many times, I will grow and learn a lot being on my own. I think I have been spoiled a lot so far. I don't even know how to cook."

"Jee, what do you think? Is it OK if Nasib stays for a couple of months?" Fatima asked me the same question I was going to ask her.

"Nasib, you are welcome to stay but only for a maximum period of two months. I am expecting that we will be respectful of each other and maintain a happy atmosphere in our home."

"And there is one other request I would like to make. There are many books on personal growth in my study room, written by some of my favorite authors, like Steven Covey, Anthony Robbins, Deepak Chopra, Wayne Dyer, Paolo Coelho, and Robin Sharma. Take one and start applying just one lesson applicable to you.

"You will discover wisdom that you would never come across accidently. It will be as beneficial as it will be humbling."

Fatima reinforced my suggestion, "Nasib, life is so complex that we need a wide range of abilities to function, and these abilities do not come naturally. My memory was very poor until I read and applied the techniques in a memory improvement book by Harry Lorayne.

"Allow me to impress you. You go and check the second shelf in Dad's study room. You will find books written by Eckhart Tolle, John Gray, Dale Carnegie, Rhonda Byrne, Richard Carlson, Jack Canfield, Jon Kabat Zinn, and Phillip McGraw *in that order*," as she raised her fist in triumph.

I smiled and continued, "Fatima, that is very impressive indeed. I have read them and reread them and have actually been able to apply some of the lessons in them. Your mother and I have read some of them together. I can tell you that we have benefitted enormously.

"I know I have asked you to read these books before, but I do not believe you have taken me seriously. This time I hope you will listen to me. Nasib, is that acceptable to you?" I asked, knowing the limited options he had.

"Yes, Mom and Dad. I appreciate all that you have done for me in my life. Dad, I will start reading one book. But now it is high time that I leave the nest," Nasib replied, obviously pleased with the outcome. "I will be back tomorrow."

"Nasib, you can stay tonight if you want to," Fatima offered.

"Mom, you are so sweet," he said while looking at me accusingly because I was not as friendly as Fatima. "I already paid for the hotel for tonight. My meager belongings are still there. I will take my laptop and a change of clothes. I will savor for another night what my bachelor life is going to be like, without Mom's cooking. See you tomorrow!"

Fatima and I breathed a sigh of relief after Nasib left. "Fatima, this is the best outcome we could have wished for. We are still talking, and we can still influence Nasib positively. And what is more, we will be able to monitor if anything untoward were to happen."

"Jee, I am still worried about Nasib's safety. Will we know if anythingbad was about to happen?"

I gave her my best assessment. "Well, I believe that nothing untoward is going to happen anytime soon. Aziz will lie low, probably for a long time. I am sure he has told Nasib not to contact him until he contacts Nasib. But, Fatima, as you well know, there are no guarantees in life . . ."

Nasib spent the next month keeping himself very busy and avoided seeing us, especially me. He would go to work very early and come home very late. I was proactively looking to engage him so that he started to see alternative ways to benefit Islam. These militants have the fierce determination, total commitment, and intelligence to succeed in their goals. I wondered what would happen if all that was to be used for the benefit of Islam.

One day he was late going to work. I was reading the newspaper with the headline which read, "Suicide Bomber Kills 45 People Applying for Police Jobs."

So I asked him matter-of-factly, "Nasib, what do you make of this operation?"

He replied as though he had thought this through. "The bomber will be remembered as a martyr. He was so committed to the cause of Islam that he was prepared to sacrifice his life."

I was not surprised that he did not mention anything about the forty-five people who were killed, looking for a job to feed their families. So I pressed him, "What about the forty-five innocent civilians who were killed? They were looking for a job to feed their families. What was their crime?"

He replied calmly, "The police are controlled by our enemies. They were going to become stooges of our enemies, carrying out their dirty work, killing our brave fighters. That was their crime."

"Nasib, each of these people who died were human beings. I wouldn't be surprised if there was a father who was working hard to earn money so his precious daughter could have a decent wedding. What about that father and daughter?"

"Dad, the father could have died in a road accident. Allah would still have made it possible for his daughter to get married. Besides, we are in a war situation. We have to drive out the enemy. All these people who died, including the suicide bomber, died in the cause of Islam. Anyone who dies in the cause of Islam goes to heaven."

Once again, I felt despondent as to how the terrorists justify the unjustifiable and how some people actually believe them. But I tried not to show that. So I decided to leave Nasib with some questions he might not have thought about. "Nasib, did you know that the terrorists are bleeding the Muslim countries much more than they are the Western countries? The Muslim countries can least afford it. Their development is being choked because precious resources are spent on antiterrorist actions. Did you know that thousands of more Muslims than Americans are being killed by the terrorists? How can that be justified?"

Nasib took a little time trying to formulate an answer. "Nasib, you don't have to answer that now. If there is a good answer, you will find it." So I left him with something to think about.

As he left, Fatima walked in. "Fatima, how about sharing with me the progress you made toward restoring the glory of Islam since we last talked?"

"Oh, I am very excited about being a volunteer at the local food bank. I went to see the manager yesterday, and she asked me if I could volunteer four hours a week. They provide training and team you up with an experienced buddy for a few weeks. The only drawback is that she would like me to work on Saturday and Sunday evenings. The job involves serving food to the poor. I hope you will not mind that I may have to miss some social engagements."

"Fatima, this is very good initiative. This is very much the kind of thing our religion asks us to contribute to. Just get started. Serving humanity takes priority over social obligations. If ever there is a conflict, I am sure you will be able to get one of your friends to fill in for that evening. What motivated you to volunteer at the food bank?"

"Jee, what I am doing is nothing new. We used to do the same in Afghanistan. It is one of the obligations of Islam. Everybody who comes from outside thinks America is a very rich country. But there are pockets of deep poverty, hidden from view. Somehow, we got so busy in America that we neglected this aspect. I want to contribute toward alleviating poverty and hunger. One other very important motivation is that since I always wear the hijab, I will be the visible, true face of Islam. This will counter the ignorance and prejudice of the American people," Fatima replied with satisfaction.

"Fatima, I am so proud of you! Once again you come up with a brilliant action," I commended her.

She added, beaming with excitement, "Who knows what this could lead to? I know that there is so much synergy that we can harness."

"Fatima, I don't know exactly what you mean, but please continue. We don't have to know the exact outcome or justify our actions if we are doing something good. You are doing great! Now let me share what massive action I am taking. But before I can do that, I need to get your concurrence," I said.

"Sheikh Jee, I am sure you are thinking of doing something good. You just said that we don't have to know the exact outcome or justify our actions if we are doing something good. It seems you are asking me for permission," Fatima commented in a quizzing manner.

"Fatima, my dear, analogies have to be interpreted in context. Once I explain to you what good deed I am thinking of doing, you will see that I need your concurrence, indeed your permission," I said smilingly.

"Sheikh Jee, don't talk in riddles. The curiosity is killing me. I think you need my reply before I die. So what are you up to?" she asked cheekily.

"Well, I am fifty now. As you know, I have been thinking of retiring for the last two years. Thank Allah, we have been rewarded financially for all the hard work we have put in. In the first year we came to New York, you bugged me, actually hounded me to buy an apartment building, live in one apartment, and rent the rest. I am so glad I followed your advice. So now we have seven apartment buildings. When we bought the properties fifteen years ago, the prices were very low. Since then they have skyrocketed.

"Meanwhile, my job as director of finance in the world's biggest pharmaceutical company has paid very well. You progressed very quickly from being a clerk at the university to becoming the head librarian. We now have a beautiful house, indeed a mansion in a very posh area."

"Sheikh Jee, I still do not know what you are trying to say," she said impatiently.

"Patience, my dear, patience! This is leading to a very significant change in our lives. Even though we have done well, we have a very delightful problem. We are asset rich and cash poor!" I said, smiling.

"I don't understand. And if you can't tell me very quickly something I can understand, the answer is no," she said sternly.

"Fatima, I want to retire within the next three months. To sustain your luxurious lifestyle, we are going to have to sell one of our apartment buildings so you can live in luxury!" I said with tongue in cheek.

"No!" she said abruptly. "You took too long. Besides, you accused me of being spendthrift. Sheikh Jee, just for that you will have to keep on working until I retire."

"But, Fatima, why don't you retire with me?" I asked, knowing that is what she wanted me to add.

"Ah, now you are talking," she relented as she smiled. "I know you have figured out the finances and the cash flow calculations. And I know you will keep yourself productively busy after retiring. I am really enjoying working right now. So, Sheikh Jee, go ahead and enjoy your retirement!"

"Oh, Fatima, I love you! Thank you for your understanding," I said, hugging her tightly. "But you did not ask me what I am going to be doing after I retire."

"Well, you have been updating me on the orphanage your friend is establishing on the outskirts of Kabul," she said.

"Yes, Fatima, the project has reached a stage where a lot of effort is going to be required to get it off the ground, just like a jumbo jet when it is taking off. I will need to work full time on that for a few months. So what I am planning to do is to retire in six months. I will talk to my vice president tomorrow. I want to part on very good terms. I have worked very hard to earn the respect of my management, peers, and workers. It is even possible that the VP may agree that I retire within three months.

"Fatima, there is one very important thing I want to tell you," I said very sincerely, looking directly into her eyes. "You will be just as instrumental as me and all the other sponsors in the success of this project. We have a wonderful vision of helping the orphans, to add sparkle to weeping eyes, getting proper schooling and contributing to the growth of our country, transforming it from a war-torn country to a country of freedom, peace, and prosperity."

"Jee, I am honored to be part of your vision. With your deep sincerity and commitment, you will succeed. This will negate all the destruction caused by the terrorists, and the resulting peace and prosperity will glorify Islam," Fatima said softly.

"Fatima, we have just taken the first steps toward our new goals. A lot still needs to be done. But let us remember that in any journey we make, the first steps are as important as the last steps," I added.

"Jee, I have one question though. Would we have set these new goals if Nasib had not helped Aziz with his operation?" she asked in a whispered tone.

"Fatima, it is quite possible that we may not have been shocked into taking action. Strange as it seems, calamities shock us out of complacency and force us into remedial action. But let us not spend energy analyzing that. We have many more important things to accomplish right now," I answered to the extent I knew.

The following day when I was alone, I was pleasantly surprised when Nasib asked me if I had some time for him.

How situations change! When Nasib and Shahnaaz were younger, they complained that I was too busy to spend time with them. Now I was the one who wished they had time for me.

"Sure, son, what's on your mind?" I asked, feeling happy that Nasib was willing to talk.

"Dad, I have a question for you. Why do you call the Afghans who are fighting against the Americans and their allies terrorists?" he asked with a straight face.

I was taken aback because I had no doubt in my mind that they were terrorists. However, I responded confidently, "Nasib, these people kill innocent Afghan civilians."

"Dad, first of all they target Afghans who collaborate with the occupying enemy. They are not innocent civilians. Innocent civilians die because these collaborators are living among them. It is the collaborators who are responsible for the deaths of innocent civilians!" he replied back, becoming agitated.

I had never even thought about what Nasib was saying, but it made me pause before answering.

Nasib continued, "I challenge you that we are freedom fighters. Of course, I understand that one country's freedom fighter is another country's terrorist. So I am not surprised that the Americans and their allies would deem us to be terrorists, but some of our own countrymen calling us terrorists, that is too much. We are freedom fighters, happily sacrificing our lives for Islam and freedom for our country!" he said passionately.

I wanted to know more about what Nasib was thinking, so I let him continue.

"I will give you an irrefutable example that we are freedom fighters and not terrorists. Dad, would you agree that it is a historical fact that the Germans occupied France during the Second World War?"

"Yes, son, I am well aware of that," I replied, expecting Nasib to build up his case. "Like you, I read about it in some American history books I borrowed from the library."

He continued, "You will note many parallels between what I am about to say and the situation in Afghanistan. During the Second World War, the Germans installed a puppet French government while maintaining total control over the French population. You may recall that this was the hated Vichy administration.

"That gave rise to the French Resistance. This consisted of the brave patriotic Frenchmen who chose to fight and died for the freedom of France. Of course, the Germans and the French collaborators called the French resistance fighters terrorists, but for the majority of French population, they were freedom fighters. These freedom fighters were armed and supported by the Allies. These freedom fighters targeted and killed German soldiers and French collaborators.

"In targeting the French collaborators and enemy soldiers, many innocent Frenchmen also died. Ask the Frenchmen today, and they will tell you that was the price of freedom, that innocent civilians died. If the same situation was to happen today, they will gladly pay the same price for their freedom. Do you see the many parallels between the actions of the French freedom fighters and the Afghan freedom fighters?" Nasib asked demandingly.

I replied very seriously, "Nasib, you have raised some very good points. I will need time to digest what you are saying."

I did not share with Nasib the thoughts that were racing in my mind at that time. Nasib had raised many questions in my long-held beliefs. Is it possible that the people that we are labelling as terrorists today will be the future heroes of freedom?

Nasib was not finished just yet. "Dad, while you are at it, I would like you to digest a few other things as well.

"Did you know that many of the groups that the Americans are calling terrorists today were known as the mujahedeen—Muslim soldiers fighting in support of their political and religious beliefs? At that time, they were fighting the Americans' proxy war against the Russians and were called freedom fighters liberating their country from Russian occupiers. It is the Americans who are responsible for the turmoil in our country.

"We are still the mujahedeen, the same Muslim soldiers fighting in support of their political and religious beliefs, this time against the Americans and their allies. We will win this time as well. We will destroy our enemies, like we did the Russians and the British before that. Islam will be victorious, and our beloved country will be free!" Nasib ended, smiling with deep commitment and looking upward at the sky.

"Nasib, I want to thank you again for sharing your beliefs with me. I will share my answers with you when I am ready, but for now let me really understand what you have said," I said pensively.

I could not help thinking about the questions that Nasib had raised. What at one time was black-and-white for me started to take on varying shades of gray. I could not deny that there were some parallels between the French Resistance fighters and the Afghan mujahedeen.

I had told Nasib that I really wanted to understand him. Instead, I found myself instinctively trying to counter Nasib's firmly held beliefs and justify my own firmly held beliefs. So I discovered, once again, that it is easier to say than to do. But this time I was determined to understand Nasib's views, knowing that understanding does not necessarily mean agreeing.

That night I questioned Fatima, "I think that the people we call terrorists will one day be remembered as freedom fighters. What is your opinion?"

As I expected, I knew her response. "Sheikh Jee, you have been talking to Nasib, haven't you?" Fatima answered my question with a question.

"But I know you want to take Nasib's position to try to understand him better. Our teacher in high school in Kabul taught us this technique to understand opposite points of view without agreeing with them. So please go ahead. I know it is very important for us to understand Nasib's beliefs. After all, he is very intelligent. Somehow, he has these beliefs which he never had before. He obviously got them from someone, somehow."

"Fatima, you have come to know me too well. So do you think that the people we call terrorists today will one day be remembered as freedom fighters?"

"Jee, there have been many true martyrs in the history of Islam. But these people are simply terrorists. They will never be true martyrs," Fatima said confidently.

"Fatima, my belief is that they will be called terrorists until they defeat the infidels. At the moment, the infidels have the upper hand and control the media. So they malign them and brand them as terrorists. If they were to win against the Americans, they will be remembered as martyrs and freedom fighters.

"Look, the French Resistance fighters were also called terrorists by the Nazis. Only after the Nazis were defeated were they called freedom fighters. History always ends up being written by the victors."

Fatima replied studiously, "My dear sheikh, you forget one crucial difference. The majority of the French population was in support of the Resistance, albeit not openly. The majority of the Afghan population is in opposition to the terrorists, albeit not openly. I believe in jihad, but this is not jihad."

I tried hard to put up some opposition to refute Fatima's reply but couldn't. "Fatima, I agree with the crucial difference you pointed out. My only problem is that the terrorists will not be as objective to reason as I am. They are implacable in their beliefs."

Fatima felt very pleased that her answer was both true and solid. "Jee, we have to do the right thing. We have to be just as determined in the truth. There is such a thing as absolute truth. Our tactics will be very different, but we need to ensure that truth prevails."

"Fatima, I thank you for putting things in the correct perspective," I replied thoughtfully. "But I have my question about history being written by the victors."

"Fire away, Sheikh Jee, I can answer any question."

"After the defeat of the Nazis, many were put on trial for war crimes by the Allies. Some were hanged while others were imprisoned for life. Some are still being hunted. While it is true that that the Nazis were guilty of atrocious crimes, the Allies committed some deeds which would be considered war crimes had the Nazis been victors.

"During Allied bombing raids in Dresden, Hamburg, and Berlin, literally thousands of people were killed in the firestorms in single nights. These were ordinary civilians who were targeted and killed!

"So if the Nazis had won, how many Allied generals would be put on trial for war crimes? And the verdict would be guilty even before the trial."

"Jee, I suppose you are right. The presently confirmed crimes committed by the Nazis would not even be brought up, and the evilness of the crimes committed by the Allies would be remembered as notoriously as the Holocaust is today. There is no room for smugness in victory. In war, the hands of victors and the vanquished drip with the blood of innocent victims," Fatima observed thoughtfully.

Then in a pained expression, she said, "Jee, I don't want to answer any more questions. It hurts me to think of the continuing inhumanity of humankind."

I tried to make sense of the current situation where Islam is branded as a violent religion. But wasn't it the Christian, Western civilization that committed the most atrocious war crimes against each other during the first and second world wars?

Yes, it hurt me to think of the continuing inhumanity of humankind.

In the meantime, Nasib was very active in finding new accommodation and making changes in his life.

But the course he chartered was very different from the one we were envisioning. So he updated all of us during the weekly family meeting.

"Well, everybody, I have some exciting news to share with you. I am going to quit my job, and I am going into business for myself!" Nasib announced.

While Fatima and I were digesting what it meant, Shahnaaz was immediately ebullient. "Wow, Nasib, that is fantastic! What business is it?"

Nasib continued, feeling very pleased with himself, "I have landed a major contract with an international bank, and that should keep me occupied for the next year or so. I won't even have to find an apartment in New York. I will be working in different American cities implementing the system."

Fatima hid her disappointment that Nasib was moving away from home while I tried to cover it up.

"Nasib, you are taking the bold risk of quitting your well-paying permanent job at the aerospace company for the potential of much bigger rewards of running your own business. We are always here to give you all the support that you may need. Son, I am proud of you!"

Shahnaaz was still very excited. "See, Dad, you have trained us well. I always told you that the apple does not fall from the tree."

Fatima and I looked at each other and smiled bravely, realizing that the example Shahnaaz innocently gave was not applicable in this case. We were advocates of peace, and Nasib was an advocate of violence.

This time Fatima kept the conversation going smoothly. "Nasib, how many people are you going to employ?"

"Mom, initially just one, and that is me! First, I need to write the software which increases the security of the banking system. After that I will need to hire more people as needed when the system gets implemented across all the branches, first in the US and then internationally."

Nasib answered a question he thought I would ask. "And, Dad, don't worry about financial viability of my business. I am being paid very well indeed. I will be able to take care of hotel, car, and meal expenses. I will even be able to pay back the money I borrowed from you within six months.

"I have planned out as much as I can know presently, but there are things I don't even know that I don't know. One thing that I do know is that there will be unexpected setbacks. However, like you always taught us, setbacks are not dead ends but stepping-stones on the path to success. I have taken the first steps on the path toward success."

I was very impressed with the wisdom and confidence that Nasib displayed. "Nasib, we are very proud of you indeed. You deserve the success you desire. May Allah be with you!"

Shahnaaz concluded a turning point in our lives. "Hurray for Nasib! Let us all give him a group ladhi hug."

That night, Fatima was feeling apprehensive instead of happy. "Jee, I can't explain it, but something is bothering me about Nasib's new business venture," she said, sounding worried.

"Fatima, I am OK with how events are unfolding, but I understand you may be sensing something darker. I do not want to dismiss your feelings. Why don't you share them with me?" I asked, empathizing with her.

"Well, he is going to be away from us for extended periods of time. We won't know what he is up to or who he is associating with. I am really worried that the terrorists will get him involved in another violent act, this time right here, in America!" she said, crying.

I held her gently, wiped her tears, and said, "My dear, let us address your fear instead of wishing it away because it is too painful to think about. Anything is possible with the terrorists. I really think they will want to keep everything normal for now, keeping a very low profile and maintaining silence. This will give us the time to win over his heart and soul with our own peace offensive."

Up to that time, none of this had occurred to me. But I remembered my grandmother saying to us when our mosque was firebombed that once we start facing our fears, Allah provides us the guidance to navigate through the unknown.

I shared this with Fatima and continued, "Even though we could be wrong, let us work with some possible scenarios. Would you like me to share with you what I believe is going on?"

"Yes. I wish and pray that your scenario is correct," she said, looking more hopeful.

I took a deep breath and started, "Fatima, I base my scenario on the safe assumption that the terrorists are extremely dedicated to their cause and too clever to fumble any opportunity to carry out their evil deeds. I agree that they have some blind spots, but they are not stupid. On the contrary, they are extremely smart and plan strategically.

"For them somebody like Nasib is too valuable to be used for carrying out a physical terrorist attack. They have many other people who they could use for those operations. I believe they are expanding their activities to attack the business and commercial infrastructures."

Things seemed to be settling down during the next few months. Nasib became extremely busy establishing his new business, but kept in touch with us by phone and e-mail. I was relieved that for the moment he would not have time for any other activity. We were very pleased when he asked us if he could visit us for a week during the Thanksgiving break.

At the table, Shahnaaz was brash as usual. "Haddy, let me sit closer to Nasib. He is the next billionaire, and I want to make sure I treat him nicely!"

She continued, "Nasib, how much does it cost to get your laundry done?"

Nasib looked puzzled but answered, "For one week's laundry at the hotel, it usually costs me one hundred dollars. Why do you want to know?"

"Wow! Nasib, I am so happy that you are earning enough to spend that kind of money on laundry," Shahnaaz said wide-eyed.

"I will make a deal with you that you cannot refuse. Every time you come home, bring your dirty laundry, and I will do it for you for half price. You will save money, and I will make money! I will make more money doing your laundry in a couple of hours than I make working for two days at Starbucks. It is a win-win situation, what do you say?" she asked excitedly.

Nasib was taken aback. "Shahnaaz, my dear little sister, I would not feel good making you do my laundry. But I will keep you in mind as a salesman, selling and marketing my software solutions. You show a natural flair for selling. You could sell sand to the Arabs and refrigerators to the Eskimos!"

"Future promises are nice, but I need the money now, brother," she pressed on.

"I am smart and multitalented. I could be your virtual assistant! You know, a lot of geeks have virtual assistants who work from India. I don't work from India, but you are definitely a geek. Hire me!"

Fatima and I laughed out loud, feeling very proud to have a daughter like Shahnaaz.

Nasib laughed sheepishly and agreed, "Shahnaaz, I never thought of that. I could free up my time if somebody reliable were to do many routine tasks for me. At the moment, I am inundated with work. Forget the laundry. Let me get back to you tomorrow with some challenging bite-sized tasks. I promise you it will pay much more than Starbucks and the laundry combined."

I hugged Shahnaaz and told her, "It is so gratifying to see how you created this opportunity out of nothing and followed up with persistence."

Shahnaaz responded, "Thanks, Dad. I love that saying from Milton Berle that I hang in my room—if opportunity does not knock, build a door."

Fatima summoned us all to the dinner table, "Let us thank Allah for everything we have in our lives and enjoy the dinner."

We had been living in America for sixteen years. We were just like any other American family enjoying Thanksgiving turkey dinner except that we believe in Islam and looked different. We had a thoroughly enjoyable Thanksgiving.

The following morning started out tumultuously.

Fatima sounded very distraught, "Jee, I just got off the phone with Salma. She was sobbing uncontrollably."

"Oh, what happened?" I asked sympathetically.

"Nasib has broken off with her. After all these years, I always thought they loved each other."

"Fatima, I don't like this development. What is the reason Salma told you for the breakup?"

"He just told her that his life has taken on a very different path, and it will be better that they break up. He said he is breaking off because he loves her too much. What a strange thing to say. Poor girl, she does not understand him. While we were having such an enjoyable Thanksgiving, she was sobbing alone!" Fatima said, almost tearful herself.

"How could he do that? Jee, please, you talk to Nasib."

"Fatima, it's déjà vu! Another difficult, unsolvable situation to resolve. Why me? Why don't you talk to him?" I protested.

"Sheikh Jee, let us not shy away from difficult situations. Let us face them. I will call him. We will both speak to him."

Somehow, it made a big difference. Facing a difficult situation together made it less daunting.

Nasib sensed what we were going to ask him but pretended nothing untoward had happened.

Fatima started, "Nasib, I just got off the phone with Salma. She was sobbing uncontrollably. What happened between you two?"

Nasib took a deep breath and started, "Mom and Dad, I could say that this is none of your business, but I believe I owe you an explanation. As you know, I have started this new business. I am going to be travelling from city to city, living from hotel to hotel. I am so busy I don't even have time for exercise. This is going to continue for an indefinite period of time.

"Salma needs a stable, domestic environment. She wants children. She does not like uncertainty. I love her too much to make her adjust to a situation that is diametrically opposite to her needs. This is why I believe it is best to go our separate ways."

He closed his eyes and took another deep breath. "I know I am going back on everything I had been promising her up to now. Believe me, I never planned things to happen this way. Events took over my life. I know it will be extremely painful for Salma, but I know she will get over the heartbreak and make a new life for herself. She is very beautiful and smart. She will survive and go on to thrive."

I summoned courage to ask Nasib a question, which was very difficult for me to ask, let alone for Nasib to answer. "Son, if you had not been involved with your extremist friends, would you still break up with Salma?" I asked, looking straight into Nasib's eyes.

He hesitated, looked down, and replied thoughtfully before walking away. "Dad, I have no idea. Now if you don't mind, I need to work on my business."

I turned to Fatima, shook my head slowly, and said quietly, "This is not good news. He was head over heels in love with her before he went to Afghanistan. And now he is cold and distant. It is not his involvement in the new business that has changed his mind."

"Jee, what makes you deduce that?" Fatima asked with a wrinkled forehead.

"Fatima, again, I could be wrong, but Nasib is preparing his social environment so that he can perform his activities in a detached way when he is needed. The terrorists brainwash their disciples into believing that you are married to your cause. They are led to believe that family ties prevent them from dying for Islam. He will abandon us in a heartbeat when the situation demands. I sense he is totally committed to his extremist views."

Fatima felt exasperated by my assessment. "Jee, we had such a wonderful Thanksgiving. The joy lasted but just one day. Salma is despondent and distraught. Nasib is cold and uncaring. And now you are painting such a dark scenario. Why can't you say something hopeful?"

I was taken aback by Fatima's charge. "Fatima, my dear, I am basing my assessment from the manner of Nasib's response. His body language gave more information than his words. When I asked him if he had not been involved with his extremist friends would he still break up with Salma, he looked down, did not answer the question, and walked away. Again, I could be wrong, but if he was not influenced by his extremist friends, his body language would have been different, and he would have answered differently."

"Jee, I am sorry. I know you are working with very little information, but I believe you are right. I just wish we did not have to deal with this problem, but I know wishing alone will not make the problem go away," Fatima noted a bit more objectively.

I continued, "If Nasib were to continue his terrorist activities, this new business venture provides a very convenient cover for him."

"Sheikh Jee, how would that help?"

I elaborated, "He can move from city to city, doing a legitimate business. He is working on security for banking transactions. He is single and mobile, extremely smart, and totally dedicated to his cause. He can lie low for an indefinite period of time while preparing subversive activities. During the cold war, the Russians used to have sleeper agents who could provide strategic information. After lying low for years, one day he could be asked to strike and cause chaos in the financial sector."

Fatima was not impressed at all by my prediction. "I think you have been reading too many spy stories. I don't believe you. Sheikh Jee, you are paranoid!"

"Fatima, I pray to Allah that I am wrong in my assessment. Look, we just celebrated Thanksgiving. For the turkey, one day was exactly the same until the last fateful day. The turkey was never expecting to be slaughtered.

"Until September 11, every day was the same. Then the unimaginable happened. The terrorists are constantly hatching very different types of plots. A terrorist cyber attack is definitely possible."

"Jee, I am getting extremely frustrated. You keep on saying what can go wrong. What are we supposed to do? And don't say you don't exactly know," she said impatiently.

Actually, I was going to say that I don't exactly know but surprised myself with the answer I had to come up with. "Well, Fatima, we have to keep Nasib engaged and talking with us even more. I will talk to my friend Sheikh Zahid who has started a project to build a self-sustaining city in the Arabian Desert. He has even named the city Al-Bahar. He is a true visionary and looking for smart people to work on the project. I will arrange for him to share his vision with Nasib."

"Thank Allah for taking some action instead of speaking in riddles," Fatima said pointedly.

"Yes, my dear, it is ten o'clock in Riyadh. I will call him now before he goes to bed."

That made Fatima happy. "Jee, I am very impressed. Usually you postpone action until the next day."

"Are you trying to be funny, Fatima? Why don't you make me a nice cup of tea while I phone Sheikh Zahid?"

"Sheikh Jee, I will make you a nice cup of tea tomorrow. Since you are on a roll with taking action, I am sure you can make the phone call and tea at the same time," she said teasingly. "And while you are at it, make me a piping hot cup of Lady Earl Grey tea as well!"

THE FUTURE CITY

Sheikh Zahid was very excited about his visionary project in the desert. He was one of a very few of my Muslim friends who addressed me by my first name. "My dear Zafar, the project is going extremely well, but it has reached a plateau of progress. We keep on finding new subprojects we need to execute within the superproject. I urgently need many bright and enthusiastic people to take full ownership of some new projects. For example, right now I need someone to head the IRN project. Do you know anyone?" he asked hopefully.

"Zahid, my friend, I admire your visionary ideas, but what is the IRN project?

"Zafar, I am sorry for not explaining the jargon. IRN stands for Intelligent Road Network. Visualize a network of highways and roads which safely control the movement of all the vehicles. These vehicles will be an optimum mixture of buses and cars, all driverless. The city will own the buses and cars, but no one person will own any car but will have full use of a car. You just request where you want to go and when you want to travel, and a car or bus will come to a point within walking distance from you and drop you within walking distance of where you want to go. There will be no traffic jams or accidents on the Intelligent Road Network!" Zahid explained with excitement and total conviction.

I was very fascinated by the boldness of his creative vision—a smooth-running transportation system with no traffic jams and no accidents! No car ownership and be able to get to where and when you want as though you had your own car! And skeptical.

"Zahid, you know I am a very optimistic person, and I truly respect you, but this idea seems almost impossible, even to me. Are you sure you can make it work?" I asked with hesitation.

Zahid became even more energetic and emphatic. "Zafar, I am absolutely convinced. I am in the business of converting vision into reality. I visualize every day flying into Al-Bahar. I see no traffic jams as we are landing. I have called ahead to the IRN, and the network knows what time my flight is landing and where I need to go and will have a car ready for me within minutes of me coming out of the airport. It will be a lot faster than the time it takes me now to catch the shuttle to the rental terminal.

"Then I just sit in the car, and the car drives me to the Al-Bahar university complex where I am supposed to give a lecture on building sustainable cities to people who have come from all over the world to learn and share their experiences."

He continued with passion and total conviction. "I visualize this every day. For me it is fait accompli."

I was very impressed with Zahid's vision and even more with his actions. "Zahid, I am sure you will succeed. Every vision which is a reality today was once just a dream. The Wright brothers' fledgling flight sparked a vision which surpassed by far the original dream, both in terms of advancement and the time it took to convert it into reality. From the first *Kitty Hawk* flight in 1903 to the passenger plane in just thirty years. Now we have the jumbo jets and Dreamliners for the masses.

"My father always said that the grander your vision, the more likely you are to succeed, because it fires your imagination and creativity. It generates its own passion and unstoppable momentum. Others join you in executing your vision. Your vision becomes the grander, collective vision. I am sure your vision will become the grander, collective vision which will become a bigger reality and will be executed much sooner than you had envisaged."

"Sheikh, my dear friend, I thank you for your encouragement. But I have not shared with you the real reason why this vision will become a reality and transform the world! Do you want to know?" Zahid asked quietly.

"Zahid, of course I want to know. But it must be very late for you in Riyadh. Don't you need your sleep?"

Zahid started slowly and thoughtfully. "What is driving me now has given me boundless energy. Ever since the bombing of the twin towers seven years ago, I have been extremely troubled. The impression that the world has of Islam is completely wrong.

"Islam is a religion of peace, and yet there are Muslims who believe it was a justified attack on the enemies of Islam. They believe that the Western world, indeed the whole world is conspiring to weaken Islam."

Zahid continued, becoming more earnest, "Sheikh, it is a view that I share privately with you. I know a lot of Muslims recognize this reality but are afraid to admit it publicly. We need to stop blaming others and take responsibility for our own weaknesses. At one time, Islam was in full glory. The Muslims were setting the course for the development of the rest of the world. They were guiding the future of the world. At one time scholars from all over the world felt privileged to attend Islamic centers of learning from mathematics to medicine to cutting-edge architecture and military strategies.

"It seems the Islamic world stopped developing at one time and fell far behind while the rest of the world raced ahead. Now we find ourselves thoroughly frustrated and powerless. Even when we are right, we do not have the might to be right. And we lash out against some real and gross injustices inflicted on the Islamic world. There are several countries much smaller than ours, without any physical resources which exert much more influence than some very populous Muslim countries."

I could not help but agree with him. "Zahid, I agree that the first step is to stop blaming anybody else and take personal responsibility. But please carry on."

Zahid continued with passion, "We need to restore the glory of Islam. Can you name any invention from the Islamic world after the seventeenth century? It is shameful that nothing comes to my mind.

"In the meantime, inventions originating in the Western and Christian world have completely changed the course of the world and determined the history and the future of the world.

"Just look at the inventions that have changed the course of the world—the bicycle, the steam engine, electricity, steel, the railway engine, the motor car, ocean-crossing ships, the machine gun, the tank, the aeroplane, the submarine, and vaccination to name just a few. Each one of these enabled the Western world to develop and grow and become economically and militarily powerful. Meanwhile, we were not even aware as to how far we had been overtaken and left far behind, literally in the dust. The Western world dominated and colonized the world. It is shameful that even once-powerful Muslim countries like Egypt, Sudan, Iraq, Yemen, Jordan, and Palestine were colonized by the British while Algeria, Syria, and Lebanon were colonized by the French."

Once again, I could not help but agree with Zahid, and I started wondering how we fell so far behind.

Zahid continued, "Zafar, things continue to get worse. The Western world has accelerated their progress by inventing radio, television, space rockets, satellites, computers, supersonic fighter jets, and atomic weapons. They pioneered and implemented industrial systems like assembly line production, breakthrough quality improvement systems, inventory control systems, and the Internet. Up to now we have been falling farther and farther behind. Just absorbing and making use of innovations has been a challenge.

"The progress that a handful of Muslim countries have made is based solely on oil and gas. Even here, the entire infrastructure is supported by Western technology. Even to know what resources they have and where to drill is determined by the technology invented in the West. The expertise to harness these natural resources is all provided by the West. Am I depressing you, Zafar?"

I replied sombrely, "Zahid, I am really trying to challenge what you are saying, but unfortunately what you are saying is painfully true. I just hope you are also going to be able to say something hopeful. I just know there are solutions for the Islamic world."

Zahid continued earnestly, "Of course there are solutions! But let me continue for a little bit longer. Were it not for the resources that these Muslim countries have, they would be just as poor as the ones that do not have any natural resources. The benefits from the natural resources stay with a very few people at the top while the masses remain poor. How un-Islamic is that? The political system of most Islamic countries is perpetuating the stagnation of progress. We are stuck in medieval times. Most of these countries have authoritarian dictatorships where nobody can challenge the ones in control.

"May Allah help the people who rely on the mercy of the mighty," Zahid continued in exasperation.

I interrupted him, "But there are several Islamic countries where there are free elections and every opportunity to voice your opposition. Look at Turkey, Pakistan, and Bangladesh! Why, they have even had women prime ministers!"

Zahid agreed happily, "Zafar, I told you that there is hope. I am always encouraged by the direction of the progress more than the speed of the progress. Of course the progress may be erratic—two steps forward and one step backward. But moving in the right direction generates its own momentum because of the benefits it brings."

Once again, I interrupted him, "Zahid, you were just talking about lack of innovation being the cause of powerlessness of the Islamic world, and now you are talking about the autocratic political system. What is the real cause according to you?"

Zahid replied immediately, "Zafar, these are not the only reasons. Allow me to cite one more—living with the social restrictions of the past. For example, what is Islamic about denying the rights of our women to be fully contributing members of the Muslim society? We are trying to succeed in the modern world with one hand tied behind our backs. I acknowledge that we have women prime ministers, but social customs deny basic human rights to the masses of Muslim women. In some countries, they have no vote and are not even allowed to drive!

"However, I like to keep things simple. I think addressing these three can solve many other causes. We can choose to work on one of them, and all the other ones will benefit. Just choose one and start taking action! Which one do you choose, Sheikh?"

Before I could answer, Zahid continued, "Sheikh, this is one very life-changing lesson I learned from you—men of action don't wait for perfection but are quick to implement correction! I have motivated many people to take action with this phrase. Words can be very powerful. I used to spend more time in planning than doing but not anymore."

"Zahid, I am thankful to Allah that I have been of some help. Now to answer your question, looking back, I believe I am taking action to improve both the political system and to renew innovation, albeit, concentrating more on the political system," I replied.

Zahid continued with excitement, "Of course, Sheikh, it is possible to do both. Looking back, I believe I am complementing your efforts, working on both but concentrating on renewing innovation in the Muslim world. We should talk more often and harness the power of synergy."

I had lost track of time and the main purpose of my call. "Zahid, earlier on you had said that you need someone to head your IRN project. Why don't you talk to my son Nasib, he is very capable and has experience in managing software projects?" I asked him without mentioning Nasib's recent terrorist activities. I was hoping and praying that Zahid would be able to engage Nasib and harness his energies toward peaceful and productive innovations.

"I will be glad to interview him, Zafar. It is very difficult to get suitable people for jobs. I am hoping Nasib has a good attitude to work and is dedicated to contribute. In my experience, technical knowledge is the least of my problems. Why don't you ask him to e-mail his resume tomorrow? After that I may ask him to call me for an interview over the phone."

The call was so absorbing that we did not realize we had been talking for two hours. It was almost midnight in Riyadh, so I wrapped up the call. "Zahid, I thank you for a very enriching phone call and your offer to consider Nasib for the IRN project. I wish you continued success in establishing the self-sustaining city in the desert. I would really like to visit it while it is still in development. It is always a pleasure to share in your vision."

Immediately after I hung up, I phoned Nasib on the speakerphone so that Fatima could hear. "Nasib, I would like to share something very exciting with you. I just got off the phone with my friend Sheikh Zahid who is heading a visionary project, establishing a self-sustaining city in the Arabian Desert. He is looking for someone to take charge of the Intelligent Road Network project. I think this could be a very exciting opportunity to create something innovative. I will e-mail you his coordinates. Why don't you send him your resume?"

Nasib was a bit cool to my suggestion. "Dad, I am sure it is a very exciting opportunity, but I have just started my own company and have my hands full."

I persisted, "But, Nasib, just sending your resume will not take time. If Sheikh Zahid is interested, he will call you for a phone interview. Remember, you have an opportunity to be a contributor of something visionary, to create innovative technology in the Muslim world!"

Nasib replied, sounding noncommitted, "Dad, you have really piqued my curiosity to create innovative technology in the Muslim world. I respect your vision for the future, so I will send my resume tonight. But I must tell you I am not looking for a job. I have just started my own business."

It was not the reply I had been hoping for but was happy to know there was still a chance that Nasib could contribute to Zahid's vision. "Son, I understand your desire to have your own business, and I truly wish you success in your enterprise. But since you are a budding entrepreneur with so much potential to succeed, there is no reason why you could not propose a business plan as a contractor, not as an employee."

Nasib replied very excitedly, "Dad, now you are talking! Who knows where things could lead to? Give me Sheikh Zahid's phone number as well. I really want to talk to him. A self-sustaining city in the desert, the innovation of the Intelligent Road Network—I am definitely interested to check it out!"

Fatima hugged me tightly. "Jee, I am so proud of you! You persevered to get your point across. I was always telling you to add emotion to reason to get your point across. And now you just demonstrated how it should be done."

"Why, Fatima, glad to be of service. It took me a long time to learn that reason and rationality are not enough to make people take action. We need to convince peoples' minds rationally and then connect emotionally with their hearts."

Fatima agreed humorously, "If you get lost during the day but return home before dusk, you are not considered lost. What reward do I get for teaching you this life skill?"

"Let me guess, you need a hot cup of Lady Earl Grey tea." Before she could say what I was expecting her to say, I added laughingly, "And I will make one for myself for my efforts."

I was exhausted and excited at the same time. "Fatima, I feel very encouraged after the phone call with Sheikh Zahid. There are people, in the midst of seemingly endless turmoil in the Muslim world, who are taking very positive actions to restore the glory of Islam and are able to generate creative, not destructive, excitement in the Muslim youth."

Fatima and I slept very soundly that night, feeling sure that we would get Nasib to talk to Zahid, and he would offer a very challenging and fulfilling job or business opportunity to Nasib. And Nasib would be so engrossed in the IRN project that after that his life would take on a completely new turn. He would renounce terrorism and dedicate his life to peace and prosperity in the Islamic world.

Hope springs eternal!

Fatima and I were waiting the next day to find out if Nasib had phoned Sheikh Zahid when the phone rang.

It was Nasib. "Dad, I would like to come to see you and Mom this evening. I had a very interesting chat with Sheikh Zahid and want to update you about that. And what special treatment will I get from you to celebrate my visit?"

I was very heartened by Nasib's call with Zahid and more so with his lightheartedness. So I continued in that vein. "Nasib, the special treatment for you is that you will have the company of your dear little sister. Shahnaaz just finished her final exam today and wants to be fussed over."

Nasib replied, "That brat! She always hogs the limelight! I have to start my own business to generate some interest in me, and she will dominate the evening with the talk of her exams. Life is not fair! But I still love her."

"Just tell Mom I am coming. At least she will cook something special just for me to redress the balance."

"Nasib, I am sure your mother will rise to the occasion and spoil you more than Shahnaaz, and I will do my best to maintain balance," I added, trying to be reassuring, knowing well Shahnaaz's irrepressible spirit.

Once again, life seemed to carry on as usual, except for the nagging feeling that everything could be immediately shattered by an unexpected and untimely event in the Umeed family.

Nasib opened the conversation eagerly. "Mom and Dad, it fills me with great pride that Dad's friend Sheikh Zahid is building a self-sustaining city, named Al-Bahar in the desert. He has the full backing of the authorities to establish this new city.

"He had a phone interview with me and was very impressed with my experience. He wants me to go and visit him in Saudi Arabia so that he can show me how the overall project is unfolding and in particular the IRN."

As usual, Shahnaaz chipped in, "Nasib, cut out your geeky jargon! What is IRN?"

"My dear sister, for those with limited intelligence, it stands for Intelligent Road Network," Nasib replied, tongue in cheek.

"I don't know who these people with limited intelligence are, but I would like to remind you that I have always gotten better marks than you ever did when you were my age," Shahnaaz said, sticking her tongue out at Nasib. "Does anybody want to know how well I did in my exams?"

As Fatima and I started to laugh at their antics, she intervened, "Shahnaaz, let Nasib finish first."

"Why, thank you, Mother," Nasib continued. "The IRN project is very exciting! The sheikh is truly a visionary. He needs people to deploy his vision, make it a reality. Just imagine a network of roads and vehicles, completely driverless and completely safe, with no traffic jams. Nobody owns any vehicle but has ready access to safe, comfortable, and reliable transportation.

"This will require cutting-edge, safe, and secure software to run the network. And the sheikh believes I have enough experience and talent to lead a team of engineers to execute the project. He wants me go and visit him in Al-Bahar next week before he decides to hire me. The pay will be twice what I was earning at the aerospace company. He will even pay for my trip!"

We were overjoyed. Our eyes lit up wide at this development. "Hurray for Nasib!" we shouted all together.

Fatima asked impatiently, "So when are you going to Al-Bahar, Nasib?"

Nasib replied with a straight face, "Actually, I have decided not to go." Exuberance gave way to dead silence as we tried to understand what Nasib had just said.

Shahnaaz cut through the silence with a pointed question, "Nasib, are you stupid, or are you arrogant? The sheikh believes you are talented and intelligent enough that he is offering to pay you for a face-to-face interview, and you decide not to even go. I think you are stupid *and* arrogant!"

Nasib replied angrily, "Why don't you stop deciding what is good for me? If you must know, Sheikh Zahid is offering me a job. I am not interested in a job. I have been running my own business for six months and doing very well, thank you! I am an employer, not an employee.

"I am thankful to the sheikh for considering me. Indeed, I am flattered that he thinks so highly of me. But my banking security business is expanding, and I need to put in a lot more time and effort. I have already hired five very experienced software engineers to help me. Why don't you all back off and let me do what I think is best for me?"

I stepped in to calm the atmosphere. "Nasib, my son, we respect your ambitions and your decisions. The way you were describing Sheikh's vision and how impressed you were with the IRN project, we assumed you would at least go for the interview."

Fatima backed me up, "Nasib, we have full confidence in your decisions and wish you success in your new business venture. I have worked very hard to prepare your favorite dishes. And I would appreciate that all of us eat our dinner in a harmonious atmosphere."

Shahnaaz smiled and agreed, "Of course, I want to tell everybody how well I did in my exams in a harmonious atmosphere. I feel sure that I will get my chartership with flying colors. I have already applied for jobs, and I am sure I will land a well-paying job soon! Thinking of jobs, Haddy, can you give me Sheikh Zahid's phone number? I am sure he could use my talents."

She looked directly at Nasib, still smiling and said, "If the sheikh makes me an offer for a face-to-face interview in Al-Bahar, I will graciously accept." Then she stuck her tongue out at Nasib.

Nasib smiled back. "If you were not my little sister, I would wring your neck! But if you are nice to me, when I phone to inform the sheikh that I cannot accept his offer, I will put in a good word for you."

Shahnaaz got off her chair and went to give Nasib a tight hug. "You are the best brother a little sister could ever have!"

Then she winked her eyes at us and said naughtily, "Mom and Dad, for the next few days, if I am mean to Nasib, please kick me to remind me to be nice to him."

I was feeling very uncomfortable about the reason Nasib would have for not taking up the sheikh on his offer for an interview but did not know if I should probe him further.

While Nasib and Shahnaaz were talking in the other room, I shared my concerns with Fatima.

She replied in a whisper, "Jee, that makes two of us. I suspect that he being too busy with his new business may not be the true reason why he does not even want to talk to Sheikh Zahid."

"Fatima, I am afraid that pressuring him further may anger him further," I responded.

Fatima continued in a hush, "Jee, we should not be afraid. If he becomes angry, we may be able to deduce that he has some other reason that he is not sharing with us. If he stays calm, the reason he is giving now is most likely the truth, but if he gets very angry, he is hiding some other sinister motive. We have to find out either way."

Then she added craftily, "Don't be afraid. Why don't you ask him?"

Before I could protest that this time she should ask him, she checkmated me by quickly walking into the other room!

For once, I was thankful that Fatima forced me to take action. There are times to think things through and then there are times when we just take action. This was time for action. But I also realized that taking action has the added benefit of overcoming fear—I did not even have time to fear that things could blow up between Nasib and me.

I asked Nasib to come into the study room and I started speaking in a neutral tone. "Nasib, when we last talked about Sheikh Zahid's projects, you were extremely excited. You also told me that you were not looking for a job. To which I replied that you should propose that you want to do the job as a contractor and not an employee.

"Did you propose to Sheikh Zahid that you would like to work as a contractor and would be willing to submit a business plan?"

"No," Nasib replied tersely.

Sensing that there would be no elaboration to the terse answer, I continued calmly, "Nasib, you were obviously very motivated by the sheikh's grand vision and the technical excitement and challenge of the IRN project. Here you have a golden opportunity and you have the ability to be at the forefront of a technological innovation in the Islamic world, and you decline the opportunity!"

I finished by lowering my head in disgust and proclaiming loudly, "What a shame, Nasib, what a shame!"

Nasib clenched his fists, widened his eyes, and replied angrily, "What do you want me to do? I have my own strategy to restore Islam to the power it once was. We have first to survive against the Western powers hell-bent on our destruction, and then we will have the opportunity to thrive. But first we have to defend in order to survive. And the best form of defense is offense. We have to destroy our enemies! Your mind is already made-up, and you do not understand, and I do not give a damn!"

I felt very disgusted by Nasib's logic and responded, unsuccessful in restraining my anger, "Nasib, you believe the terrorists are our saviors, but the terrorists have only the negative powers of obstruction and destruction. They terrorize thousands of times more Muslims than non-Muslims. The progress of every Muslim country they believe they are helping regresses by decades."

I stopped Nasib from interrupting me and continued, "Let me finish, Nasib. They torture our brothers and sisters out of anger with their enemies. They blame the West for all the deficiencies in the Islamic world. But the very uncomfortable truth is that we are responsible for our weaknesses. We are angry at our own helplessness, our own impotence to influence any outcome in the modern world."

Nasib looked away, his forehead wrinkled with anger and nostrils flared as I continued, "Even when Muslims are victims of gross injustice, we do not have the minimum power to make justice prevail. And believe me there have been historic injustices committed on the Islamic countries, on Islam itself, and continue today."

Nasib finally got a chance to intervene, "Thank you, Dad! These injustices are what we are fighting against! You see our enemies have succeeded in weakening Islam and will not stop until we are completely defeated. There has always been a conspiracy against the Islamic world since the age of the Crusades. We have to destroy them before they destroy us!"

I closed my eyes, took a deep breath, and decided to become calm before continuing, "Nasib, look we both have the same passionate, burning objective—restoring the glory of Islam so that it can shape the destiny of the world. Our strategies to do that are fundamentally different. I have a few questions to ask you. You do not need to answer them if you do not want to. After that you will have the opportunity to explain why you believe your strategy is better."

I added very sincerely, "I promise to listen to you with an open mind. If your strategy makes sense, I will join you. I promise."

Nasib nodded, smiled wryly, and replied, "I don't doubt your sincerity, but I don't believe you will ever join me. But go ahead and ask me anything."

"Nasib, can you name me one innovation originating in the Islamic world in the last three centuries that has changed the course of the rest of the world?" I paused to make sure Nasib had the time to understand the question.

I continued solemnly, sharing the conversation I had with Sheikh Zahid, "Nothing comes to my mind! At one time, the rest of the world gravitated to the Islamic world to learn and benefit from our innovations, our culture. We were at the forefront of medicine, astronomy, mathematics, chemistry, physics, and architecture. We were at the forefront of innovation and were setting the course of the world and shaping its future.

"The Islamic world pioneered the windmill, the pinhole camera, the parachute, distillation, anesthesia, surgery, inoculation, torpedoes, and hundreds of other scientific discoveries.

"We implemented the system of checking which improved and expanded the business systems around the world.

"We opened vast and new horizons of exploration by sea and land with breakthrough navigational aids like the sextant."

I ended wistfully. "And then after the seventeenth century, we stopped! It is as though we went into hibernation. Meanwhile, the Western Christian world went into overdrive of innovation, development, and domination. They left us far behind in the dust.

"Nasib, let me ask you again. Can you name me one innovation originating in the Islamic world in the last three centuries that has changed the course of the rest of the world?"

Nasib retorted angrily, "The Western civilization has enslaved the rest of the world and continues to be the perpetrator of gross injustices in the rest of the world. This is why Islam needs to take the lead in stopping this madness. They will not stop out of realization of the destruction they have caused in the rest of the world. We have to destroy them before they cause any more damage. Then we will have a new world order and run the world according to Islamic principles of peace and justice for all mankind. Dad, you cannot reason with them!"

I felt very exasperated by Nasib's evasiveness in answering my question and the charge instead that we cannot reason with the West. "Nasib, perhaps I can reason with you! Even if the West is so terrible that it needs to be destroyed, how will you get the resources to destroy the West?"

Nasib replied calmly, "From within."

He gave another evasive and meaningless answer. I could not contain my anger. "Nasib, it is the terrorists, not the West that we cannot reason with. The terrorists have no answers for deploying their strategies after they defeat the West. All they have is the ability to cause mindless destruction. They punish and harm their own brethren thousand times more than they punish their deemed enemies. They have zero hope of military victory. To them, avoiding defeat is a victory. It is really pathetic!"

My angry response stung Nasib, and he clenched his fists. Before he could speak, I continued, "Nasib, for Allah's sake, stop blaming others for our own deficiencies! Let us open our eyes and see what other countries have done to deal with the Western powers.

"Japan was literally bombed into destruction and was forced to swallow shameful submission. But within three generations, not only had they recovered but went on to prosper. They have no natural resources. They used their ingenuity and innovation to lift themselves up by their bootlaces. They changed their political system to consolidate their advances. They became an economic powerhouse and delivered dignity and prosperity to their masses. They did not dwell on their past, and most important of all, they did not blame their past enemies or themselves.

"Nasib, they had a clear purpose, unshakeable determination toward peaceful progress, and they succeeded, as a nation, within living memory. Nobody could stop their rise to power!"

And then I became silent, giving Nasib time to digest what I had said.

Nasib looked stunned and did not know what to say.

Then he started thoughtfully, "Islam will succeed beyond our dreams, I promise you."

Then Nasib added forcefully, with angry conviction, "It will be within our lifetime, I promise you."

I wanted to end the tense exchange at a reasonably amicable moment. "Nasib, we have the same objective. Let us figure out the best means to achieve our objective. It is late now, and we are both exhausted. Wise decisions are made when we are relaxed and calm. We will continue next time we meet."

Progress on the Bumpy Road

"Jee, it's been six months since we saw Nasib. We hear very little from him. I hope he is alright," Fatima said one evening as we went out for a walk in the park. "Every time I hear news of some terrorist bombing in Afghanistan, I hope and pray that Nasib is no longer involved with any terrorist organization."

I shared my own thoughts, "Fatima, unfortunately, terrorism has become international. Do you remember when a month after Nasib came back from Afghanistan, there was the terrible bombing of the Taj Hotel in Mumbai in November 2008? Well, the first thing that came to mind was that Nasib may be involved. Mercifully, he was not."

"Jee, how can I forget? I cried that day. For a year we lived near the hotel and used to see it every day on our way to pray at the mosque. I have very fond memories of living in Mumbai in 1994. That was the hopeful year when we got US immigration."

I continued sombrely, "Fatima, my dear, I have now come to the realization that we have been spending too much effort on what the terrorists should not be doing. We just shake our heads in helpless disappointment. The terrorists are pretty effective at what they believe they should be doing. What about the rest of the peaceful Muslim majority? Are we effective at what we should be doing?" I started walking faster.

"Do we even know what we should be doing?"

Fatima held my hand to slow me down. "Sheikh Jee, you are asking very profound questions. I must say I have been guilty of exhausting myself with worrying about the actions of the terrorists, the bad image they portray of Islam. How can I divert my energy toward purposeful activities?"

I was very impressed with the question Fatima asked. I answered enthusiastically, "My dear, we should all be asking that question every day and answering it with actions every day."

As soon as I had finished, I knew what would come next, and sure enough it did. "Jee, what happened to your plan to sell one of our apartment buildings we own and retire so that you could devote your energies to help the charities run by your friends in Afghanistan?"

I confessed to my inaction sheepishly, "Fatima, this is another reason I love you. You always hold me accountable! You do not let me procrastinate! I planned everything about retiring but did not take any action."

Fatima stopped me at the nearest bench in the park and sat down, looked me straight into my eyes, said nothing but just smiled at me. I knew I had to take action.

"So, Fatima, tomorrow I am going to give one month's notice to my boss. As far as selling one of the buildings is concerned, I have decided not to sell it."

Before she could ask, I added cheekily, "But don't worry, dear, I have a plan B to have cash flow to maintain your lifestyle."

"Sheikh Jee, I am very concerned about your plan B. Please go ahead and elaborate," she said, tightening her lips.

"Plan B is to put up one of the properties as collateral to the bank and get a loan against that. That loan will be our cash flow. This was the recommendation of our accountant. Incidentally this was what Nasib said when I discussed with him about selling the property. Although property prices have risen manifold since we bought them, they are depressed currently, and we will have to sell at a lower price. The time it will take to sell is also unpredictable. To get cash flow using the property as collateral can be done within a month."

Fatima smiled and hugged me. "Sheikh Jee, Plan B is better than Plan A! I am so proud of Nasib for suggesting that to you."

I winced when she attributed Plan B to Nasib but was relieved that Fatima was happy.

"Fatima, it is very easy for mundane activities to take over and crowd out the time we need to spend on the important, challenging, and fulfilling things in our lives. If you find I am procrastinating, will you remind me?"

"Oh, it will be my pleasure," Fatima replied gleefully. "But, Jee, if these things are so important to you, why do you need to be reminded?"

"My dear, even the best athletes who know very well that they need to practice regularly feel like skipping sometimes. Just the thought of the coach admonishing them is enough to make them wake up on a cold, rainy morning when they would much rather just curl up and go back to sleep."

Then I added jokingly, "In my case, the wrath of Fatima will prevent me from procrastinating!"

I was expecting a stinging comeback from Fatima but was surprised when she admitted in a disappointed tone, "Jee, I have been guilty of the same procrastination. It has been more than six months since I visited the food bank to find out how I could volunteer. I had grand plans to make a difference, but they remained just that—plans."

She looked earnestly into my eyes and asked, "Why don't you be my coach and hold me accountable to my plans?"

"Fatima, my dear, I will be honored to be your coach," I said encouragingly. "My foreman Gunther in Germany used to have a favorite expression—a gram of action weighs more than a kilogram of planning."

"So here is my action plan," she said emphatically.

"I will phone the food bank today in order to start volunteering one day a week. Please ask me every week to make sure I follow through with my commitment."

"And, Fatima, will you ask me every week what actions I have taken to make sure I do not procrastinate?"

"It will be my pleasure, Sheikh Jee. But do you want to know the secret to prevent procrastination? Whichever day you feel like procrastinating, postpone it to the day after!" she said smilingly, answering her own question.

"Why, thank you for your witty words of wisdom," I said, hugging her tightly.

"Jee, I think it would be a very good idea to share our action plans with Shahnaaz after our family prayer on Sunday. We have not talked to Nasib for more than three months. I will persuade Nasib to call us at ten, and we can connect with him on the speakerphone. Distance should be no barrier to communication. Only our unwillingness to communicate with each other is the barrier. We even talk to our relatives and friends in Afghanistan, Germany, Scotland, Australia, and Canada for free on Skype. In fact, I will ask Nasib to call us on Skype. I don't want us to drift apart."

"Fatima, that is a very good idea. I can just imagine Shahnaaz and Nasib gleefully hauling us over coals if we do not progress on our goals."

Fatima added thoughtfully, "Jee, I think it is more likely that they are privately and silently going through similar struggles in their own lives. It will give them an opportunity to share their experiences and struggles. They may need some coaching in their lives. If they ask, we can offer our help. Just brainstorming with us may show them a way forward."

I smiled as I looked at her. "Fatima, you have reminded me of another reason why I love you. You put clearly into words what is going on in peoples' minds."

"My dear, I did not know I had that ability. Thank you for pointing it out. What a rare observation! Since you seem to be on a roll, what other reasons do you have for loving me?" she asked with a naughty grin.

"Fatima, I must confess that there are long periods of drought in between the feast of compliments I shower on you," I replied sheepishly without answering her question. "In the future I will make sure you do not suffer from feast or famine of compliments. They will be evenly spread out."

"Sheikh Jee, I forgive you!" Fatima said, laughing out loud.

Feeling puzzled, I protested, "Fatima, what are you forgiving me for?"

"For all the past mistakes you made but did not apologize for," she replied, this time laughing so hard that tears streamed down her eyes.

I shared in her laughter, and when she had quietened down, I continued, "Fatima, I also appreciate that you are keeping channels of communication open with Nasib while he and I are in a tense situation."

Fatima acknowledged my compliment cheerfully, "Jee, this is the right strategy. As you say, there is always hope if we keep on talking. So I am balancing your toughness with my mollycoddling."

I responded in agreement, "Fatima, I am not sure I like the way you're putting it. You are making me the tough cop, and you are being the good cop."

Fatima replied smartly, "Jee, being the tough cop is the role you appointed for yourself. You seem to be doing a good job. Keep at it. And you just said that you like the role I am playing. So what's the problem?"

This time I pleaded audaciously, "Fatima, there is no problem, just one request. I have made several compliments to you lately. Can you credit this compliment in the future when I forget to make one?"

I was surprised when later that day I received an e-mail from Nasib asking me if he could talk to me on Skype that evening. I was feeling good that Nasib had contacted me after more than three months and at the same time apprehensive about what he wanted to discuss with me.

"Nasib, when did you start to grow a beard and mustaches?" I asked, looking surprised and added, "You look very distinguished."

Nasib replied, smiling broadly, "Thank you, Dad. I guess I am a chip off the old block."

Feeling relieved that we had gotten off to a good start, I continued, "You looked smart and handsome before you grew your beard, and you look smart and handsome with your beard."

Suddenly, Nasib looked very serious and started, "I have started to grow a beard and moustaches in solidarity for thousands of militant martyrs who are being killed every day by our enemies. The last time we talked, you were lamenting the lack of innovation and progress in the Islamic world. It is as though you were ashamed of being a Muslim. I am proud to be a Muslim, proud of the accomplished achievements of Islam, and hopeful of the future. I forecast that the glory of Islam will be restored within our lifetime. I will tell you how. Are you ready to listen?"

I hid my sigh of exasperation and replied, "Nasib, let me make one thing very clear. The Muslims who do not agree with the militants are also very proud Muslims and also very hopeful of the future. Their methods and approach are different. But they are just as passionate. Now, I am most interested in how you believe the militants will assure the glory of Islam within our lifetime."

Nasib spoke passionately, "To begin with, the success and prosperity of the Western powers was founded on exploitation and subjugation of the rest of the world, including the Muslim world. They are morally and spiritually bankrupt. Their downfall is imminent. And we are going to speed up their downfall. We need to cleanse the world of Western decadence and replace it with a moral and just society."

I interjected impatiently, "Nasib, these are mere wishes and pronouncements. How are you going to practically do what you say?"

Nasib replied immediately with a prepared response, "Dad, your problem is that you are too stuck in conventional and rational thinking. If you keep on thinking like that, you will never progress beyond your self-imposed boundaries of possibilities. There is no way to calculate the power of passion and determination of our martyrs. You know as well as I do that there is a limitless supply of fighters who are willing to sacrifice their lives for Islam. Compare their commitment to the commitment of the Western soldiers who are impatiently counting the number of days before they finish their tour of duty and go back to their cozy decadence."

I quickly realized that Skype is not a secure site, and any secret agency could be listening in if Nasib was on their watch list. I concluded that Nasib was either unaware or unafraid or stupidly arrogant. I decided not to intervene and bring this to his attention.

Maybe I was hoping that he would get caught before he progressed from seething anger to taking violent action on American soil. Then I would not have to make the perpetually postponed decision of reporting him. Life is so complicated!

I interjected before he could continue, "Nasib, many times more Muslims are being killed by Muslims. Do you realize that the Taliban kills and maims thousands more Muslims than Western soldiers? And we are destroying our own progress and infrastructure. Where is the sense in that?"

Nasib retorted angrily, "There you go again! You are still stuck with rational calculations. The price of freedom is martyrdom. We have to pay the price. And Muslims are prepared to die for their freedom."

Once again, I was both deeply dismayed and impressed with how the terrorists are able to brainwash intelligent people to believing that the only path to freedom is violence.

I followed the advice my father often gave me when dealing with stubborn people. So I took a deep, calming breath and started with a question, "Nasib, what if I were to propose a strategy for Islamic victory which is guaranteed and peaceful? Would you at least listen?"

"I am listening," he replied with laconic cynicism.

"Good. Let me give you an actual example of a once-downtrodden, impoverished country which rose to power within our lifetime. China was occupied by the Japanese from 1931 to 1945. It went through internal turmoil, famines, and political and social upheavals and has become a superpower in less than fifty years. Within our lifetime!

"They lifted themselves up by their bootlaces. They made their progress steadily and silently, and when they broke onto the world scene, they were unstoppable."

Nasib seemed to be digesting my example thoughtfully so I continued, "They were once treated with derision but now command respect. They have changed the world order. If they can rise from impotence to omnipotence, why can't we? Why don't we?" Then I stopped, waiting for Nasib's answer.

After a long pause, Nasib started to answer hesitatingly, "China is the most populous country in the world. They have natural resources. Their sheer size gives them the base to build up on."

I continued calmly, "Nasib, you may be right about that. But what about a very small country like Singapore? They have no natural resources. After independence, the Singaporeans lifted themselves out of poverty and built a smooth-running, industrially advanced, and affluent country. They did all that by harnessing their brainpower. For the size of population, they exercise disproportionate power and influence in the world."

Now he answered a little more confidently, "Well, Dad, there are small Muslim countries that exert disproportionate power. Look at Dubai and look at Kuwait."

I nodded my head in agreement. "Yes, Nasib, you may be right there. I don't want to take anything away from that, but you realize their affluence has been based on natural resources. How much progress do you think they would have made if they had no natural resources?"

Now Nasib became very annoyed. "Do you have any other examples to put down the accomplishments of the Muslim world?"

I replied very calmly, "Nasib, I am giving these examples to make us realize how great we could be. So let me give you another example of another downtrodden, poor country which has risen to power during our lifetime—South Korea. It has progressed from being a virtual colony of Japan to become an industrial powerhouse. Again, very few natural resources but harnessed the intellect and creativity of its people."

So my challenge to the Muslim world is, "Why can't we? Why don't we?" I asked, thumping the table with my fist. "Let me put it bluntly but positively. There is a big gap, indeed a chasm between where we are today and where we need to be. How do we bridge that chasm?"

Nasib became very agitated and angry, "Dad, you fail to realize the imminent danger Islam and Muslims all over the world are facing. We need to fight back or else we will be totally defeated.

"The Western Christian world is hell-bent on defeating us. They are occupying and controlling our countries. We have to hit back, and that is the only language they will understand. There is no reasoning with them!"

"Nasib, the painful truth is that there is no reasoning with the terrorists. They have hijacked Islam, and the path they are taking us to will lead us to a dead end. The ordinary Muslims do not want that, but they are being dragged along forcefully. I am telling you that they are going to get control of their true destiny to greatness through peaceful effort.

"However, I am not going to convince you to change your direction and to walk the path of peace and prosperity. To be honest with you, there have been many periods in Islamic history when it was justified and necessary to fight violence with violence. Countless *shaheeds* have sacrificed their life defending Islam, and I deeply respect their sacrifices. I will even grant you that the present-day terrorists are sincere in their beliefs. In the future, they may indeed be remembered as *shaheeds*. The people we revere as *shaheeds* today were very likely deemed as terrorists by their enemies and indeed even by Muslims of that time.

"The terrorists have their own mission to fulfill and are going about it with single-minded zeal. The majority of the peace-loving Muslims need to fulfill their own mission as passionately as the terrorists. So we have a lot of work to do and do not want to waste any effort trying to convince the terrorists."

Nasib wanted to continue the discussion, but I stopped him before he could start.

ACTIONS AND SYNERGIES

"Jee, thank you for bringing me to Vermont during the fall season. It is so colorful and peaceful—and romantic. We definitely needed this personal retreat. It is good to get away and recharge our batteries, celebrate our successes, check the direction our life is taking us toward, and set new objectives," Fatima said softly as we were sitting on a bench beside the calm Lake Champlain.

"Yes, Fatima, I was feeling very exhausted and was getting frustrated because it seemed we were getting too busy to enjoy our lives," I said, agreeing with her. "We can't be so occupied that we forget to refuel and only find out when the tank is nearly empty."

"Jee, I am very excited to share my experience at the food bank. What really helped me succeed was weekly planning of my overall activities. Sometimes I fell behind, but because of weekly monitoring, I was able to rearrange some tasks and recover. Aren't you proud of me?" Fatima asked with beaming eyes.

"Fatima, you took action on the plan you had charted out. You have already been volunteering at the food bank for two months. Of course I am proud of you!" I answered enthusiastically.

"And I want to thank you for being proud of me after two months of waiting," Fatima replied, tongue in cheek.

I realized I had come up short on an unknown expectation Fatima had of me. "Oh, I am sorry, Fatima," I replied sincerely this time, learning from the past futility of trying to fathom her mysterious expectations.

"OK, Sheikh Umeed, this time I will forgive you. Next time, be more immediate and generous in your genuine praise," Fatima replied smugly.

"Immediate, generous, genuine praise—I can definitely do that. I am sure it will motivate whoever receives it. Come to think of, I would be more motivated," I responded thoughtfully. "In the meantime, I have booked my ticket to Jeddah to visit my friend Sheikh Zahid in Al-Bahar, the self-sustaining city being built in the Arabian Desert," I added, feeling pleased to report the progress I had made on my plans.

Fatima was very warm in praising my progress. "Sheikh Jee, I am very proud of you. Since you declared your plans publicly to me, you have taken massive action. You have secured a line of credit against one of the properties to give us the cash flow for funding our goals. You retired from your job so that you can devote more time for your altruistic interests, and you have hired a manager to monitor all our rental properties."

"Fatima, to tell you the truth, we have both motivated each other by our actions. It is so true that action generates its own momentum, and you often end up achieving more than you had planned," I observed.

"Do you want to know about a very positive development since I started working at the food bank?" Fatima asked excitedly and continued without waiting for my reply.

"Well, I was a bit apprehensive about how I would be received by the people because I wear the hijab. But most people have been very good. I have received some uncomfortable stares, but they have been overcompensated by some very heartwarming comments. One elderly man came up to me as I was about to leave and confessed that he held deep hostility toward the Muslims after the 9/11 bombing, but that he now knows that he should never judge all people by the actions of a tiny minority."

"Fatima, this is very good indeed. This is an excellent example of how we can show the true face of Islam," I commented, feeling very heartened by Fatima's experience.

"But I have more to share, Jee!" Fatima continued with wide eyes. "The coordinator at the food bank is a jovial lady with wise perception. One day I was overwhelmed with a lot of food baskets to prepare. She sent a young man, about Nasib's age, to help me out. We got along very well together, and now we are planning some new recipes at the food bank. Normally that would not be so remarkable, but this time it is. You see the coordinator is black and Christian, the young man is white and Jewish, and I am brown and Muslim. And we all get along so well together."

"Fatima, my dear, this is refreshingly welcome. Christians, Muslims, and Jews have coexisted peacefully among each other and with other religions and races for centuries. There have been short periods of violence, and we are passing through one of them now. It is hard to imagine the sun shining when we are in the middle of a thunderstorm. But this thunderstorm will pass, and clear blue peaceful skies will prevail—within our lifetime. All of us have to have faith and take the kinds of actions you are taking now."

"Jee, I hope you are right in your prediction. Meanwhile, I have not heard from Nasib, have you?"

"Yes, Fatima," I replied wistfully. "He is becoming even more militant and extremist. He has grown a beard in solidarity with the militants. I really do not understand him. He is very capable and very intelligent but very misguided. I have given up on convincing him to change his path toward peaceful means to restore glory to Islam. Now I do not want to waste my energy on him."

"Would you like me to talk to him? No offense, Sheikh Jee, but it is possible that Nasib has tuned out to what you are explaining," Fatima said, trying to be helpful.

"Fatima, I will be very happy if you are able to direct Nasib toward the path of peace. It is the message that is important, not the messenger," I replied, feeling grateful that my personal exhaustion with Nasib was not the limiting factor. "Fatima, there is only upside to your suggestion. If you succeed, it will be absolutely brilliant. If you don't, we will be no worse off than we are now. Please go ahead!"

After realizing the scope of her offer, Fatima took a deep breath and replied, "Jee, I will have to figure out how I can connect with Nasib. To offer help is easy, but to actually help requires effort. It will be good homework for me. No matter what the outcome is, I will have grown. Can I share one more thought with you?"

"Of course, my dear," I replied, expecting more synergies resulting from our personal retreat.

"I have also started planning for my retirement. As you know, I am working on a plan to build a new girls' school in the village my family came from. It is encouraging to know that many new schools are being built in the larger villages, but ours is a small village in a remote part of Afghanistan. As you well know, a good education is the best preparation for advancement of women's rights. My childhood friend Wazeera is running the current school in a dilapidated hut and needs help and encouragement. Poor woman, her husband was killed by the Taliban as punishment for teaching girls. During your next visit to Afghanistan, can you please visit her?" Fatima asked earnestly.

"Fatima, I was only planning to go to Afghanistan next year, but, yes, I will extend my trip from Jeddah to Kabul. I will be able to visit my friend Muhsin and his wife Mahnoor who are running a charity I am funding in Afghanistan and monitor the progress they have made. Of course, I will visit Wazeera. In fact, I will go with Muhsin and Mahnoor. They have a very extensive network to get things done," I replied, feeling very useful. "My dear, I feel even more encouraged and rejuvenated by our brainstorming."

"Jee, thank you very much for your offer to visit Wazeera. With a little idea from me, you created many synergies. You deserve to be rewarded for that," Fatima replied, laughing out loudly.

I sensed some cheeky suggestion from Fatima, so I made my own request, "Fatima, I deserve a romantic dinner in the restaurant by the lakeside."

"Sheikh Jee, please, I had something much grander in mind for you. I will treat you to a romantic dinner in Jeddah! All you have to do is to book my flight with you!" Fatima continued, now laughing so hard that tears started flowing down her glowing cheeks.

I shook my head gently, acknowledging her craftiness and hugged her. "My dear Fatima, I will book your ticket. We will go to Jeddah together and visit my friend Sheikh Zahid in Al-Bahar."

Fatima smiled with satisfaction and continued, "How many times have you wished to go for hajj? Sheikh Jee, now is the time to convert our dreams to reality. It is every Muslim's duty to make the religious journey to Mecca at least once during their lifetime. What do you think?"

It suddenly struck me that I had been postponing some very important events in my life. We could have gone on hajj on several occasions before but allowed other activities to provide excuses for postponing hajj.

I replied boldly, "Fatima, the best time for hajj was twenty years ago. The next best time is now. I will book our hajj for this year. Yes, November 2011 will be the most memorable time of our lives!"

"I am so thankful to Allah. We are going to hajj!" Fatima shouted with glee.

"Sheikh Jee, I have one more request," Fatima said with a sweet smile. "This is a very opportune time to stop at a very happy juncture. Let us just enjoy this present moment. You have a tendency to continue on and on, and we sometimes end up feeling frustrated. This present moment is a gift we have been given to appreciate and savor!"

"Fatima, my dear, you are absolutely right. This is a beautiful, romantic night. We have a delicious dessert with a cherry on the top. Let us enjoy our just dessert," I replied as we retired for the night, embracing each other.

The next day I followed up on an important task.

"Fatima, we are a month away from our hajj. You offered to talk to Nasib to change his path toward peace. Have you had the opportunity to do that?"

"To be honest with you, I have thought many times, but it is such an awkward topic to bring up. I have been thinking so much that I have not done anything. I have feared the outcome and failed to act. If you had not reminded me, another month would have passed thinking and feeling guilty of inaction. I will call him right now!" Fatima affirmed confidently.

"Good for you, Fatima. I am sure you will feel much better after talking with Nasib and probably wonder why you didn't have the courage to call him earlier. Do you want to know how I know that?" I asked her and then answered my own question.

"Fatima, I have faced such situations myself and have always felt much better afterward, no matter what the outcome. That is the reward we get for facing our fears."

"Jee, you always look so confident and action-oriented. I did not realize that you struggle as well," Fatima said, looking very serious and sincere.

"My dear, the biggest battles are fought silently in the battlefield of our own mind," I observed quietly. "At one time, I just visualize a victorious outcome and charge ahead."

Fatima stood up erect and walked to the kitchen and dialled Nasib's cell phone. "I visualize a victorious outcome after taking action to talk to Nasib!"

After what seemed an eternity, Fatima returned smiling and looking smug. "Guess what, Nasib is coming with us to Mecca!"

"Fatima, I am very proud of you," I responded, trying to sound excited. I was expecting a detailed commentary of how Fatima reasoned with Nasib and what his response was.

She continued excitedly, "He is going to talk to Shahnaaz to ask her to come with us! Glory be to Allah! We are going to hajj as a family!"

It was not the outcome I had visualized but decided it was an even better, unexpected outcome. "Fatima, that is fantastic. This is the dream of every devout Muslim, and it is becoming a reality for us!"

Still I could not help but ask Fatima about the assigned purpose of the call. "Fatima, did you also try to change Nasib's path toward peace?"

She replied very frankly, "Jee, I know that was the purpose of my call. But our conversation took a different turn, and I never discussed that topic. I was too pleased with the unexpected dream of our hajj as a family.

I did not want to spoil that dream. Now we have a choice—rejoice that we are going on hajj or feel frustrated that we were not able to change Nasib's path toward peace. My choice is to rejoice. What is yours, Sheikh Jee?"

I held her hand and smiled broadly. "Fatima, going to Mecca is also a path toward peace! I will call Nasib to work out the details of our spiritual journey."

"Jee, may I if I remind you of something very important? Planning for the journey is part of the excitement of the journey. Our hajj has started now, not when we reach Mecca!"

Once again, I was startled by the delay and disconnect between our efforts and results.

I remembered when I was twelve years old my grandfather gave me an example of how life unfolds.

"Zafar, life flows like a long, winding river. For example, we all know that the River Nile flows north into the Mediterranean Sea. When you set out for the very first time at its source to reach the Mediterranean Sea, your boat will flow north as you expect. However, along the way, you will sometimes start travelling east and sometimes west. You will start doubting yourself but will rationalize that you will reach your destination. But then at places it starts flowing south. Now your resolve will be severely tested. Are you headed in the right direction? It is then that you will need to have faith and perseverance and just keep rowing. If you don't get discouraged by your doubts, you will reach your destination."

I felt encouraged and knew that I needed to keep rowing.

The following morning I received the anticipated call from Nasib, sounding very excited.

"Dad, I am so happy that we are planning to go to Mecca! I have already spoken to Shahnaaz, and she is just as excited to go. I have already checked out the flights and accommodations. I have a friend I met in the madrassa during my first visit to Afghanistan, and he will make all the arrangements for our hajj once we are in Mecca."

I hid my apprehension that Nasib seemed to have made many connections from his visit to Afghanistan.

"Son, I am very impressed that you have taken the initiative to check out the flights and accommodations. I will buy Shahnaaz's ticket since she has not started to work yet and has her big education loan to pay off."

Nasib surprised me by his reply, "Dad, that won't be necessary. I have already bought Shahnaaz's ticket and paid for her accommodations! We will meet you one day after you have landed in Jeddah. I am grateful to Allah that my business is doing extremely well."

"Wow! Nasib, I am very impressed by your accomplishments," I said, beaming with pride. "And you are very generous to buy your sister's ticket."

"Dad, to be honest with you, the ticket is not exactly free. I wish she would just let me pay for her trip, but the way you have brought us up, I know she would not let me just buy her trip outright. So I proposed to her that she would repay me by becoming my virtual assistant. I offered her a part-time job. She is happy now that she is earning her trip."

"Nasib, I am very proud of you. Share that with your mother. She will be equally proud. Parents are very happy when they see results of their efforts in their children," I told Nasib while thanking Allah.

Then my mind became overcast with dark thoughts about Nasib's friend from the madrassa in Afghanistan. Is he merely religious or a militant Islamist?

"Nasib, who is this friend of yours who has arranged our accommodations?" I asked, fishing for information.

"Oh, Dad, his name is Jaffar. He has become a very learned scholar of the Koran. I would be very happy to introduce him to all of you. I know you will be very happy to know him," Nasib answered confidently.

"That would be very nice. I am looking forward to meeting Jaffar," I replied, silently admonishing myself for assuming the worst about Nasib's friend who I did not even know.

I became less sure of interpreting signals I was getting from Nasib. Sometimes it seemed he was definitely becoming more militant and scheming and then seemed to surprise me with his normality. Maybe there were no signals other than in my imagination.

But at the same time, I felt very confident in my intuition that I would catch anything of substance among the confusing fluff.

First Impressions of Saudi Arabia

"Jee, I never imagined Jeddah would be so exotic and beautiful," Fatima said softly as she gazed at the starlit sky as the moon shone brightly lighting up the sea below.

"I have not seen a five-star hotel as luxurious as this in New York. This is a new standard for a five-star hotel."

"Yes, Fatima, we have seen enough abject poverty in Afghanistan. Here we are in the lap of luxury. It is so refreshing to see a Muslim country doing so well," I said in admiration of Saudi Arabia.

"We have one more day to ourselves. Tomorrow Nasib and Shahnaaz will be joining us. What happened to the romantic dinner you promised in Jeddah?"

"Of course, Sheikh Jee. I will order the dinner, and you provide the romance! Remember, you need more practice," Fatima replied teasingly.

After a very enjoyable dinner, we went out for a walk on the beach, savoring every experience in a beautiful and safe country we had never visited before. Instinctively, Fatima held my hand as we walked.

"Fatima, I know we have been living in the United States for many years now, but we have to respect the customs and sensitivities of Saudi Arabia," I said after gently releasing my hand. "Showing affection in public is just not done here."

"I am sorry, Sheikh Jee. I felt so comfortable and at home here that I forgot. All the women either wear the hijab or abayas. They look so elegant. I will be more careful from now on."

"Fatima, all we have to do is show genuine respect for the local customs. Any accidental transgression is forgiven by the respect shown."

"Sheikh Jee, customs and sensitivities are one thing, but what is your opinion about rights, especially Muslim women's rights?"

"Fatima, I can always count on you to bring up profound and painful questions.

"I am afraid there are no quick solutions. But collective awareness of exercising women's rights is very necessary as a catalyst for change. Remember, bringing about change requires painstaking patience. Even when change happens suddenly, it is a long time in coming.

"We savor the fruit of change long after the seeds of change were planted."

"I wonder if the women in Saudi Arabia are frustrated that they cannot drive, have no vote and can be divorced at the whim of their husbands," Fatima said in a sad voice.

"Fatima, looking in from the outside, you will see gross injustices. Many Saudi women who are educated feel the same way as you do. But most women have no other reference point. They don't even know that they don't have these rights. Unfortunately, for them ignorance is bliss." I took a deep breath as I started to rationalize.

"Some just accept the injustice, and it stops hurting them. But a few really suffer and seethe in anger because they cannot change centuries-old customs in the foreseeable future," I added sympathetically.

"But, Sheikh Jee, I believe this denial of rights is fundamentally un-Islamic," Fatima protested.

"Fatima, I could not agree with you more," I replied indignantly at the injustice.

"We cannot let social customs hide behind the shield of Islam. We can't let the patriarchs stuck in the past and fearful of losing outdated, absolute authority, and privileges stop the progress of Islam. Their narrow worldview should no longer limit the infinite horizons of possibilities for progress of the Muslim world."

"Oh, I did not mean to make you angry, Jee," Fatima said, trying to calm me.

"Look at the progress made by women in many Muslim countries. Why, we have elected women presidents and prime ministers. Look at Megawati, Benazir Bhutto, Khalida Zia, Sheikh Hasina, and Tansu Ciller. There are many women members of parliament in most Muslim countries."

I persisted in my pessimism, "Fatima, what you are saying is true. Superficially, we claim to treat women equally, but the reality is much different. There is a huge gap between paper constitutions and reality for the masses of women."

"Sheikh Jee, the gap is narrowing each day. I suggest you look at the distance travelled so far than be exhausted by thinking of how far we still have to travel."

It felt strange that Fatima had a more positive view of women's progress than I but finished with my thoughts.

"Fatima, in the past, we were trying to row hard with one hand. Now we need to give full and meaningful freedom to Muslim women so we can row ahead with both hands—and row in a straight line."

Fatima smiled and nodded. "That was in the past. Now we are headed in the right direction. If I remember correctly, you are the one who said direction is more important than speed."

"Yes, Fatima, I am also the one who said that bringing about change requires painstaking patience. But I am confident that the seeds of change have already been sown. Every day women have started to exercise their rights and push the envelope. Now let us just enjoy the pleasant walk back to our hotel and sleep soundly. Nasib and Shahnaaz are going to arrive at the hotel tonight and meet us for brunch tomorrow morning."

"Hello, Mom, hello, Dad! I am so happy to see you," Shahnaaz said as she rushed to our table in the morning.

"Shahnaaz, we are very happy to see you too. Where is Nasib?" I asked as Fatima and I got up to embrace her.

"He will be down in an hour. He is lazy and slow. It takes him time to warm up. Meanwhile, I wake up to make the sun rise and start smiling on the world," she replied, grinning.

"Now, now, Shahnaaz, you should be more respectable toward your brother," Fatima said, coming to Nasib's defense in his absence.

"He is a very capable person. A lazy and slow person cannot establish a very successful software development business and employ his little sister so that she can earn enough money to pay for her hajj."

"Oops, I am so sorry!" Shahnaaz replied sheepishly. "Of course I am grateful to Nasib, but he is so ponderous and figures out everything before proceeding. He never does anything spontaneously. Meanwhile, I believe in taking quick actions and making corrections if things go wrong. Why doesn't he do like I do? He will progress much farther, I tell you. He is such a geek, but I love him!"

Fatima and I glanced at each other and smiled. Fatima had often complained about me being so ponderous, so I let Fatima respond to Shahnaaz.

"Shahnaaz, there are situations where it is much better to think things through before proceeding. But each of us is hardwired to make decisions in a certain way, and we do that for all situations. For Nasib, it is unnatural to make quick and spontaneous decisions just as it is unnatural for you to make fully analyzed decisions. I don't think it is possible to say which decision-making process is better. Jee, what do you think?" Fatima questioned as she cleverly put the ball back into my court.

"Would you like a spontaneous or a properly thought-out answer?" I answered smartly with a question.

"Shahnaaz, Sheikh Jee here is trying to be very clever. He just gained time to formulate a thought-out answer," Fatima said, rolling her eyes.

I tried to answer a question that has puzzled me for a long time. "Life is delightfully contradictory. I am sure you have heard the expression 'The early bird catches the worm.' You may have also heard the expression 'Decide in haste and repent at leisure.' Both expressions are valid. In my life, I have benefitted when I have made quick decisions, and I have paid dearly for not taking the time to think things through.

"Similarly, I have benefitted from thought-out decisions and lost out on opportunities when I have taken too long to analyze.

"What I have learned so far is that we have to be aware that different situations require different answers. Just this awareness guides us to take the right approach in most cases. We should always pay attention to our gut feelings. This helps us to overcome our otherwise hardwired response. I am still learning and improving."

Shahnaaz and Fatima listened very intently trying to digest what I had said. "So, Dad, are you saying that just being aware of the difference between quick decision making and slow decision making will guide us to decide which process is appropriate for a particular situation?"

"Yes, Shahnaaz. You have learned very quickly what took me a long time to understand," I replied, feeling very good to have put into words what was in my mind.

Fatima added her own vote of confidence as Nasib joined us at the table. "Jee, what you said makes sense to me now. I will start being more aware now."

Nasib looked very refreshed and relaxed as he sat down at the table. "I thank Allah for giving us the opportunity to perform the hajj. I am sorry for being late, but I got up early to arrange our accommodations in Mecca with my friend Jaffar. So, is everybody ready for the ride to Mecca this afternoon?"

Shahnaaz cleared her throat and quickly recovered. "Nasib, Mom and I were just commenting as to how accomplished you are to establish a very successful software company and how grateful I am that you have employed me. And you did not sleep in but got up early to make all the accommodations for us. I am so proud of you!"

But it was her next comment that startled Fatima and me. "Nasib, since you have done so much for me, I will help you by driving all of us to Mecca."

Nasib was quick to complain, "No, you won't. Mom and Dad, I warned her that women are not allowed to drive in Saudi Arabia. She could easily get caught, and we could all be put in jail. This could ruin our hajj. She is so impulsive and reckless!"

Shahnaaz retorted immediately, "And you are so ponderous and cautious. I don't know what I have done wrong. I took the initiative to show my American driving license and asked the car rental agent to list me as an additional driver, which he did. So I am allowed to drive our rental car."

"My crazy little sister, you do not understand. A car rental agent cannot give you the right to drive in Saudi Arabia. He was probably new at the job and made a mistake to list you as the additional driver. I let you drive last night because it was dark and no one would notice a woman was driving the car. If you drive during the day, it would be too risky."

"Nasib, I am not crazy. I know exactly what I am doing. Every day Muslim women need to exercise their rights and be assertive. You should be helping me, not repressing me. You have been associating with the Taliban fundamentalists too much. What kind of an Islamist have you become?"

Fatima and I glanced at each other and smiled, recalling what I had said just the day before about women pushing the envelope to exercise their rights.

Finally I intervened, "Nasib and Shahnaaz, we are faced with choosing between two rights. Nasib, you want to make sure that our hajj goes ahead smoothly. Shahnaaz wants to exercise her right to drive in a country where women cannot even get a license to drive. Choosing between two rights is a lot trickier than choosing between right and wrong."

Shahnaaz started to justify her action. "Listen, everybody. I am very respectful of the local customs and sensitivities. I am happily complying with the local dress code for women. I even bought an abaya in New York that I wore before I boarded the plane. I do not smoke and do not drink. I am a very responsible visitor. But a woman not being allowed to drive has nothing to do with customs and sensitivities. It is against their fundamental human rights. I have a small opportunity to exercise that right safely. It would be a lot riskier for a Saudi woman to drive because women cannot even get a driver's license. I have a valid driver's license. I believe all of you should support me," Shahnaaz concluded by thumping on the table.

Nasib's forehead wrinkled as he asked, "What happens if you are caught by the police? We could all be arrested, and our whole hajj could be jeopardized. What do you say to that?"

Shahnaaz replied with a cheer, "I will smile, show my American driver's license, apologize to the policeman, and hand over the keys to you. I just want to push the envelope, not upset the apple cart!"

Nasib put his arms around Shahnaaz's shoulder and smiled. "What am I going to do with my feisty sister? Mom and Dad, if you are willing to take the risk, so am I."

I gave my support to Shahnaaz. "Exercising rights always carries risk, sometimes very grave risk. However, I believe there is very little risk for us especially because we are American citizens on hajj. It would not be good publicity to detain us during the hajj season."

Fatima gave her blessing. "Shahnaaz, I like the idea that you just want to be assertive and not upset the apple cart. There is already overwhelming support for women's rights in the Muslim world. It takes time for laws to reflect public support for changing centuries-old customs. I believe in this case women will succeed by just being assertive, not aggressive."

Shahnaaz clapped her hands with joy. "Thank you all for supporting my small gesture of support for my Saudi sisters. Fasten your seat belts, and let me drive you to Mecca. I am so excited and overwhelmed. Mom and Dad, you sit in the back and relax. I will be your chauffer in Mecca."

Nasib took out his cell phone and started to call his friend Jaffar. The rest of us were aghast to hear Nasib speaking in Arabic!

Fatima was the first to express her surprise, "Nasib, I am very impressed. When did you learn to speak Arabic? You sound very fluent!"

"Why, thank you, Mom. I learned a little bit when I was in the madrassa in Afghanistan. When I started my own business, I figured I would learn Arabic in order to expand my business in the Arabic world. Jaffar has been helping me a lot. He is my Arabic tutor."

Shahnaaz was very impressed, "But, Nasib, your friend lives in Saudi Arabia. How did he tutor you? Can you read and write as well?"

Nasib tried to get back at his sister, "Shahnaaz, have you ever heard of Skype? It is the best way to teach remotely. It is free. And yes, I can read and write Arabic very well. It took me just one year. And I was running my own business as well. You accuse me of being slow. I am a very quick learner. Even Mom and Dad marvel at my fluency. Do you want me to teach you Arabic for free?"

As usual, Shahnaaz stuck her tongue out at Nasib and fired back, "I suppose being a geek has its advantages. But geeks are modest, and you are arrogant. Just for that I will not take free lessons from you. I would rather pay Jaffar to teach me Arabic."

I looked at Fatima and squeezed her hand and thanked Allah for being parents of children who both love each other and love to hate each other.

Fatima and I felt very happy that Nasib was participating fully in the experience of hajj. He seemed very relaxed and normal.

This was a far cry from the Nasib of late, retracting into an angry and isolated shell where we did not know what dangerous concoctions were brewing in his mind.

Was it because his new business was doing so well? Had he really renounced militancy?

During a stop on the way to Mecca, I took Fatima to one side and asked her about Nasib's unusually cheerful demeanor.

"Sheikh Jee, you are too suspicious. Nasib is a very honest person. You see that he is very happy. Are you implying that he is putting on a happy face to hide his anger?"

I answered uneasily, "Fatima, with all the external signs of normality, I cannot explain why I still feel that Nasib is still an angry person, scheming revenge against those who he believes are enemies of Islam. I know I should not be thinking this way, but I cannot help it."

Fatima hissed her reaction, "Sheikh Jee, did I ever tell you that you are paranoid?"

I replied very sombrely, "Fatima, I pray to Allah that you're right!" Meanwhile, Nasib announced. "There is a small change to our plans.

I just received a call from my friend Jaffar that we will go to his house to freshen up and eat. We will park our car at his house, and he will take us to our hotel in his van because it is very difficult for a foreigner to drive near the Kaaba."

"Wow, Nasib, what a chic neighborhood! Your friend Jaffar has a palatial home," Shahnaaz gasped as she slowed down as the guard smiled and opened the gate.

Two little girls who looked to be five years old ran gleefully toward our car and greeted us in English! Behind them was a tall, handsome young man who rushed toward Nasib, greeting him in Arabic and hugged him tightly. We were very moved by the genuine affection between them.

"Mom, Dad, and Shahnaaz, this is my dear friend Jaffar," Nasib said as he proudly introduced him. "We spent one of the roughest, the toughest, and the best time of our lives in the madrassa in Afghanistan. Jaffar, do you remember how excited we were when we found out that Gosama bin Baden was going to give a lecture to us and how disappointed we were because our enemies bombed the only bridge to our madrassa? And we still won because the next day we listened to the lecture recorded on a tape thrown across the bridge.

"During our stay at the madrassa I learned a lot from you and have deep respect for your knowledge and reverence of Islam."

"Uncle Jee, Auntie Jee, and my sister Shahnaaz, my family and I welcome you respectfully into our humble home," Jaffar said, feeling a little embarrassed, speaking in fluent English. "Nasib flatters me a lot. Come, let me introduce you to my daughters Nagma and Shabnam."

Uncle, Auntie, and sister! Accentuated by the formality and respect of "Jee"! We were being addressed with as much respect as if we were back in Afghanistan. Fatima and I looked at each other, acknowledging approval of the first impressions of Jaffar as we walked behind him.

Meanwhile, Shahnaaz tugged at Nasib and pulled him back and asked in a gushed whisper, "Nasib, does Jaffar have a younger brother as handsome and wealthy as he is?"

Presently, Jaffar led us into a large compound with a beautifully manicured garden around a large pond. We never envisioned such lush affluence in the middle of the desert. There were two women in veil sitting on a bench under the shade giggling.

"And these are my wives, Tahira and Sajjda," Jaffar announced, smiling at us.

Shahnaaz's jaw dropped as she looked at Nasib. She did not say anything, but we could read her lips as she said, "Forget it!"

Jaffar continued proudly, "Tahira is my first wife, and Nagma is her daughter. Sajjda is my second wife, and Shabnam is her daughter. Nagma and Shabnam were born one day apart! Allah has blessed us with a very happy family life."

Shahnaaz chipped in with caustic sarcasm, "We have a lot of blended families in the US as well but not quite like yours."

Nasib glared at her as Fatima tried to defuse the situation by going forward to hug Tahira and Sajjda. "Allah bless you both, and may Nagma and Shabnam bring you continued joy."

I was very impressed with Jaffar's peaceful and dignified demeanor. He had obviously done very well financially, but what impressed me most was his humility.

"Uncle and Nasib, it is time for prayer now. After that, let me show you around the house while Tahira and Sajjda prepare the meal for us. Auntie and Shahnaaz can talk with Tahira and Sajjda. Unfortunately, they speak only Arabic. But the maid who helps with the cooking is from Pakistan and can speak Urdu, Arabic, and English. She will be happy to translate."

The dinner table and the meal were lavishly set. Nasib was feeling very happy because at least Fatima and I were feeling very comfortable in the Jaffar household. Everything seemed to function effortlessly and smoothly.

We all had a delicious dinner while the maid was dutifully serving us. I guess we had lived in the US so long that it felt strange for a maid to be serving meals in a home.

Jaffar looked at Nasib and announced, "Uncle, Auntie, and Shahnaaz, you must be tired after a long journey. I will drop you at the hotel. Nasib and I have a lot of things to catch up on. I will drop Nasib at the hotel afterward."

Jaffar's brand-new and sleek nine-seater Toyota van was waiting just outside the compound. I was surprised when Jaffar took the keys from his Filipino chauffer and drove us to the hotel.

"Here you are, please make sure you rest well tonight. It is going to be a very exhausting day for you tomorrow. Sajjda and I will accompany you on the first day of hajj tomorrow. Don't wait for Nasib. We don't know when we will be back. We have a lot to catch up on."

As soon as we checked into our luxurious hotel room and we were alone, Fatima spoke with apprehension, "Sheikh Jee, I am very puzzled. I felt very comfortable at the Jaffar household. But the very close friendship between Jaffar and Nasib makes me feel very uncomfortable. Jaffar seems a very gentle person, but he exercises great influence over Nasib.

"I am wondering if Nasib's Islamic militancy is based on his close association with Jaffar. After all they were learning together at the same madrassa. Now Jaffar has taken Nasib away from us. I don't know what they are up to. All I can say is that I feel very afraid!"

"Fatima, I must say that I am puzzled as well. It is very unusual that Jaffar would drive since he has a chauffeur. Perhaps he speaks both English and Arabic and Jaffar and Nasib do not want anybody to know what they are discussing. I don't know what they are up to either, but, Fatima, I do not feel afraid."

Fatima's forehead showed a pained look. "Sheikh Jee, now I am even more puzzled. We have observed the same situation. You have always told me that our inner feelings or intuitions are generally a good indicator of the truth. I feel afraid, and you don't. So what is the truth in this case? We can't both be right, right!"

"Fatima, to be honest I do not know the answer to your question. Let us not dismiss each other's feelings. I am sure we will get another hint to confirm whether we need to worry or not. In the absence of any other information, let us always choose to be fearless."

Fatima held my hands, looked into my eyes, and smiled. "Sheikh Jee, you just said that you did not know the answer. But you just gave the answer!"

My jaw dropped at this realization. "Fatima, I thank Allah for this moment of instant enlightenment."

We heard a knock at our door and were surprised to see Shahnaaz. "Mom, I am very puzzled! I thought Muslim women had no rights in Saudi Arabia, but they are treated very well. They are exercising a lot of influence in shaping their future and that of their country."

Fatima stroked her hair and said, "Sit down, Shahnaaz. What we read in the Western press is a very segmented and skewed view of women's rights. They are not deliberately skewed, but they are viewed through the Western lens and compared to Western standards. However, I must admit that even though they are exaggerated, they are mostly correct about the lack of women's rights in Saudi Arabia.

"But coming back to the Jaffar household, I am very puzzled as well. I am wondering if their life is typical of the Saudi Arabian women. Sheikh Jee, why don't you enlighten us?"

"Fatima, thank you for flattering me. My batteries are beginning to run down with all this enlightenment. Shahnaaz, what makes you believe that women are exercising a lot of influence in shaping their own future and that of their country?"

"To start off with, they are running Jaffar's manufacturing facility. Tahira runs the factory employing five hundred people, and Sajjda takes care of the logistics. Did you know that their factory makes the most advanced and efficient solar panels available in the world today?"

"How do you know all that, Shahnaaz? You were only with them for a couple of hours, and they don't speak English," I asked.

"Dad, but they understand, read, and write English! They don't speak it because they do not have to. All their employees speak Arabic even though they are from different countries. I asked my questions in English, and they replied in Arabic which was translated into English by their maid."

She continued enthusiastically, "They are very capable and very confident and have big plans. They have invited us later on this week for a factory tour. In some ways I envy them."

Fatima's curiosity was now aroused, "Oh, why is that, Shahnaaz?" "Well, they don't have to do any housework! No laundry, no cleaning, no gardening, no making beds. Even cooking is so easy for them. The maid does all the preparation. They have all the quality time for their children. Life is not rushed. Their life is a lot less stressful than ours, Mom."

Fatima agreed with most of Shahnaaz's observations. "But, Shahnaaz, for them there is no driving and no vote."

Then Shahnaaz's eyes lit up with hope. "But they have awareness, and they have an action plan! They believe very firmly that within one generation, they will have both. The plan is simple—education. The way Tahira and Sajjda explained to me was that every mother will make sure that their daughters get full education, learn foreign languages, and be full participants in the information age. Even though they cannot drive, they will make sure their daughters will drive. The vast majority of parents think this way now. So it will happen!"

I wondered if what Shahnaaz was envisioning was naivety or near-future reality. "Shahnaaz, I sincerely believe that what you say will happen. But every social change requires overcoming the inertia of status quo. The ultraorthodox mullahs still exert enormous influence and will not relinquish their power easily. So the types of action you are taking to constantly push the envelope are part of the journey toward winning women's rights.

"But now I really need to sleep. This has been a delightfully exhausting day. Let us continue tomorrow. We will meet for breakfast at half past five tomorrow morning. I hope Nasib comes back early from his visit with Jaffar. We start our hajj at half past six. Jaffar asked us to be very punctual."

EXPERIENCES OF HAJJ

As usual, Nasib and Shahnaaz were late joining us for breakfast.

"Hello, Mom and Dad, did you have a restful night? Remember today is our first day of hajj," Nasib startled us by sitting at our table just as we were about to leave.

Fatima, as usual, was the first to respond, "Nasib, yes, we are well rested. I am glad to see you looking refreshed and in a cheerful mood. What time did you and Jaffar come last night?"

"Now!" he replied, grinning broadly.

"Now? It is quarter past six in the morning. What were you doing all night?" Fatima asked with a mixture of curiosity and worry.

"Mom, Jaffar drove me to an oasis about one hour from here. We had so much to catch up on. We spent the whole night talking, gazing up at the stars. The stars look so bright in the desert.

"We were so absorbed reminiscing about our memorable experiences at the madrassa in Afghanistan that we lost track of time. Then we picked up Sajjda and Tahira. On the way back, we watched the most glorious sunrise. Dad, you should see the desert sunrise."

I could see the discomfort and unease on Fatima's face and tried to deflect attention from her worries. "Nasib, I have seen many a glorious sunrise in many different settings but not in the sandy desert where the dunes are as high as hills. Fatima, do you remember when we woke up very early to see the sun rise above the Grand Canyon?"

Fatima was still aloof from the conversation, so I continued, "Whenever we connect with nature, it gives us serenity. It could be a sunrise, a sunset, a meadow, a beach, a lake, a river, a forest, or a park. No matter what the situation in our lives is, connecting with nature invigorates us and helps us to think clearly."

I tried to bring Fatima into the conversation. "And of course, if you are with someone you love, it is very romantic. Fatima, do you remember me telling you that time stood still when we were watching the sunrise atop the Grand Canyon?"

There was an embarrassing silence from Fatima, so I continued, "Nasib, I would love to take you up on your suggestion to see the desert sunrise. Why don't you take your mother and me to the oasis one day after we have completed our hajj?"

Nasib smiled as he replied, "Dad, you will have to romance Mom alone. Besides, I have many things to discuss with Jaffar after the hajj. I can ask Jaffar to arrange for his driver to take you there."

Fatima stood up and left without saying a word. Nasib looked at me and smiled. "Haddy, I am so glad I don't have the problem of soothing Hummy's feathers. Good luck!"

At least Nasib and I were communicating. I shook my head as I smiled. "Nasib, it is not a problem, it is a challenge. Why do I have so many challenges in life? We don't want to start our hajj with one person sulking."

As I took the elevator to our hotel room, I sighed as I visualized Fatima's anger.

I was saved the effort of asking Fatima what was wrong as she asked angrily with clenched teeth, "Sheikh Jee, you are so naive! Nasib has spent the whole night hatching out some terrorist plot with his terrorist friend, and you are talking about romantic sunrises. How can you be so blissfully ignorant while I am terrified?"

"But, Fatima, I don't believe there is anything malicious going on," I replied calmly, hoping that she would not get angrier.

Fatima continued to seethe, "We have come for the most joyous experience in our lives, and something keeps on going drastically wrong. Why can't we just be like millions of other pilgrims and simply enjoy the hajj? Is that too much to ask of Allah?"

I was tempted to start explaining rationally that it is up to us what we see and experience. But one thing I had learned through fruitless previous attempts is that humans are emotional creatures. Reason alone does not work. So I started to explain rationally while searching how to connect emotionally.

"Fatima, my dear, please come here and sit down. I understand your anger that Nasib spent the whole night alone in the desert with Jaffar. We cannot be sure what they discussed. It may be very innocent. Do you remember when your friend Afsana came to visit you from Afghanistan? You took her shopping and did not return till very late. We were supposed to take her out for dinner that night. Your cell phone was turned off and we had no way of contacting you. While we were worried, you two were so engrossed chatting like little schoolgirls that you lost track of time. Perhaps the same thing happened between Nasib and Jaffar . . ."

This comment diverted her attention momentarily away from her anger as she smiled faintly. "Sheikh Jee, we had met after thirty years and were indeed reminiscing about our childhood memories. We had so much fun that night. We are planning to meet again next year."

I tried to capitalize on a small opening. "So it is very possible that Nasib and Jaffar were reminiscing—"

Fatima interrupted by clenching her teeth again, "We were not plotting anything subversive. These two could very well have been. Don't you see the difference?"

I felt I was not only not making any progress with Fatima but that she was putting up even more resistance and becoming even more unreasonable. I felt I was failing to counter her emotions.

"Fatima, I care as much for the well-being of Islam as you do. Let us just suppose they were planning something subversive which is totally opposed to the principles of Islam. What would you want me to do? What would you do?"

Fatima became a little quiet and pensive. "If I knew what to do, I wouldn't ask you, Sheikh Jee. All I know is that I wish we never had this constant fear about the actions of Nasib lurking in the background."

"Fatima, I have these fears too. If you wish I can share a suggestion about what you can do to enjoy your hajj. After all, this is one of the noble duties of Muslim. And isn't it true that we have all come here to fulfill one of our most important dreams?"

This approach seemed to be getting some traction. "Yes, I am prepared to listen," Fatima replied hopefully.

So I tried to connect with my heart rather than with my brain and started passionately, "Fatima, we do not know what Nasib and Jaffar are up to. Our dreams are under our control. All I know is that we will not let them sabotage our dreams. Let us just concentrate on the present. We are in the holiest place of Islam. Allah will protect us all. It is the will of Allah that we fulfill our duty as devout Muslims and experience the deepest spirituality of Islam."

Suddenly Fatima stood up and proclaimed boldly, "Yes, Jee, you are absolutely right. Our dreams are ours alone, and nobody can steal them from us. But maybe it is just our imagination that someone is stealing our dreams. In any case, I want to enjoy my hajj, and I don't want to spoil everybody else's hajj by being a stick in the mud. Let us go down to the lobby where I hope Nasib and Shahnaaz are waiting for us."

I felt very relieved and thankful to Allah for showing me a good example of how to resolve many serious situations by reasoning combined with emotional appeal.

I was even beginning to feel a little smug when Fatima commented, "Sheikh Jee, I still think you are burying your head in the sand."

"Yes, Fatima, my dear. At least it is in the holy sand of Mecca!" And we hugged each other tightly, thankful that we were going to start our hajj for the first time in our lives on a cheerful note.

As we entered the hotel lobby, we saw a huge crowd gathered around a television set. We joined the crowd with curious trepidation and saw the breaking news headline: "American Forces Kill Gosama Bin Baden in Pakistan."

Everybody watched in shocked silence, and nobody stayed around too long. Some muttered and cursed and left in anger and disgust.

Nobody does instant interviews of ordinary citizens of Saudi Arabia to find out what they think of the killing of the best known Muslim religious freedom fighter or the most hated terrorist.

Fatima tugged at my shirt and whispered, "Jee, I wish this didn't happen during our hajj. I hate to think how Nasib would react."

I whispered back, "I wish the same as well. But we will deal with whatever his reaction is. Let us go outside where Nasib said Jaffar and his wives will be waiting."

Shahnaaz caught up with us as we were going outside and was much more animated in her response when she greeted us.

"Oh my God! They killed Gosama bin Baden. I hope there is no trouble here. I don't want anything to spoil my hajj."

Before we could say anything, Nasib came to us, looking very sombre.

"Our enemies will pay very dearly for this act, I promise you. They think they have killed Gosama bin Baden. Instead, they have created a true martyr of Islam, a true freedom fighter for Islam. He was an inspiration for all Muslims to fight for their dignity and their freedom. In his death, he is even more of an inspiration."

He continued speaking calmly and clearly as though he was giving a rallying speech. "A million Gosamas will convert his message into action. Millions of Muslims will join forces to defeat the infidels who are occupying our lands and bent on destroying Islam. It is a good omen that Gosama bin Baden, our most revered freedom fighter, has been martyred at the start of our hajj. Millions of Muslims will vow to avenge his martyrdom."

He finished by announcing as we approached the van, "Today, I am not sad because I have been reinspired and reenergized. Allahu Akbar!"

Jaffar and his wives Tahira and Sajjda came out of their van and greeted us very warmly. There was no mention at all about the death of Gosama bin Baden. It felt very strange that we all knew and yet chose to say nothing. Our silence highlighted that we had very different views on his death.

Fatima and I were surprised that Jaffar and both his wives were going to accompany us for our pilgrimage.

Fatima showed her appreciation. "Jaffar, we really appreciate that you are going to be our guides, but I hope all of you being away from your business does not cause any problems."

"Auntie Jee and Uncle Jee, quite the contrary! Tahira had suggested that she would stay behind to mind the business, but Sajjda persuaded us that we should take this opportunity to gauge how mature the business is. In addition, we have to thank you all for giving us the opportunity to go on our second hajj."

It was a pleasure to get used to the formality and respect of the "Jee," but I was surprised that it was only the second hajj for Jaffar, Tahira, and Sajjda.

Tahira and Sajjda spoke to Jaffar in Arabic and started to giggle while he translated for us. "Tahira and Sajjda are saying that the business runs very well without me, but they were curious if it could run without them. But they do not trust me to run the business if they were not there!"

We all laughed as we thanked Allah for a happy start to our hajj.

Jaffar asked us to sit in the van as we were already a little late. As his driver started the van, he started to speak. He had a strong but gentle personality and commanded respect.

"I would appreciate your attention for a few very important minutes. Please listen carefully to what I have to say and you will get full benefits of the most important and the most spiritual experience of your lives.

"I can see that you are all well prepared. One big mistake that most hajjis make is to carry too much. Even one gram extra becomes a tiresome burden over the days. The only extra thing to bring with you is patience, lots of patience."

Shahnaaz was too excited. "How far is our miqat from here? How far is Kaaba from there?"

Nasib glowered Shahnaaz down to silence. "Didn't you hear Jaffar? The only extra thing to bring with you is patience, lots of patience. Just shut up and listen. Stop showing off!"

Jaffar closed his eyes, raised his hand, and brought it down slowly to signal everybody to remain calm and continued, looking mostly at Shahnaaz.

"Our miqat where you prepare yourself for hajj is Yalamlam and is about one hundred fifty kilometres from here. From Yalamlam to Kaaba is fifty kilometres. However, it is more useful to talk in terms of time and not distance. I estimate Yalamlam is about two hours from here and from Yalamlam to our hotel near Kaaba will probably take us two and a half hours at that time. Remember what I said about patience. With traffic, it could easily take more than double the time. The Masjid Al-Haram is within walking distance from the hotel. The Kaaba is in the Masjid Al-Haram complex. Normally it takes ten minutes to walk to the Kaaba, but expect huge crowds of pilgrims, and the actual time could be a few hours. It will be a physically exhausting but a spiritually uplifting experience. Any questions so far?"

Shahnaaz as usual was the first to speak, "Brother Jaffar, thank you for answering my questions. I don't have another question for now, but I would like to propose how we can keep in touch with each other and not waste time finding each other."

Jaffar was expecting to continue with his instructions but was genuinely appreciative of Shahnaaz's initiative. "Sister Shahnaaz, do explain to us how we will keep in touch with each other."

"Well, Tahira and Sajjda will be escorting Mommy and me, and you will be escorting Daddy and Nasib. Tahira has her Blackberry and will use it only for texting if need be. Either you or Nasib can use your Blackberry for texting only."

Nasib volunteered his services as everybody snickered, "As the designated geek of the family, I will use my Blackberry but only in case of emergency. I do not want any unnecessary disruption of my hajj."

Jaffar continued with his explanations, "What we do at Yalamlam is the most important preparation. It is called *ihram*, which means physical and spiritual cleansing. Physical cleansing is easy. You bathe yourselves and put on the simple white cloth called *ihram*. The women can wear the new long white dresses, which cover your ankles and wrists and the white hijabs you brought with you. All this time you will be chanting the invocation."

Then Jaffar became very serious and solemn and looked directly at each of us as we listened ever more intently.

"The much more challenging aspect of *ihram* is the spiritual cleansing. Each one of us must take this opportunity to elevate ourselves spiritually. Start with practicing the forgiveness and reconciliation. Other requirements will surface as we go along."

Then Jaffar broke into a smile, "I know I am taking longer than I thought, but practice some of your patience on me please. Investing a little more time in preparation makes the rest of the journey more productive and fulfilling.

"I will give you just the logistics of what comes next, but these will be the experiences which cannot be described but which you will remember for the rest of your lives. You will feel them. They will connect with your spirit and soul.

"Once we have checked into our hotel near Masjid Al-Haram, we will walk to the Kaaba which is in the Masjid complex. We will perform *Tawaf al-Qudum*, going anticlockwise seven times around the Kaaba, followed by reciting two *rakkats* behind Maqam Ibrahim and drink water from the Zamzam spring.

"By this time you may be feeling exhausted, but there is still the ritual of Sa'iy to be performed. This is where we commemorate the desperate search for water by Hajar, Ibrahim's wife, by running seven times between the hills of Safah and Marvah. The spring that Allah brought forth for Hajar and her baby son, Ishmael, is called Zamzam, and flows copiously to this day.

"At the end of the Sa'iy ritual, we undergo the ritual of Halaq, which is cutting of the hair. Uncle Jee, Nasib and I will get our heads shaved. Auntie Jee, Shahnaaz, Tahira, and Sajjda just need to cut a short length of their hair. This is the end of *ihram*.

"From there we will walk to the tent city of Mina, which is eight kilometers away. We will reach there in the early evening and sleep overnight. We will need to forget about material comforts and get used to a Spartan life for the rest of the hajj.

"Now even I am getting tired and would like to have a power nap as Nasib and I have been up all night. I will update you on other details as we reach Kaaba. In the meantime, I suggest we listen to some CDs of Talbiyah. I will update you about the ceremonies at Mina. But let me summarize what we have covered so far.

"From here to Yalamlam, it will take us about two hours. Performing *ihram* at our miqat in Yalamlam will take about one hour. From Yalamlam to our hotel, it will take two and a half hours. We will unload our luggage and check in at the hotel. From the hotel to Kaaba, it will take indeterminate time, but expect at least one hour. At

Kaaba we will perform *Tawaf al-Qudum*, going anticlockwise seven times around the Kaaba.

"The first time you set your eyes on the Kaaba will be the most memorable experience of your lives. Most people start crying with happiness that they experience but cannot explain.

"This will be followed by reciting two *rakkats* behind Maqam Ibrahim and drinking water from the Zamzam spring. From there we will walk to Mina, the tent city, which is about eight kilometers and will take us about three hours. We will stay overnight in Mina. Travel light and have a lot of patience. It will be a very exhausting day and night, but I promise that you will enjoy the immensely holy experience of hajj and the exhilaration of exhaustion."

"This is absolutely ridiculous," Shahnaaz protested indignantly as she returned to the van after performing *ihram* at Yalamlam.

"It took so long waiting to go into the washroom. My feet are killing me. Why can't they make more toilets? There is a total absence of planning. They know how many people come here every year!"

Nasib, who, up to this time, had been calm, looked angrily at Shahnaaz. I spoke before he could say anything.

"My dear Shahnaaz, I understand your frustration. I know it comes as a shock to you because you are used to things being planned and organized in the United States. But there is much more at play below what we see superficially. This is not an excuse for lack of planning, but let me share with you what I observe.

"Can you hear the sweet chant of Talbiyah, the prayer of sincere conviction that the people sing to proclaim they have prepared themselves to perform the hajj?

"Can you see that everybody looks the same? There are millionaires and there are paupers. There are masters, and there are servants. No one can tell the difference between them.

"You can see people of all colors, all races, and all languages, and they are all equal in the eyes of Allah. Islam is truly a religion of peace and equality.

"Yes, there is chaos, but if we choose to sense it, this is a uniquely peaceful and an overwhelming experience. Let us not let the superficial chaos rob us of the spirituality of *ihram*."

Shahnaaz suddenly realized her shortsighted view of hajj but was halfhearted in acknowledging her misguided frustration. "Oh, I suppose I should be more patient."

Nasib joined in with stern admonishment of Shahnaaz while Fatima, Jaffar, Tahira, and Sajjda looked on uneasily. "You are just a spoiled brat, my little sister! There are literally millions of people here who are less fit but more patient than you, and they are patiently enjoying the experience of *ihram*. Just suck it up and shut up!"

Tahira and Sajjda looked at each other and started giggling. Jaffar started to laugh out loud, and then we all started laughing, except Shahnaaz and Nasib, as Tahira spoke to Jaffar.

Jaffar translated for us, "Tahira thinks we can all learn from Shahnaaz by being more patient and from Nasib by being more compassionate."

Jaffar continued, "Remember, the physical part of *ihram* is very simple. It is the spiritual part that is much more important and much more challenging. This is a perfect opportunity for all of us. If we can exercise patience and compassion for the duration of the hajj, we will plant the seeds of improvement which will flourish after the hajj."

Nasib was the first to realize the improvement he had to make and spoke sincerely, "I will be more compassionate from now on."

Shahnaaz replied humorously as we all smiled, "And from now on, I will be more patient than Mother Teresa."

Fatima hugged them both. "I am so proud of you. You recognized your shortcomings and are willing to improve.

"Allow me to share what my grandfather told me after he returned from his hajj. He told me that each one of us has many weaknesses, some that we know of and some that we are afraid to admit even to ourselves. We are ashamed of some weaknesses we know we have. We hide them. But they always remain with us and limit us.

"And then there are weaknesses that we never knew we had. He said that during hajj, all these weaknesses become exposed, and we have a golden opportunity to improve ourselves without beating up on ourselves. Remember, Allah is the most merciful and wants us to succeed."

As we all sat in the van to go to Mecca, Shahnaaz asked Jaffar, "How long will it take to reach our hotel in Mecca, and how long will it take to go to Kaaba?"

Jaffar smiled and looked at me to answer her question.

I took a deep breath and started. "Shahnaaz, my dear, there are times and places where our planning and control apply and are useful and necessary. But then there are situations that have their own rules and rhythms. Hajj is one of these experiences. I know it is going to be difficult, but for this experience, let us just go with the flow. All the logistics and planning you are used to will work out by itself. We will get there when we get there. Let us just be in the present moment and enjoy the experience."

Shahnaaz looked perplexed, "Mom, do you understand what your husband is saying?"

Fatima's forehead wrinkled as she replied, "No, I don't really understand what Sheikh Jee is saying."

I nodded my head. "For me being in the present moment has been the most difficult concept to understand. Even now I do not fully understand it. I suppose some things cannot be adequately explained in words alone. But your spirit knows them and wants you to enjoy them. I get fleeting, transitory experiences of being in the moment and want to experience them again. However, I don't exert myself but just leave myself open to them. When I experience them, I enjoy them immensely.

"Just because we cannot understand some things does not mean they do not exist. We can enjoy them even if we cannot understand them."

As Fatima and Shahnaaz sighed in unison, I continued, "I am afraid I cannot explain what I would like to. Why don't you be on the lookout for a time when you are feeling extremely peaceful and tranquil and realize afterward the joy you just experienced? That would have been a present moment. But don't worry if you don't experience any present moments. After all we have lived our lives up to now without being consciously aware of them."

I was relieved from continuing my awkward explanations by the honking of horns at a bus in front of us, which had just stalled.

Jaffar asked the driver to load the CD player with CDs of *nasheeds* and *naats*. "We can all benefit from listening to songs about Islamic beliefs, history, and religion, as well as current events."

As we started listening to the *nasheeds* and waited in the gridlock that developed in minutes and could take hours to resolve, Fatima whispered to Shahnaaz, "Here we are sitting and waiting in our comfortable and air-conditioned luxury van. Millions of people are waiting in stifling heat."

"Yes, Mommy. I feel so lucky that you and Dad have provided us with all the luxuries and comforts of life. But I do feel very sorry for the people who have so little in life. I feel guilty for being so well-off compared to all these poor people. How can Allah give so much to so few and so little to so many?"

Jaffar overheard Shahnaaz and told the driver to turn off the CD. "My little sister is asking a very important question. During the hajj, we are going to be experiencing a lot of extremely jarring, in-your-face situations. We can ignore them or learn from them. Hopefully we can learn from them. If I may, let me tell you what I learned from the extreme poverty I saw during my first hajj.

"Our family was not poor, but by no means rich. My parents were very devout Muslims and worked hard and honestly to provide for us. They could barely provide for our needs, and we had no luxuries. I remember very vividly the physical discomfort of all these people stuck in the traffic jam.

"I also remember very vividly praying to Allah to give me the ability and strength to work hard and become financially wealthy so that I could give my family a better life and be in a position to help those less fortunate than me. And I thank Allah every day that I am able to provide for all the needs of my family and help in my small way those who are less fortunate.

"It doesn't exactly answer Shahnaaz's question 'How can Allah give so much to so few and so little to so many?' but that is all I have to say."

Nasib, who had been reserved after feeling chastised for his outburst at Shahnaaz, offered his response, "This is the first time I have ever seen such extreme contrast between affluence and poverty. Being so sheltered in the West, I could not have imagined this contrast. Just seeing television images does not prepare you for the harsh reality. However, I think if we start asking why Allah gives so much to so few and so little to so many removes all responsibility from us. I think this is a wrong question to ask. It leads us to a path which does not yield any constructive answers."

I felt very happy and proud of Nasib's answer. "Nasib, I agree with you wholeheartedly. I would suggest that we replace Shahnaaz's question with 'What can I do to alleviate this situation?'"

Shahnaaz's eyes lit up. "Wow! I never thought of this question. The hajj has just begun, and I am already learning so much of what I need to learn."

Once again, I felt very happy and proud of Shahnaaz's response. "My dear, it is extremely necessary to ask questions. It is also easy to ask questions, but to answer them takes a lot more effort. It requires deep self-reflection and discipline to metabolize the resulting self-improvement."

Fatima chipped in as she asked the driver to restart the CD player, "Sheikh Jee, I think you are giving us all an improvement overload. I think this is enough homework for now. I would like to listen to some very delightful Urdu *naats* that I remember from our stay in Pakistan and India."

It was dusk when we came out of the hotel to go to see the Kaaba. The excitement of our first glimpse of the Kaaba was so intense that none of us felt tired at all.

Never have I seen such huge crowds of humanity buzzing with expectation moving slowly in unison toward the Al-Masjid Al-Haram. As we were getting closer to the Kaaba, the *lubaikh* got louder and louder, and my heart started to palpitate uncontrollably. And yet, it was the most wonderful and comforting feeling I had never felt before.

Then suddenly I caught my first glimpse of the Kaaba. Tears of joy started flowing down my cheeks. The splendor and the solemn majesty of the Kaaba were spellbinding. My throat choked as I could only absorb the heavenly scene but could not speak. How could I describe the indescribable? How could I quantify the unquantifiable? That day I experienced the gap between description and experience.

I lost track of time, and it was only when I came to mundane consciousness did I realize the enormity of what I had just experienced. I had experienced peace and tranquility that I had never experienced before. I had experienced total solitude while being connected to millions of people. I experienced total silence in the midst of the loudest chanting of prayers. Everything happened without any conscious effort. I realized I had performed the *Tawaf* but did not know how many times I had been around the Kaaba. I had been praying and thanking Allah. I wanted to stay perpetually in this state of peace and tranquility.

I felt a firm tap on my shoulder. I turned around and saw a relieved Nasib. "Dad, we have been looking for you. Everybody is waiting for you near the gate to go back to the hotel. We thought we had lost you! Let's go!"

On the long walk back to the hotel, we all related our experience of the first glimpse of the Kaaba and performing *Tawaf*. Everybody ran out of superlatives trying to describe their individual and emotionally overwhelming and beautiful feelings of their hajj so far.

Before retiring to our rooms, Jaffar spoke to all of us, "Let us all meet at seven o'clock in the hotel lobby so that we can get a good start to walk to Mina."

Jaffar translated what Sajjda said, "Sajjda says she is too excited and would like to know if we can leave at six o'clock. She thinks she will not even be able to sleep."

Shahnaaz responded quickly, "Brother Jaffar, I have a very different problem. I am asleep before my head hits the pillow. The difficulty I have is to get up early in the morning. I get up late and then get stressed to be on time for school or work. I really need to break this bad habit. So I will use the hajj experience for cultivating the good habit of getting up on time. Count me in. I will get up early so we can leave at six."

Nasib joined in, "I must admit I have the same problem of getting up late in the morning. I sleep very late. Since I started my own business, I have realized the benefit of the old expression 'Early to bed, early to rise, makes a man healthy, wealthy, and wise.' I am not sure about becoming healthier or wiser, but whenever I do get up early, I am able to prepare for my business meetings, and that early planning and preparation has landed me some very good contracts. And in case things get delayed during the day, I still have time to recover. If I get up late and things get delayed, I run out of time to do anything about it. I will use my hajj experience to make getting up early the habit rather than an occasional necessity."

Upon hearing Shahnaaz and Nasib's pledges, Fatima burst out laughing, "Sheikh Jee, how many times have you and I tried to convince them of the benefits of getting up early? I think we should have brought them to Mecca ten years ago!"

"Fatima, I am too tired to laugh but only too happy to hear their pledges. Let us keep on looking for many more improvements for which hajj will be the catalyst. But we don't need to wait for hajj to do the right things. Islam is a way of life, and whoever practices it sincerely will become an exemplary human being. Remember, just being born a Muslim is not enough, and just reading the Koran is not enough. We have to practice the teachings of Islam."

Everybody was ready at six o'clock to set off to Mina. Nasib was feeling very relaxed, and we were bonding very well after some tense exchanges during the past year.

The women were also bonding very well which made me curious as to how they were overcoming the language barrier with Sajjda and Tahira.

Jaffar was eager to provide the answer and asked Sajjda and Tahira, "Please explain to Sheikh Jee how you overcome the language barrier. After all, you speak only Arabic, and Shahnaaz can speak only English and Farsi. And Auntie Fatima can speak only English, Farsi, Pashto, and Urdu."

Tahira and Sajjda smiled as Jaffar translated their response, "Tahira and Sajjda say there is no language barrier. They have learned to ask just one sentence in English. 'Do you speak Arabic?' If the answer is 'yes', they know that the person can speak English and Arabic and they are in business. With this one question, they have made several friends from many different countries who have become instant translators for them to communicate with Auntie Fatima and Shahnaaz. They are having so much fun!"

I was very impressed with their resourcefulness. "Tahira and Sajjda, that is simple and brilliant! It is true that once we have the willingness, we can overcome all barriers. On top of that, you transformed the seeming barrier to work to your advantage and you reached out to people you would normally not have spoken to."

I turned to Jaffar and Nasib. "We can learn from the women. We have been talking mostly among ourselves. Let us talk to people from many other countries in the world. I am sure I will find some Muslims from Germany, Afghanistan, Iran, Pakistan, and India."

Nasib complained lightheartedly. "Whenever I speak Farsi or Arabic, people reply to me in English. I really need to improve my fluency in Arabic and Farsi.

"But, Dad and Jaffar, I am very overwhelmed by the sheer number of people. There are literally millions of people of every color, of every race, and from every country. They speak so many different languages. There are billionaires, and there are people who do not have two pennies to rub together. Islam makes them all equal in the eyes of Allah."

Jaffar agreed, "And wearing the *ihram* makes everybody look visibly equal. It is only our good actions and what we are inside that differentiate us."

At times we were together, and at times we were making new friends. Walking seemed effortless because we felt as though we were being carried by a tide of millions of hajjis, singing and praying as they were walking. I did not even notice the scorching sun. We all had plenty of water from the Zamzam spring to keep us hydrated.

One thing that was noticeable was the difference in accommodations. There were hajjis who were housed in relatively comfortable accommodations and then there were a lot who were too poor and who would end up sleeping under the bridges. Shahnaaz's unanswerable question came to my mind. *How can Allah give so much to so few and so little to so many?*

I had lost all sense of time and did not know how long it took us to walk from the Kaaba to Mina. It seemed to me that I was carried effortlessly by the current of a river of millions of people.

Mina was another manifestation of the grand scale of the hajj. In the flat valley of Mina, there were white tents as far as the eye could see. As usual, the queues for toilets, food, and water were on a grand scale as well, resulting in occasional sparks of anger and frustration.

However, I was surprised with how much patience and acceptance the vast majority of hajjis displayed to sometimes glaring incompetence in planning and caring by the authorities.

As our host, Jaffar often felt apologetic. "Uncle Jee and Nasib, it is embarrassing that after hundreds of years of hajj and billions of hajjis, the authorities still overlook some fundamental requirements of the hajjis. And there is no shortage of money to make improvements. It is deeply disappointing."

Nasib put forward his explanation, "I believe that what we see as lack of planning is more a sign of how many more hajjis are coming nowadays compared to even a decade ago. Air travel has made it possible for literally millions of more people to fulfill their obligations. The most effective and the simplest way to make hajj a smoother experience would be to restrict the number of people performing hajj. But that would be wrong. We cannot prevent Muslims from fulfilling one of the most important obligations of our lives.

"I have not been to any other place where millions of people go, but I have read in the news of hundreds of pilgrims of other religions being trampled to death. They cannot even provide for basic security, let alone comfort. I think the authorities here are doing a very good job considering the tens of millions hajjis who come for just six days. In every event of this magnitude, there are bound to be errors, some of which could be categorized as incompetence."

Jaffar felt somewhat satisfied with Nasib's explanation, "I suppose you are right. There have been a few Olympic games where even the facilities were not completely ready in time. They had all the time and money to plan everything, with fewer people to handle, but this is Islam, and I do not want to compare it with Olympics. I believe we could still do a better job . . ."

I put forward my observation, "In my opinion, it is not helpful to overlook our shortcomings in comparison with other religions or other events. Whenever we compare ourselves to others, we can be motivated to do better, or we can be tempted to justify ourselves by saying that we are not that bad compared to others. Sometimes we compare ourselves and gloat at how much better we are than others. Other times we become very angry when we find out that we are a lot worse than others and lash out against ourselves or others. There is only one good way to progress— compare in order to motivate and improve, not to gloat or punish."

Jaffar seemed genuinely impressed, "Uncle Jee, I believe this is a very wise approach. If we are on a quest to continually improve ourselves, there is no blame assigned—we acknowledge the deficiency and spend all the energy to improve.

"Once again, we can learn from the women. Sajjda and Tahira have used this approach to improve the quality of our factory. We have a very diverse workforce, and all of them have become motivated to improve the quality of our products. When something goes wrong, there is no blame assigned, and our workers identify the root cause and implement actions to prevent that from happening again. They really take ownership to continuously improve. This has greatly increased the output of the factory, and we have increased our customer satisfaction."

"Jaffar, you cite a very good example of continuous improvement. If I may add, this is the tip of the benefits iceberg. You see, when we improve one aspect of our lives, we improve several other aspects. This is a very powerful and natural positive feedback life cycle. I am sure you will agree that your workers have also started to apply this technique to other areas of their lives. Once continuous improvement becomes a way of life, it improves life."

As we approached our tent, our conversation was interrupted by some loud shouting and arguing in the adjacent tent.

We went straight into our tent, not wanting to get involved in any arguments as one of the requirements of *ihram*. We were all too tired and just wanted to get peaceful sleep to set out early for Arafat the next day. But the shouting and arguments got louder.

I was surprised but not shocked to see that even during hajj, some people flout the fundamental teachings of Islam. It was a sobering reminder of the thin line between reason and misguided emotion.

Nasib was the first one to make a move. "All of you stay in the tent. I will go and find out what is going on."

Feeling responsible to make sure Nasib did not get into trouble, Jaffar followed him.

After a few more minutes of shouting, everything became very quiet. We did not know when Nasib and Jaffar returned, but we breathed a sigh of relief, prayed, and fell sound asleep.

We all set off to Arafat at the appointed time of six o'clock.

"What was all the commotion about last night? What time did you come back, Nasib?" Shahnaaz asked the question we all wanted to know the answer to.

Nasib was quick to reply, "There was this man from Afghanistan who was arguing with everybody and said he was happy that Gosama had been killed. Can you believe that? He said that his two brothers had been killed by a bomb which exploded near the queue for enlisting as policemen outside the main police station in Kabul. He said that the bomb was planted by Al-Qaida or Taliban. One hajji was extremely upset with him and wanted to beat him up and rightly so."

"But, Nasib, why do Al-Qaida and the Taliban target their brothers who are trying to earn an honest living?" Shahnaaz asked pointedly.

"Now you are arguing just like that man from Afghanistan. Don't you know? These people become instruments of our enemies. These policemen merely enforce the wishes of our occupiers. I know it sounds cruel to bomb our brothers, but they have been given ample warning by the Taliban not to become stooges of the enemies," Nasib tried to rationalize.

"Yes, but why did they want to beat him up? Surely, he is entitled to his views. How would you feel if someone killed your family?" Shahnaaz continued.

Nasib became agitated, "It is sacrilegious to be disrespectful to Muslim martyrs. They pay the ultimate price to defend Islam against our enemies. We have to accept that some innocent people will die, but that is a small sacrifice we should be ready to pay as Muslims."

For once Shahnaaz did not continue to argue, "Nasib, what you are saying does not make sense to me, but you are entitled to your opinion. Let us not argue with each other lest we spoil our *ihram*. Remember, we are required to practice forgiveness and reconciliation. Islam is the religion of peace. Let us all have a peaceful hajj. Who knows, by the end of hajj, I may start understanding your point of view or you may start understanding mine."

We all felt relieved that the flames of last night's argument did not spread any further and started walking briskly toward Arafat on a cold and crisp early morning.

Surprisingly, even at this time there were thousands of people walking, mostly silently.

In the peaceful silence, I started wondering if Nasib would really change his way toward peace or become even more hardened in his stand. One thing I felt sure of was that no one who was peaceful now would go toward the path of violence. Was this just hopeful or wishful thinking on my part?

After a while, Jaffar caught up with me. "Uncle Jee, correct me if I am wrong, but you and Auntie Jee seem to be extremely worried about Nasib's behavior. If you wish, you can share your thoughts with me. After all Nasib and I are very close, and we did spend one year together at the madrassa in Afghanistan. I may be able to help you."

I was taken aback by Jaffar's offer and did not know what I should do. His offer seemed very genuine and sincere. Of course, his observation about our worry was very accurate.

My instinct was to open up immediately and fully, but my heart felt that I should proceed with caution. As I had learned through experience, I decided to follow my heart.

"Jaffar, what is your opinion about the death of Gosama bin Baden?" I asked, gaining more time and getting more information to base how much I should open up. At the same time, I was thinking whether I should consult with Fatima before opening up to Jaffar.

"Uncle Jee, I do not advertise my opinions for obvious reasons, but I am very categorical about the path Islam needs to follow. Muslims need to renounce terrorism immediately, stop blaming everybody else, and start working on improving ourselves.

"That Afghani had the courage to say loudly and openly what the vast majority of the Muslims think. Now I am not happy that Gosama was killed. He sacrificed a lot at one time for Islam, and we should give credit for that, but after a certain point, his terrorist strategy became disastrous for Islam."

We looked at each other to know if someone could overhear us and then continued. Strangely, we both felt that the combination of the noise surrounding us and the constant flux of people around us made it safe for us to be discussing this controversial topic.

So Jaffar continued very solemnly, "At one time I was prepared to do what terrifies me today. Even thinking about what I was thinking makes me shudder. I prayed every day that I would be trained and chosen to die for Islam. I was totally brainwashed. I thank Allah every day that circumstances allowed me to escape the whirlpool of death and destruction. Today I am convinced of two things—the path of violence leads to the destruction of Islam, and the path of peace and progress leads to the victory of Islam. I speak through my actions. If I used words, I would be silenced, indeed killed by the extremists. So I have conceded a minor victory to the terrorists so that I can contribute to the real victory for Islam."

I thanked Allah for this moment and put my arm around Jaffar's shoulder. "Jaffar, I am extremely impressed with your actions and courage and wisdom to return to the right path. I will share my worries and my dreams with you later on. I am sure we will be able to brainstorm and reach some tangible solutions."

Once we reached the base of Mount Arafat, it was breathtaking to see literally hundreds of thousands of pilgrims gathered at the foothills. I choked with emotion at the greatness of hajj, at the greatness of Islam. The sight is unimaginable until one sees it. Then it becomes unforgettable, forever etched in one's memory.

Later that afternoon, Fatima caught up with me.

"Sheikh Jee, you have been very scarce. Just because we are on our hajj does not mean you should neglect me," Fatima said half seriously and half in jest.

"Fatima, my dear, I always cherish you. Even when I am away from you," I replied cautiously, hoping that I was not guilty of not meeting some unstated expectation of me.

I felt relieved when she lightened up. "Are you saying that you cherish me only when you are away from me? You seem to have been spending a lot of time with Jaffar. What were you two talking about?"

"Fatima, during our hajj I was just *expecting* some breakthrough on how to guide Nasib toward peace. I did not know from where or when or how this breakthrough would come about. But I just knew it would come, and now it has!" I said excitedly.

"What, you just *expected* it, and it came?" Fatima asked incredulously.

"Yes, Fatima. I have come across this many times now. Initially I succeeded accidentally, but now I expect consciously and invariably I succeed. I must say I succeed mostly partially, but it gives that little break which can be capitalized upon. The hope generated by the little break makes me put in the effort which leads to the actual breakthrough."

"Jee, that is very interesting. I will try it and let you know. But how does it work? On second thought, don't tell me. You take too long. I will just believe what you say. So what is the breakthrough you are so excited about?"

I smiled broadly and started, "After Nasib's proclamation that we should accept that fact that some innocent Muslims will die as a result of terrorism, Jaffar sensed our deep worry. He offered to listen if I wanted to share my thoughts with him."

"And you call that a breakthrough?" she questioned disappointingly. "Patience, my dear. He told me that he has totally renounced violence and is working toward peace. He has spent a lot of time with Nasib in Afghanistan and knows exactly how Nasib has been brainwashed. Nasib looks up to Jaffar and trusts him. Through Jaffar, we have the best chance to influence Nasib. What do you think?"

"Jee, we do not know Jaffar well enough. I am not sure we can trust him. He may just be nosey. Besides, Nasib is too stubborn. Jaffar may not be able to change Nasib's mind. I am not sure we should share our deepest worries with someone we just met."

I persisted, "But, Fatima, there are very few instances in our lives where we know enough to make good decisions. In fact, some of the most critical decisions have to be made with very little information, indeed with contradictory information. We may not know Jaffar intimately, but I feel he is a very sincere man. If he is not that, he is either a very good actor or extremely conniving and deceitful. Surely you would have sensed his deceit a long time ago." And then I paused.

"Sheikh Jee, you are right that I would have sensed immediately if he was deceitful. But can we trust him?"

While I paused, I remembered what Fatima was always complaining about me—that I try to convince with reason alone, but to succeed, I needed to add emotion.

"Fatima, if he is not conniving and deceitful, he is trustworthy. We can make a decision on partial information. After all, we have a golden chance to influence Nasib positively and live worry free. We are on our hajj, and we should seize this opportunity. Can you imagine how much good Nasib can do to further the cause of Islam if he took the path of peace?" I pleaded emotionally this time.

"Jee, I agree with you. We need to enlist Jaffar's help. Have you shared our worries with him?"

"Fatima, I always consult with you before I take any significant decision. Remember you are the one who said that by being aligned, we both go in the same direction."

Fatima lightened up with hope, "I expect this small break to lead to a big breakthrough. Even if you had started the dialogue with Jaffar unilaterally, I would have supported you. If you are doing good, no permission is required, but I do appreciate you consulting me." And respecting the customs and values of Saudi Arabia, she stopped just before she hugged me publicly.

We continued to reflect silently on our lives and pray to Allah for mercy and renewal until dusk.

On the way to Muzdalifah, while Nasib was busy talking with a group of hajjis from Afghanistan, Jaffar and I continued our talk. After alignment with Fatima, I felt very confident and free to share our worries and hopes for Nasib.

I took a deep breath and started, "Jaffar, our constant fear is that while everything seems normal on the surface, Nasib may be involved with planning some terrorist attack in America. Our worst nightmare is to suddenly, one day, find out that our own son has carried out a terrorist attack and killed thousands of innocent people. We don't know what to do and what not to do."

Jaffar started thoughtfully, "Uncle Jee, I know how tormented you and Auntie Jee must feel. This is not what any parent plans for nor should they. To be honest with you at this time I do not know what to do either. All I know is that even to think about killing innocent people is totally against Islam. Since I am convinced that the only way for the Muslim world to progress is through peace, I would like to do everything possible to promote that. We have had enough bad publicity in the past two decades."

Then he became very emotional, "The noble name of Islam has been dragged in mud. This is most distressing for me. I am motivated to present the true face of Islam to the rest of the world."

"Jaffar, I thank you for your offer to help. Even though individually we both do not know what to do, once we join forces, we will come up with actions we can do individually and together. This is the power and beauty of synergy."

"Uncle Jee, thank you for enlightening me. I feel very encouraged that by putting our hearts and minds together, we will be effective. I also do feel responsible for Nasib's actions. After all, we both spent a year together in the madrassas and training camps in Afghanistan. We were both indoctrinated the same way."

We were getting off to a very good start.

"Jaffar, you have renounced violence completely whereas Nasib still thinks it is his duty to obey whatever orders he is given by his handlers. The battle is between the Muslim terrorist planners and the proponents of peace. Nasib just happens to be the passive instrument of the terrorist planners."

"Uncle Jee, I am thankful to Allah that I escaped from the devilish clutches of the terrorists. I could easily have ended up thinking and acting like them. But do you know what allows these terrorists to control their protégés?"

I was curious to know about the experience of a would-be terrorist, but at the same time, I was hesitant.

"Jaffar, I would like to know, but I do not want you to divulge any information that would put you or me at risk with the terrorists. I am sure there must be some things the terrorists made you swear not to tell anybody else."

Jaffar straightened up to continue, "It is true that there are many things that we were sworn not to tell anybody else. But now, I have to choose between what I swore at one time and what I now know to be true. I can be bound by a false sense of duty not to divulge anything or be free to do and say what I believe is right.

"I know I can be severely punished by people who trained me, but I choose to be fearless because of my love for Islam. Of course, I will not be stupid to advertise my changed course, but I am fearless. Allah will protect me because I am working to restore the glory of Islam.

"Uncle Jee, I am very selective with whom I share my deepest thoughts. I am sharing these with you because I know we can both work together for a shared cause and because I trust you and Auntie Jee."

I was moved and impressed with Jaffar's way of thinking.

"Jaffar, you show great wisdom and courage. I appreciate that you trust us completely, and I would like you to know that we trust you completely. I completely agree with you that we need to do everything discreetly but fearlessly. There are no set rules by the terrorists, and they can decide on a whim who they deem to be enemies of Islam."

I was taken aback by Jaffar's next response, "Uncle Jee, you seem to use the word *terrorist* to refer to the Taliban and Al-Qaida. But to get the correct picture, you have to know that the authorities perpetrate many terrorist acts as well. In fact, many of the people who gravitate toward the Taliban do so because they become fed up with the corruption, incompetence, and arrogance of the authorities. They arrest people arbitrarily. There is no justice system, and many innocent people are tortured every day. These terrorist acts are happening silently every day, and nobody hears the anguished screams of the innocent victims. Nobody talks about them because these acts of violence are committed by the government. Imagine the son or brother of someone who is being tortured. He has no recourse to justice and so turns to the Taliban. Please remember that terrorist acts are committed both by the government and by those who people usually refer to as terrorists.

"Jaffar, I agree with you that several governments all over the world commit terrorist acts directly or through their proxy terrorists. It is true that some Western governments do that as well. Remember, at one time the United States was arming and supporting some terrorists who were committing terrorist acts against the Afghani government and the Russians to drive them out of Afghanistan. At that time, they were called freedom fighters. Now those freedom fighters are called terrorists because they are fighting against the Americans. It is so very confusing."

"Instead of trying to find cause and effect and justify or condemn anybody's actions, let us just concentrate on making Islam great again and restore dignity to Muslims all over the world."

STONING THE DEVIL

We were so completely absorbed in our exchanges that we did not notice our arrival at Muzdalifah at dusk.

Nasib approached us excitedly, "Dad, Jaffar, we have been looking for you. Let us collect the pebbles to stone the devil."

He had one other hajji with him. "Let me introduce my friend Rashid. He is the hajji who wanted to punish the man who said he was happy that Gosama bin Baden had been martyred. Rashid, can you tell my father Sheikh Umeed and my friend Jaffar why you wanted to beat up that man?"

Rashid immediately started weeping uncontrollably and started blurting out his sorrow incoherently.

Nasib gently calmed him down until he stopped sighing. Jaffar and I were deeply moved by his genuine grief.

Sensing that he was from Afghanistan, I spoke sympathetically to Rashid in Pashto, "Please tell us what is hurting you so much."

Rashid started slowly, his eyes staring blankly downward. "They tortured and killed my father. They raped my sister and mother in front of my father and me. I do not know if they are still being raped. I do not know whether they are dead or alive. I hope to Allah that they are dead. They were torturing me before I was freed from the prison by the brave *shaheeds*. I am forever indebted to them."

Jaffar could not understand Pashto but did not require any translation. He understood Rashid's agony.

Nasib asked Rashid to elaborate further, "Rashid, how did you get captured? Who tortured you and your father, and who raped your mother and your sister?"

"It was two years ago when one dawn the Americans stormed our tiny village near the Pakistani border. They separated the men from the women and children and started questioning them through some Afghani interpreters. They wanted to know if we were hiding some Al-Qaida fighters who had planted a roadside bomb just outside our village. Apparently one American soldier had died in the blast.

"Some men were freed, and some men were further detained by the Americans because the American officer in charge was not satisfied by their answers. At that time my father and I were not worried when we were not released because we knew we were innocent.'

"We were shocked when the Americans started roughing us up. We had never had contact with the enemy soldiers before, but their behavior was much worse than we had ever imagined. And the few Afghani traitors they had with them relished in shouting their orders. Our hands were tied behind our backs, and our feet were tied, and we were forced to lay face down from the moment we were captured until midday. We were treated worse than animals, but worse was to follow.

"My father was a simple farmer but a very proud and very devout Muslim. He was the first to be questioned. He told the Afghani traitor to tell the American officer that he was a barbaric infidel and that none of us would talk until we were untied and given water to drink.

"At that, the American officer started shouting and swearing. He kicked my father's head, and his turban went flying off. He turned his face upward and started laughing. Can you imagine the insult of having your turban removed?

"Two other American soldiers came running and turned him around so that they could look at my father's face. I feel ashamed of telling you of the further indignity they inflicted on my proud father."

Nasib patted him on the back and encouraged him to carry on. "Rashid, I know it is very painful to describe, but the world needs to know. We only know of a very few cases of Western brutality which cannot be hidden. But every day, Muslims are silently tortured and tormented out of sight by our enemies. We need to publicize their personal stories which expose the truth about the most inhumane acts against the Muslims by the self-proclaimed Western and Christian civilization. The world needs to know the real truth!"

Rashid started crying again and described the ordeal. "While the officer was laughing and cursing, the other two started urinating on my father's face. The American officer told the Afghani traitor to tell us that this was the payback for killing one of their soldiers. I cannot ever forget that humiliating scene. My innocent and proud father reduced to total helplessness!"

Nasib looked at me ruefully. "Dad, this really happened. How would you feel if that happened to you? How do you think I would feel to see you humiliated like that?"

I was too shocked just listening to what was obviously a true heartbreaking and spirit-breaking story. "Rashid, this is very bad and very sad. No human being should be subjected to such inhumane treatment. I am outraged that the Americans could be so cruel. They claim to be civilized but obviously not all of them are."

Nasib was expecting more than mere acknowledgment of the Americans' cruel behavior. He looked at Jaffar for condemnation of the Americans. "Jaffar, why don't you tell my father of the countless similar stories we heard during our training in Afghanistan?"

Jaffar replied painfully, "Uncle Jee, it is true that we heard of countless true stories of torture by the Americans. This is what motivates the mujahedeen to kill and drive out the Americans and their allies."

"Dad, you keep on asking me why the Taliban kill their brothers and sisters. Rashid, please tell us what happened next."

Rashid started to whimper but wanted to carry on. "They took us to a prison where they handed us over to the government soldiers. We were expecting better treatment from them. They were even more cruel and calculating.

"My father pleaded with their chief that we were completely innocent and to release us. Surprisingly he said he believed us and offered to inform my mother to come and take us home.

"We started to feel hopeful. Little did we know what their evil plans were."

He broke down, sobbing uncontrollably and blurting out incoherently, "In front of my father and me, the animals . . ."

Nasib tried to comfort Rashid and, with seething anger, finished what Rashid could not say, "They raped his mother and sister in front of him and his father!"

All four of us started to cry. I closed my eyes as tears overflowed down my cheeks and hugged Rashid to comfort him.

Rashid's face became full of rage as he vowed. "Allah will give me the strength. I am going to kill them all, the Americans and their puppets. They are traitors to Islam and Afghanistan.

"And may Allah bless the Taliban and their brave allies who risked their lives and broke into the prison and released many of their comrades and us.

"My father was killed during the escape. I do not know what happened to my dear mother and my beautiful sister, who was soon going to be married. I pray they are both dead."

Then he said very coldly, "I am thankful that my father died during the escape. He would not have wanted to live after seeing what he saw. Allah saved me so that I can avenge the injustice and the indignity my family has suffered. My only wish now is that I die defending Islam and killing the devils. And I have been well trained to do just that."

Nasib finished the episode of Rashid's heartrending story by announcing, "Rashid, let us go and collect the pebbles to stone the devil!"

Jaffar and I looked puzzled. There was no denying the suffering of Rashid and thousands like him. In war and in normal life, there is more than enough guilt for one side to condemn and demonize the other—to justify actions against our enemy, which normally we would abhor.

I broke the uncomfortable silence, "Jaffar, the real purpose of stoning the devil is to overcome the devil within us. But it is easier to externalize and see the devil in others. If we do just that, then the whole purpose of stoning the devil is lost.

"I do not know about you, but I really thought that every hajji would go away purified and peaceful. I can see that for some this pilgrimage will justify, affirm, and confirm their anger and condemnation of others. We all come to the same place but go away with different experiences.

"I thank Allah for not putting me to such an unimaginable test like Rashid had to face. I feel very sure that I would not become vengeful, but emotion can easily overwhelm rationality. It is easy for us to judge the terrorists, but we do not know their individual stories of desperation and motivation."

Jaffar was brutally honest. "Uncle Jee, I used to torment myself thinking about justice and revenge during my training in Afghanistan. If my sister and mother had been raped in front me, I would seek revenge. Just listening to other peoples' stories made me seek revenge.

"It was too painful, so when I returned to Saudi Arabia, I took the easy way out, decided that I would find a peaceful and purposeful way of restoring Islam to power."

My heart filled with elation. "Jaffar, you have not chosen the easy way out. You have chosen the wise way forward! This is the true message of Islam, and I am convinced this is the way to restore the glory of Islam!"

"Thank you, Uncle Jee. For me, life has become simple and joyful. I am working extremely hard to improve myself, provide a better life for my family, grow my business, and develop my country. I have simply redirected my energies to peaceful progress. This is the best way to help Islam. This is the simplest and the surest way. I do not blame Rashid for seeking revenge, but I am as fiercely determined in my way as Rashid is in his way."

"Jaffar, this is wonderful. This was the same conclusion that Fatima and I had come to. Do not spend energy to condemn or reform the terrorists. Be even more determined in your peaceful way to truly help the cause of Islam and benefit personally in the process. I know millions of other Muslims are coming to the same conclusions, and their peaceful way will overcompensate for the actions of the terrorists. Here come the women with pebbles in their hands. Let us collect some pebbles and stone the devil inside us."

As we approached one of the pillars representing the devil, Shahnaaz shouted above the deafening din, "Dad, I had never imagined this scene. Look at the surging masses of passionate people! I am so happy to be here. This is so exciting!"

Meanwhile, I felt I was suffocating, and my eyes bulged with fear. Fatima just laughed at my helpless predicament and made unmistakable lip movements. "Go with the flow."

It felt like the terrifying experience for me and the exhilarating experience for Fatima during our first roller coaster ride in Disneyland.

I felt grudgingly grateful for another forced lesson during hajj and another example of different experiences from the same situation.

After the first day of stoning the devil, I felt very relieved. Initial disappointment at my own inadequacies gave way to hopefulness that I would overcome them this time.

Then doubt crept in. After all, I had felt that I would be able to overcome temptations and procrastinations many times before and failed after a short time. What would be so different this time?

In a moment of enlightenment, I knew the devil I had to pelt the next day. Doubt was the devil!

That evening all of us gathered and shared our experiences of stoning the devil. As expected, Nasib was the first to speak out, "I have stones for all of the devils that are threatening Islam. Today I feel rejuvenated because it has been reconfirmed to me who the devils are and to stone them until they lie down."

And as expected, Shahnaaz was there to challenge him, "Nasib, I was told that we are to focus on the devil within us. You are just fixated with revenge. If you were a tool, you would definitely be a hammer. To you everything is a nail to be hammered in. I am getting fed up and annoyed with you."

Even Tahira and Sajjda were taken aback by Shahnaaz's attack.

Nasib kept very calm as he explained, "You did not hear what Rashid told Dad and Jaffar. Let me ask you, would you want to take revenge on someone who pissed on Dad?"

"Ugh, that is so gross! Of course I would want to punish whoever did that to Dad," Shahnaaz replied, looking disgusted.

Nasib continued, "And would you want to punish someone who laid his hands on Mom?"

Shahnaaz closed her eyes as she replied, "That is disgusting. Of course, I would want to punish him. I would kill him if I got my hands on him."

Nasib announced with grim satisfaction, "Well, everybody, this is what the Americans and their traitor Afghani dogs are doing to innocent Muslims. So please stop maligning those who have the courage and take action to teach our enemies lessons not to mess with Muslims."

Fatima had been listening intently and responded, "Of course it is extremely wrong for anyone to do that. But I don't think we can lash out against everyone. Nasib, you framed the questions in such a limited context which forced a predetermined logical answer. I do not know how to explain it, but my conscience would not allow me to be focused on revenge alone."

Jaffar translated what Sajjda wanted to say, "We are on our hajj, and these are very important and complicated issues. We will have plenty of opportunity to discuss them afterward. May I request that we continue our hajj in peace?"

Tahira observed Nasib feeling alienated and sympathized, "Brother Nasib, we understand your anger. I don't think we should just ignore and meekly accept injustice. I know you have enough wisdom to realize the difference between revenge and justice."

I felt very pleased in my heart that Sajjda and Tahira defused the situation and simultaneously made Nasib question his dogmatic belief. Hearing similar responses from Fatima or me would have sounded like lectures and would have just angered Nasib more. I thanked Allah for small mercies.

Jaffar looked at me and laughed with relief as he had been saved from contradicting Nasib in front of everybody. He had gained some more time to work on Nasib. "I agree with Sajjda and Tahira. Having one wise wife would have been enough, but I am blessed with two. How can I ever go astray?"

Everybody burst out laughing, including Shahnaaz, for whom Muslim men being allowed to have four wives was a very sore subject.

Nasib tuning out and becoming angry by my reasoning reminded me of when I used to become angry when my father kept on badgering me to mind the till in our shop so that I could learn to deal with the public. It is a very good life skill to acquire, Zafar, he used to say.

Later on, he told me how he succeeded in getting me to work in the shop. He got his brother who I respected a lot to relay the same message. And I complied with the same message delivered by my uncle and benefited. But other than Jaffar, I could not ask anyone else to convey what I wanted Nasib to understand.

Meanwhile, the following day I vowed to pelt the devil of doubt at the largest wall. Looking back, I realized that I had forgotten some fabulous dreams, which I was convinced I could convert to reality.

I had started working on my dreams with great enthusiasm and sincerity. However, when I encountered the first difficulties, doubts crept in. Was this a dream really worth pursuing? Will it ever become a reality? Do I have the abilities to make my dream a reality?

Because I had not succeeded in my dreams, I just got busy with humdrum life. Without knowing it, I had stopped dreaming! But no more!

Whenever the devil of doubt appears to steal my new dreams, I will pelt it with stones and make it disappear. My current dreams will become realities.

I visualized the orphanage I was funding helping the orphans to become cheerful and confident women and men with bright futures.

We all decided to go very early in the morning to pelt the largest wall, Jamrah of Aqaba, so that we could focus on conquering the biggest devil troubling each one of us.

As we were walking together toward Jamrah of Aqaba, Fatima spoke in a hushed voice, "Jee, the devil I want to pelt today is fear. You may find it strange but looking back I have been fearful of success."

I was very puzzled by her experience. "Fatima, I have always been fearful of failure. What do you mean you have been fearful of success?"

"Well, in Afghanistan, men always dominated positions of power. Mercifully, our family always encouraged women to succeed. But a lot of men resented women having authority over them. I chose not to stand for election in the neighborhood council in Kabul. I felt I had more capability than any of the men standing for election. If elected, I would have had men report to me.

"I know things are very different now, and there are women elected to the Loya Jirga, the Afghani parliament. Back then I was afraid of how once I was elected, I would overcome structural constraints against the women in the Afghan society. I self-censored my ambitions through fear of success."

"Fatima, my dear, I wish you had shared this with me at that time. I would have encouraged you to go for it. I would have supported you and helped you to succeed."

"Yes, Jee, I wish I had talked about my fear to someone I could confide in. I could have saved a lot of guilt and anguish. I am sure that you for one would have helped me.

"Looking back, I sometimes let my pride stop me from asking for help. I always thought self-sufficiency was paramount!"

"Fatima, I must say I have also sometimes let my pride get in my way to progress. I fumbled for a long time before admitting I needed help, and that it is actually beneficial to seek help. You can get faster to your destination by asking for help. Now I can usually tell the difference when I need to continue trying myself and when I would make faster progress by asking for help."

"Sheikh Jee, you always say that in order to convey your message, it is better to give an example. Why don't you give me an example of how you overcame your pride?" Fatima asked curiously.

"You know that I have always been a very proud person. This is why it stung me so painfully the way I was treated by some people when I first went to Germany. Let us fast-forward to when I was promoted to the post of account manager at BMW. I started encountering difficulties when learning the new accounting software.

"I used to spend hours at night learning functions I did not understand during the course. I knew that the new graduate Gabriele could have saved me a lot of time and effort if only I could ask her. But she was a lot younger than me, and she was a girl! What would the rest of the department think? After all I was the manager who was expected to know everything and answer other peoples' questions.

"I persevered for another week before I became exhausted and forced myself to ask her for help. Then I kicked myself for letting my pride get in the way of success.

"It is what happened afterward that convinced me to ask for help earlier rather than later. Would you like to know that?"

"Sheikh Jee, you better answer that before my curiosity kills you!" Fatima added half in jest and half in threat.

"Fatima, Gabriele was very helpful and became a power user of the software. Soon a lot of other people from other departments and some even older than me came to her for help. Of course, she felt very good about this and became one of the best employees in my department. A multitude of successes followed after I stopped my pride from stopping progress."

"Sheikh Jee, I am very impressed that once you really learned the lesson, you applied it in other situations as well," Fatima said with a grin.

"What makes you say that, Fatima?" I asked, sensing some other bad habit Fatima had wanted me to overcome.

"Well, last month you lost your way going to your friend Avrum Goldbloom's new country cottage in Connecticut. It used to be that because of stubbornness or pride, you would not ask for directions, but you stopped at the first opportunity and asked for directions. As a result, we got there on time, without stress. I want to thank you from the bottom of my heart," she said, this time bursting out laughing. "My heart did not have to accommodate the instant peak in my blood pressure at your stubbornness."

I thanked Allah and nodded in agreement and relief that indeed I had been applying the lesson in other situations, some trivial and some very significant.

"But, Fatima, my constant challenge has always been the devilish doubts that often prevent me from succeeding. Doubts have sometimes made me want to give up on my goals right in the beginning. It is possible that I did not even dream some dreams because of doubts. How do I overcome my doubts?" I pleaded.

"Sheikh Jee, I think it is your fears that make you fail. I think doubts and fears are the same devil in different guise. But everybody has doubts and fears, and some people succeed anyway. You can too!

"However, there is one thing that puzzles me. You come across as being very confident, and you have succeeded at many endeavors. You had to flee Afghanistan with nothing. You were the first Afghani to become an accounting manager in BMW. You are now the well-respected and influential imam of our mosque in New York. You have retired early because you have seven apartment buildings, and you are very wealthy. For someone who is that successful, how can you be dogged by doubts and fears?"

Once again, Fatima put things into perspective for me. "You are right on all counts, Fatima. I agree that doubts and fears are the same devil in different guise. I am also very thankful to Allah for all that I have been able to accomplish in my life. Most of all, I am thankful to Allah for you, Nasib, and Shahnaaz.

"Still, I hide a lot of fears and doubts from the public, but they are always there with me, lurking. I need to banish them for good."

"Sheikh Jee, why don't we share our fears with each other?" Fatima asked sympathetically. "We may succeed together where we have struggled individually and failed."

"Fatima, how ironic is it that one of my fears has been to share my fears! I have been ashamed to show my weaknesses, but I want to thank you for providing a safe opportunity to discuss them."

I took a deep sigh and started, "Right now my biggest fear still is that our lives will come crashing down if Nasib commits some terrorist act. Everything that we have worked for, every principle that we have stood for will be shattered."

"Jee, but this is our common and constant fear, and we are working on it by taking action. Why don't we start with a fear that you have not shared with me, hopefully less challenging. We can get more familiar with the process of overcoming fear with an easier one and then apply it to a more challenging one."

"Yes, of course, Fatima. It makes perfect sense to start with a lesser challenge, learn from it, and apply it to a bigger challenge. But fear has the capacity to paralyze us and prevent us from thinking clearly.

"My other fear is for my safety when I visit Afghanistan to oversee the building of the orphanage that I am funding. You know very well that we have enemies who would relish harming us. To be killed by them would be better than to be kidnapped by them. Knowing how well-off we are, they would demand a huge ransom. While trying to do a good deed, I could put myself and my family in great distress and danger. Sometimes this fear makes me question if I should even continue this project. Sometimes I just want to quit!"

Fatima listened very intently and gave a much-unexpected answer, "Sheikh Jee, doubts and fears are good!"

"Good? What do you mean good?" I asked indignantly.

I realized she was trying to get me out of the rut of fearful thinking by jarring me out of my current state of thinking. This is a technique my father taught me to use when I was having difficulties in school and convinced myself that I would never be good at maths. I was thankful that Fatima kicked me out of the rut that I did not even realize I had fallen into.

"Sheikh Jee, let me explain. You are so mesmerized that you don't even realize that it is you who taught me that fear is for our protection and not for our paralysis. We must be aware not to cross that fine line between them.

"So it is right to listen to your fear of safety and figure out ways to protect yourself. I am not trying to minimize the threat, but hundreds of thousands of people visit Afghanistan every year and come back happy and safe. It is true that when we hear the news in America, we get a very negative perspective of the safety situation. Your friend Muhsin and his wife Mahnoor who are running the charity are living there. Surely, they are much more aware of the situation and will guide you and make sure you are safe. You will be able to sense any potential danger and adjust your life to make it perfectly safe. It is like going into a rough neighborhood in any large city in America."

Then she became silent and looked straight into my eyes so that I could register what she had said.

"Fatima, I love you! You brought me back from paralysis to protection. I could not have done that myself. Now I will go forward confidently. My motivation to help the orphans is much stronger than any fears I used to have!" I proclaimed solemnly.

"Jee, I am glad to be of service. Like you often say, even doctors cannot treat themselves. They need other doctors," she said, beaming and stopped herself again just before she was about to hug me publicly.

"My dear Fatima, I am ready to stone the devil of doubt and fear. Let us end on a good note and savor this present moment."

BREAKTHROUGHS WITH SETBACKS

I did not sleep at all that night. The relief provided by hope that this time I will finally conquer my fears for good opened up vast vistas of possibilities. I was reenergized and fired to go forward again.

The next three days were spent performing *Tawaf* and stoning the pillars and praying. I lost track of time, and as Fatima had suggested, I went with the flow.

All the suffocation and trepidation I had felt before completely disappeared, and everything became effortless.

Meanwhile, we all had plenty of opportunity to share our experiences of hajj and the future of Islam.

Sajjda and Tahira came to see Fatima and me and brought along Jaffar for translation.

"Uncle Jee and Auntie Jee, we want to thank you for giving us a second opportunity for performing hajj," Sajjda started shyly. "It gave us a forced break from running our business."

Tahira spoke next, "Sajjda and I would like all of you to come and stay in our home for a few days after the hajj. It will be an honor for us to host you. We have learned a lot from you, and we still have a lot of things we would like to share with you, especially on the role of women in Saudi Arabia and some other Muslim countries."

Since I had not had a lot of conversation with Sajjda and Tahira, I replied, "Sajjda and Tahira, Fatima and I would like to thank you both and Jaffar for everything you have done already and really appreciate your offer to stay with you for a few days, but we already have plans to visit my friend Sheikh Zahid. You may know him. He is establishing a self-sustaining city in the desert called Al-Bahar."

This brought a lot of excitement from Jaffar, Sajjda, and Tahira. "Uncle Jee, Sheikh Zahid is one of the leading visionary people in the world today," Jaffar chipped. "Our company is manufacturing the most advanced solar panels that Sheikh Zahid has invented."

Tahira was eager to share her involvement, "Sajjda and I spent three months at his research facility and were trained to manufacture the solar panels. The sheikh came to visit our factory and was so impressed that he wants us to set up another manufacturing facility in Mali."

Fatima was full of genuine praise for Sajjda and Tahira's accomplishments. "You wanted to discuss the role of women in Saudi Arabia and some other Muslim countries. I am extremely impressed that women have already started to take the initiative. You are breaking new ground and are the pacesetters in your country."

I shared my perspective, "What Jaffar said about Sheikh Zahid being a visionary is very true. In my discussions with him, he has the vision of Islam in full glory once again, making the world peaceful, prosperous, and equal. Islam is a religion of equality. Somehow, social customs of extreme patrimony in some societies have used Islam to perpetuate their hold on power, but he uses any and every opportunity to promote women. You could call it reverse discrimination for women, and I would support that wholeheartedly to redress the injustices of the past. You could call it offensive action on behalf of justice."

"Would you mind if I conveyed a message to the Umeed family?" Sajjda asked and continued as we nodded our heads in anticipation.

"Muslim women living in the West must be proud of their religion and identity and show it by wearing the hijab—like Shahnaaz and Auntie Jee. This has the built-in power of self-assertiveness and personal advancement."

Fatima was eager to agree, "I am glad that I am the beneficiary of the built-in advantage of wearing the hijab on a personal level and helping my religion by showing the true, peaceful face of Islam to the rest of the world. I feel so good helping at the food bank in New York."

I felt reinvigorated by Sajjda's request. "As the imam, I have always implored Muslim women and men to be proud of their Muslim identity. But I will convey your personal message to our congregation and to all the other imams in the area to convey to their congregations."

Tahira was next. "And I have one message as well from all the women in my country. You have been living in the West for a long time, and your understanding of the women's rights in Saudi Arabia and some other orthodox Muslim countries may be unintentionally skewed.

"We have many challenges to overcome, and we always appreciate moral support from the West, but we need an independent, internal Islamic solution, and we are fully assertive and capable of implementing that.

"We are in the midst of a fast evolution of implementing women's rights. We need an internally regulated evolution, not an externally forced revolution."

Fatima and I looked at each other a little bewildered before Fatima replied, "You are absolutely right, Tahira and Sajjda. You do not deny but accept that there are many challenges to overcome. And we have already seen firsthand the difference between our distant perception and the reality on the ground.

"Both of you are independent and assertive in shaping your family's and country's future. I am sure there are many other women like you. I can visualize their daughters and your daughters Nagma and Shabnam benefitting from your efforts.

"It is very possible that the Islamic solution to women's rights minus the current deficiencies of the West could become a new model for the world."

I reinforced Fatima's observation, "And these solutions will be based on Islamic principles and be in harmony with values and customs of each individual country. Islam will deliver to women freedom without decadence."

Jaffar joined in with a question he knew the answer to but wanted to make sure we all understood, "Uncle Jee, what is the difference between principles and values?"

"Thank you for a very good question. The principle we are talking about is equality between men and women. The values and customs we are talking about could be how we dress. Unfortunately, like what happened in my country Afghanistan, the extremists deemed how men and women dress as being an Islamic principle to be enforced. They turned values into principles.

"They turned the clock back and even banned women from studying, voting, and driving. Where in Islam is that allowed? So the principle of equality would ensure men and women would have equal opportunity to education, political office, and mobility. How men and women dress would be governed by local values and customs.

"The sad truth is that in some countries granting these fundamental rights is considered progress!"

As everybody nodded their heads in sadness, I remembered what my father had taught me—always end on a positive and hopeful note.

"Fortunately, this is an exceptional and a temporary setback. Let us maintain faith. Freedom and equality are as irrepressible as flowers blossoming in spring." And I saw everybody smile as we retired to our tents to rest for the night.

I reflected on the miracle of how millions of hajjis had been fulfilling their duty. Despite sporadic administrative deficiencies, the authorities were able to deal with everything confidently. I became less critical and more complimentary as the hajj progressed. After all, there was no precedence in the world for being able to organize logistics for millions of people concentrated in one city for approximately three weeks every year.

Everybody seemed to have developed the strength and the stamina to endure and overcome the physical demands of hajj.

I was surprised that I did not feel tired at all even though I had slept for only a few hours some nights.

The spiritual reward overcompensated for the physical demands.

For me the biggest accomplishment was the freedom I felt having stoned the devil of fear. I felt as if a huge burden had been removed from my shoulders.

I did not know at that time, but my newly found freedom from fear was about to be tested.

Early the following morning, Jaffar came into my tent looking very sombre. "Uncle Jee, I am very worried about Nasib. Let us go for a walk.' "Nasib and I had an almighty row last night after discussion with you and Auntie Jee. We are not talking to each other. He accused me of being a traitor to Islam!

"I know I offered to help you, but at this moment, I am at a complete loss. I know you were counting on me as the one person who could persuade Nasib to renounce violence.

"And I was convinced that I could reason with him. I am very sorry to have let you down."

We walked in silence for what seemed to be an eternity while I digested what had happened and what the implications were.

Then the fear crept in.

In my mind, I saw headlines of a terrorist attack on a jumbo jet en route to New York being blown out of the sky. And a few days later Nasib being named as the suicide bomber who carried out the attack.

Fatima and I were weeping and distraught, feeling responsible, as to how our son could carry out such a heinous crime, the authorities grilling us for not reporting . . .

Then I stoned the devil.

I was not sure if I succeeded in making the fear go away. I cleared my throat and started despondingly, "Jaffar, it is true that you were the one and the only person who I thought could transform Nasib. And now that hope is gone. I cannot say that I have experienced this kind of situation before and that afterward things turned out for the better. At this moment I am at a total loss as to what to do next."

Jaffar momentarily jarred me out of my despondency. "Uncle Jee, you just said *at this moment* you are at a total loss and earlier I remember clearly that I told you that *at this moment* I am at a complete loss. Do you think that even if our brains cannot figure out what to do, in our hearts we are hopeful? Do you think we should listen to our hearts?"

I straightened up and replied, "That is a brilliant observation, Jaffar! I think we should use this phrase more habitually. Words indeed have great power.

"As far as listening to the heart is concerned, I have never quite understood what it means. But I still believe in listening to the heart and analyzing with the brain. However, the brain cannot analyze the heart. Intellect and intuition are our allies. We need to use both. They give us the whole scenario on which to base our decisions and solutions.

"But, Jaffar, what led to Nasib calling you a traitor to Islam?"

"Nasib is very incensed about the death of Rashid's father and the rape of Rashid's sister and mother by the Afghani authorities. He wanted me to help him take revenge on them and teach them an unforgettable lesson as he described it.

"I had been hesitating all this time to ask him to renounce violence and use his energies in a peaceful way. I was afraid of how he would react, but this time I was courageous and told him right away that it was the wrong thing to do. I asked him to forget about revenge and violence.

"He was convinced that I would agree with him. After all, we had both been brainwashed during our training in Afghanistan to defeat the enemies of Islam by whatever means necessary and whenever possible. It was our duty as devout Muslims to punish, defeat, and kill the infidels.

"So when I told him that we had been brainwashed to carry out the evil deeds of totally misguided terrorists, he accused me of being a traitor, which is exactly the description used by them to keep us under their control.

"He accused me of turning my back on Islam and being selfish and only interested in personal comfort. He told me to seek comfort in my wives' beds while he sacrifices his life for Islam.

Jaffar choked as he finished, "Uncle Jee, this was too much for me. He is too blind to see the truth that he is terribly wrong in his belief. I am sorry that I cannot turn him around. I am so sorry . . ."

I put my arm around his shoulder and tried to console him, "Jaffar, you did the right thing to tell Nasib that you will not support him. You had the courage to go against all that you had been initially convinced was right and to follow what you personally believe to be right. Please do not blame yourself, and I want you to know that I certainly do not blame you. On the contrary, I want to thank you sincerely for your efforts so far. I believe that there is still a lot you can contribute. I would like to brainstorm some scenarios with you."

Jaffar composed himself and continued, "Thank you for your vote of confidence in me. I hope I will be able to help you even if it is indirectly."

"Let me start with a question, Jaffar. This will provide some answer even if it is partial or raise more useful questions. What do you think about reporting Nasib to the authorities?"

"Uncle Jee, what authorities? The Saudi authorities? The American authorities? I for one would not do that. I would consider that betrayal of my friend. No, I would never betray my friend.

"Besides, there is no immediate danger. Even if Nasib were to plan something, it would take a long time. We still have time."

I did not tell Jaffar that Fatima and I had come to the same conclusion before. "Jaffar, I agree with you. There is no immediate danger. We will monitor the situation and take action if needed. We still have time on our side. I would also like to point out that it would be my responsibility to report Nasib to the authorities. I would never ask you to do that, but I am glad we are making progress."

Jaffar looked a little confused. "Perhaps I am missing something. What progress are you referring to?"

I was eager to share my newfound hope with Jaffar. "We have precious time on our side. There are other dynamics at play here. I don't know how it will happen, but I can see that one of the women will sense the tension between Nasib and you and will hound you both to make up. It will be some irresistible female force for good."

We both lightened up. I felt better as I saw the devil of fear limping away.

Jaffar replied sheepishly, "I don't know about Nasib, but the tag team of Sajjda and Tahira has always been able to knock me into submission."

I smiled and gave Jaffar another scenario, "And you may get to witness the piercing eyes and the sharp tongue of Shahnaaz silencing Nasib's rationalization. She is able to lambast Nasib and get away with it. Fatima and I could never do that!"

I can just picture her ordering Nasib, "We don't want to know what happened between you two. We are on our hajj. Don't you dare spoil it for all of us. I want you to take the initiative and make up with brother Jaffar."

Jaffar looked at me, bemused, "And he will actually obey her? I don't understand."

"Jaffar, I don't understand how things sometimes work, but somehow they do. According to us, they should not, but they do. I think you and I always analyze and plan everything very meticulously and even then some things do not work out.

"Now don't get me wrong. If Shahnaaz were to do this regularly, she would fail soon enough. We still have to do the right things. I am sure we also take risky shortcuts in our communications without realizing it. There is always some forgiveness for doing the right things."

Jaffar was only too happy to agree, "Uncle Jee, why was I so afraid? I pictured many dark outcomes. I pictured Nasib telling our old comrades about me being a traitor to Islam. I imagined them blackmailing me and threatening to kidnap and hurt my precious daughters. None of this will actually happen. I can visualize Nasib and I reconciling. Uncle Jee, I let fear torment me for nothing!"

I empathized with Jaffar, "We are all continuously tested by the demons of fear. They keep on inventing and exaggerating phantom fears and making them real for us. So we have to keep on fighting them.

"But the good news is that once we recognize that, we will be able to prevail until the next time. It is very encouraging—we just need to get up once again. We just witnessed the proof!

"Jaffar, I want to thank you for one lesson I learned, again. Progress is not linear. Yesterday, I thought that stoning my devil of fear once would be it forever. But success seldom comes at the first attempt, and even after we have succeeded a few times, we could falter. Two steps forward and one step back is more like how real life works. Let us remember that and persevere instead of panic when we have to take one step backward."

And we parted thanking Allah for energizing us.

I was pleasantly surprised when Jaffar came back that evening looking very happy. "Uncle Jee, you will not believe what happened. Nasib apologized to me!"

"Why, Jaffar, that is very encouraging. Are you satisfied with his apology?"

"Uncle Jee, I am less concerned with the apology but happy that we are civil to each other. The good news is that he did sincerely apologize for calling me a traitor to Islam. The bad news is that I have no influence to turn him around toward peace. We have agreed to disagree and be civil to each other. I can live with that."

"So, Jaffar, there is no bad news. If you are civil to each other, that could still lead to lasting peace between you two."

Jaffar smiled. "Uncle Jee, with respect, I think you are forcing optimism. We were supposed to get together for a few days of extra bonding after hajj. I don't see that happening now. Nasib will come up with some excuse why he has to leave immediately after hajj. You will see."

All of us got together the last night before we were to end our hajj to share our experiences.

Everybody ran out of superlatives to describe their experiences. Everybody became emotional and tearful when they ran out of words. We all agreed that we would want to come again.

As we were packing our belongings for the farewell *Tawaf*, Nasib came to see me.

"Dad, I have some very good news for you. You will be very happy. Where is Mom? She needs to hear this too."

Fatima overheard him and came running before Nasib could call her. "Nasib, I can't wait to hear what you have to announce."

Nasib beamed his good news. "You know how you wanted me to see Sheikh Zahid. Well, last night I e-mailed him and asked if I could see him after our hajj. Guess what, he replied that he would be very happy to talk to me. So I will be coming with you after we end our hajj tomorrow."

Fatima shouted with joy while I remembered Jaffar's prediction. "Nasib will come up with some excuse why he has to leave immediately after hajj. You will see."

Hearing Fatima shouting with joy, Shahnaaz came running as well. "What am I missing, my familia?"

Nasib was too eager to reply, "My little sister, you wanted me to arrange an interview with Sheikh Zahid. Well, I asked him if you could come with Mom, Dad, and me. Guess what, he will be very happy to see all of us. He may even give us a personal tour of Al-Bahar, the self-sustaining city of the future being built in the desert.

"I took the liberty of booking our flight to Riyadh and delaying our flight back to New York by one week. Is that OK with my little sister?"

Shahnaaz literally jumped with joy. "Nasib, I just loveded you. I will never call you a geek again!"

We were all overjoyed.

I wondered if this was the breakthrough Fatima and I were looking But this time I remembered that even if it was not, we would persevere once again instead of being disappointed once again. And I thanked Allah!

The final *Tawaf* around the Kaaba was the culmination of joy for all of us.

We said our emotional farewells to Jaffar, Sajjda, and Tahira and promised to meet again. Fatima and Shahnaaz had bonded very well with Sajjda and Tahira, and I had bonded very well with Jaffar.

I was pleased to note that Jaffar and Nasib were polite to each other although it was not outwardly apparent that their relationship had changed forever.

I observed very carefully if Nasib had apologized to Jaffar with Shahnaaz's intervention and was happy to conclude that he had apologized voluntarily.

I could not get over the immensity and marvel of hajj. I saw millions of Muslims from different parts of the world, of different colors, speaking different languages developing new friendships, and learning to respect each other.

I felt sure in my heart that they would carry these experiences with them and promote harmony with the rest of mankind. They would become better human beings for having come here.

Of the trillions of seeds of personal growth sown during hajj, billions may wither on stony ground, but millions would surely flower as time goes on. We may never be able to quantify the benefits of hajj because they are too huge to be counted.

Glory be to Islam, the religion of peace! Tears of joy flowed down my cheeks just thanking Allah for giving us the opportunity to fulfill our hajj.

A COMPELLING VISION

Sheikh Zahid came personally to Riyadh airport to greet us. I was very proud to introduce him to Fatima, Nasib, and Shahnaaz. He was dressed in the traditional Saudi Arabian *thobe* and headdress and even at his age had a long jet-black beard. He stood tall and looked very fit and trim for a fifty-year-old man. He had a commanding presence.

He was very generous in praising us, "Congratulations on completing your hajj. I am honored to meet all of you. My friend, you have a beautiful family. May Allah always bless you with happiness!"

I reciprocated in admiration, "Zahid, we are much honored to meet you. I am always very proud to speak of you and your vision of the self-sustaining city of the future with my family. I am sure they will come to discover that I have described only a small fraction of your dreams."

Fatima spoke about what she knew of him from me, "Brother Zahid, Sheikh Jee has told me so much about you that I feel I already know you. I am really looking forward to spending the next week in Al-Bahar."

Nasib was eager to speak at the earliest opportunity he got. "Uncle Zahid, I wish I had come to see you when you first invited me. I checked out your website, and I am extremely impressed. I know there are many things in very early stages of progress, but I truly believe your vision is reality in the making."

Shahnaaz had been restraining to jump in but for once politely waited her turn and then started with a broad smile, "Uncle Zahid, I am overjoyed to be here. I have just graduated from the university in New York with a master's degree in media and communications, and I am bursting with energy to use my talents to benefit my employer. My resume is fully up to date." And she then handed it to him!

We all watched aghast until Sheikh Zahid broke into a hearty laughter, "Shahnaaz, I don't think I will need to read your resume, but since you took the trouble to hand it to me, I promise I will read it this evening."

As we approached Sheikh Zahid's van, he asked Nasib to sit in front with him while Fatima, Shahnaaz, and I sat in the back. I was expecting that he would have had a driver, but he drove the van himself.

As we drove off, he started speaking thoughtfully and deliberately, "Nasib and Shahnaaz, I am already impressed with both of you. When I look at you, I see the future of Islam, and I feel very hopeful. You are the children of modern Islam, and the future of Islam is in your hands. I hope I do not frighten you with my expectations of you. After your stay here, I will let you know if I can use your talents, and of course, you will decide if you want to work here.

"My vision is a world with a peaceful, prosperous, and glorious Islam. Establishing the self-sustaining city of Al-Bahar is just one of the means."

And then he spoke to Fatima and me, "I congratulate both of you for raising two beautiful, intelligent, and decent children. I have been too busy with my projects to get married and raise a family, but if I had a daughter, I would like her to be like Shahnaaz. And if I had a son, I would like him to be like Nasib."

Fatima and I half smiled with perplexed looks and politely accepted his compliments about raising good children. I started to have grave reservations about Sheikh Zahid's ability to assess the true character of people.

Was he naively believing in the good in all humans and perilously ignoring the evil in some humans? Or was he unconsciously so confident that once anyone starts working with him, he will be totally transformed by his vision?

It created doubt in my mind about Zahid's judgment of human nature.

As I was about to stone the devil of my doubt, I stopped. Was this a genuine, helpful doubt? I felt deeply exasperated. For the first time in my life I had doubt about doubt!

In about two hours, we got out of the van. Sheikh Zahid pointed to the huge sign proclaiming in Arabic and English. "Welcome to Al-Bahar, the Self-Sustaining City."

The sheikh started explaining very proudly, "Within the boundary of Al-Bahar, no private vehicles are allowed. We will walk to one of the designated stops where a car I have ordered in advance will be waiting for us. It already knows our destination. Come, let us try it out."

"Wow, this is great. I already love it," Nasib beamed enthusiastically as a female voice greeted us in Arabic. We just understood the words Zahid and Umeed.

Sheikh Zahid was impressed when Nasib translated from Arabic into English. "She said that this car has been reserved by Sheikh Zahid. Welcome to Sheikh Umeed and his family. Please be seated. You will be arriving at the university visitors' campus in three minutes and thirty-seven seconds."

We were incredulous! There was no driver. There was no noise. It was air-conditioned and very comfortable. Nasib started timing the journey. "Fantastic! We reached five seconds earlier. Now she is saying that we should check in at the reception center, which is signposted and is two minutes' walk. Thank you for using our services, and we look forward to serving you again."

We all clapped our hands in delight and congratulated Sheikh Zahid.

Sheikh Zahid was very gracious and humble in accepting the accolades. "Glory be to Allah! I am just a tool in Allah's hands. Thousands of very passionate and dedicated people who share my vision of Islam have made this possible. What started off as my vision has become the shared vision.

"The best news is that this is just the beginning. We are on the verge of realizing the benefits of many exciting discoveries."

Then he looked directly into Shahnaaz's and Nasib's eyes and asked passionately, "So who would like to share in the common vision of peaceful, prosperous, and glorious Islam?"

Of course they were moved to action after he added emotion to logic.

Nasib spoke immediately, "Uncle Zahid, I am very excited to contribute to your vision. I cannot wait to start. I can already see so many features that can be added. For example, we could already be automatically checked in and directed to proceed straight to our room."

Fatima and I again glanced at each other in suspicion. Did Nasib really understand the shared vision, or did he conveniently overlook the word *peace* in his enthusiasm for technical improvement?

Sheikh Zahid nodded his head and smiled. "Nasib, I really like your thought process. I usually give very few guidelines and let people use their creativity in my projects. But one of the guidelines I have given is to make sure that technology does not remove humanity from humans. I think the current designer of this portion of the IRN project wanted to make sure that there is deliberate human contact to ensure an overall human experience. We call it the human speed bump to slow down technology. Let me know tomorrow if you still think we should automate the room check-in."

Fatima showed her own fascination with Zahid's guideline. "Brother Zahid, I never thought of purposely slowing down technology, but it really should be taken into account more often. I feel frustrated when some automated phone-answering services leave you abandoned. By the way, what is the IRN?"

Before Zahid could answer, Shahnaaz volunteered brashly. "Mom, it stands for the Intelligent Road Network. I still remember the loving manner in which Nasib explained it to me."

She was going to stick her tongue out at Nasib before Fatima stopped Shahnaaz with a stare.

Meanwhile, I was still dazed in doubt about Zahid's judgment of human character. I could not get out of my mind that he would say he really liked Nasib's thought process. I wondered if I was wrongly endowing Zahid with an ability he did not possess nor claim to possess.

I saw another cresting wave of hope of influencing Nasib through someone else crashing on the rocks of real life.

As we approached the reception desk, we were greeted very warmly in Arabic by a girl wearing the hijab who showed us to our condominium.

Sheikh Zahid asked us to sit down in the living room and explained what to expect during our one-week stay. "Al-Bahar is a physical as well as a social model of the city of the future. As first-time visitors, you have a unique perspective that can help Al-Bahar evolve in the best way.

"Ideally if you are able to function next week without noticing any difference in the way you have lived so far, it will be very good news. But please be very honest and constructively critical to help us improve.

"This condominium is for a family of four, and the typical energy consumption is currently about 80 percent of what is generated in the complex by solar and wind energy. You will be able to read the meter which measures your net energy consumption so that you can adjust your activities."

Shahnaaz was very impressed. "That is great. We are already consuming less energy here than we are generating."

Sheikh Zahid sighed slightly. "Shahnaaz, I wish that was enough. But we are consuming much more energy in the transportation sector. The objective is to have an overall positive regenerative impact on the environment. Some sectors may consume more, but then other sectors have to consume a lot less.

"It requires a combination of technological breakthroughs and lifestyle changes. And lifestyle changes are much more challenging than technological breakthroughs.

"Al-Bahar is a very complex and delightful project but is surely being tackled steadily step by step. This is why a lot of human ingenuity and cooperation is required."

I was surprised at how much Sheikh Zahid had accomplished so far and his certainty for the future. "Zahid, I see you have progressed more than I had imagined. Well done!"

"I wish to thank you all for the encouragement. Now if you can excuse me, I need to attend a very important progress meeting. Why don't you all come to my office at eleven tomorrow morning? I won't give you any instructions how to get there. It will be a good test of the IRN if you arrive on time without any questions. In the meantime, I would suggest that this evening you take a relaxing walk in the park surrounding the lake."

While Nasib and Shahnaaz were busy investigating and assessing the technological marvels, Fatima and I walked to the park.

Fatima was immediately impressed. "Jee, this is a very beautiful park. I never imagined such lush vegetation in the middle of the desert. I am surprised there are so many people in the park, and yet it seems very spacious. Do you think this is an artificial lake?"

I was too absorbed in judging Zahid's lack of judgment of Nasib's character to answer Fatima. "He would like to have a son like Nasib. Can you imagine that? How would Zahid deal with his son?" I asked quietly.

Fatima replied sympathetically, "Jee, let us sit down. I know you are deeply disappointed. You had high hopes that Sheikh Zahid would be able to engage Nasib and turn him around. I am just as disappointed as you.

"But don't you think you are projecting your hopes on the sheikh unfairly? After all, he does not even know what you are expecting from him. Anybody who looks at Nasib is bound to be very impressed. I mean our son looks very much like you. He is very handsome, intelligent, eloquent, confident, and successful. You should be proud!"

I answered wistfully, "Yes, Fatima, I am very proud that he looks like me. I just wish he would also think like me."

Fatima became very angry with my gloominess. "Sheikh Jee, it seems you came with immediate expectations of solutions that others would provide. Now you are blaming them for your problems, which they don't even know they are expected to solve for you.

"I think you are tormenting yourself for nothing. You are the one who says to have faith and patience. I am sure Sheikh Zahid will sense if he has been wrong in assessing Nasib. And you always have the option of pointing out Nasib's dark thoughts if you feel the need to. Everything is still under control. At worse this is a setback which we will be able to overcome."

Then she lightened the atmosphere and commanded in jest, "Sheikh Jee, nothing has changed except in your imagination. Have faith and patience, right now."

"Fatima, I wish to thank you for lifting, indeed shocking me out of my self-created gloom," I replied sincerely. "If you had not done that, without realizing I would have submerged myself into the whirlpool of my own fearful thoughts and stayed there for only Allah knows how long. However now I feel very hopeful, relieved, and pleased."

I had not been able to update Fatima about the falling out between Nasib and Jaffar. The one hope that I had of Jaffar reforming Nasib had vanished, but I knew that even if I had updated her about that dashed hope, her answer would have been the same.

I rediscovered that plans seldom work out the way we plan them and rarely ever when we expect them to work out, but looking back, invariably they do work out.

I rediscovered that any one step backward is no reason to panic. It can always be overcome by taking two steps forward.

Fatima was not quite finished with me yet. "Jee, you really surprise me. You are the wise one and coach me and guide me when I feel down and tell me to follow the same advice I am giving you now. Why can't you just follow your own advice?"

I replied with a smile, "Fatima, thankfully I am only human. It is good to be humble and heed advice from people you respect and trust. Even coaches need coaches!

"Allow me to give you an example. As you may recall our family was going through an extremely stressful period after our house was burned down, and we had to flee to Pakistan. When I first arrived in Germany, I started to smoke for the first time in my life. Even though I knew it was harmful, I started to smoke because it gave me immediate relaxation from my stress.

"I realized that I had become addicted only when I wanted to give it up. My health was deteriorating, not to mention the money I was wasting on a packet of cigarettes every day. I could send that money to my family instead of ruining my health. I had the full motivation to quit, but I was now addicted.

"Do you want to know how I quit smoking?"

Fatima rolled her eyes. "I don't think I have a choice. Go ahead, I will look for another lesson you learned."

"Why, thank you, Fatima, for your enthusiasm," I started after imitating the rolling of Fatima's eyes. "Well, I joined Smokers Anonymous in Germany. I became friends with Walter who was addicted to nicotine and alcohol. I was extremely surprised to find out that he was a doctor!

"He appointed me as his coach to quit smoking and drinking. He insisted to be accountable to me—volunteered accountability to ensure success is the way he described it. Can you imagine that? A doctor became accountable to me for improving his health!

"He would joke with me that I was twice as good as him because I only had one vice. He said he was envious of me because he had to work twice as hard.

"In turn I volunteered to be accountable to him. I failed many times and wanted to quit quitting smoking, but he always persuaded me to persevere. You only have to work half as much as me, he would admonish me.

"Whenever I faltered, he would say it is only one step backward. Just take two steps forward! You know you will succeed!

"Fatima, it sounded so simple, but it was so difficult. I must have failed at least a dozen times, but in one year, I had permanently given up smoking and regained my health. That really built my confidence and enabled me to overcome many other challenges in the future. In a strange kind of way I am thankful I became addicted to nicotine.

"Fatima, the moral of the story is that even coaches need coaches."

Fatima seemed genuinely impressed. "Sheikh Jee, I am very proud of you. What happened to Walter?"

"Ah, Walter was much more disciplined than me. He faltered only two times with smoking but succeeded the first time with giving up alcohol. He made my job quite easy."

Fatima was very curious about Walter's bull's-eye success with alcohol. "How did Walter succeed the first time with giving up alcohol?"

"Well, he was very convinced that he succeeded the first time because he made up his mind to stop drinking totally and immediately. He said that if he were to quit smoking again, he would stop smoking totally and not in stages.

"The last time I phoned him a year ago, he was proud to say that he had not smoked or drank alcohol again."

Then I added cautiously, "But he did admit that he may be addicted to coffee."

That comment gave Fatima another opening. "Jee, how many times have I told you to stop drinking so much coffee?"

I replied cheekily, "Fatima, when I gave up smoking, it boosted my confidence immensely. I only started to drink a lot of coffee so that the next time I would need to boost my confidence again, I would stop drinking coffee."

As expected, Fatima had the last word, "Sheikh Jee, just for that, I am going to hide coffee from you for the one week we are in Al-Bahar."

And we walked back to our condominium. I felt relieved about Zahid's opinion of Nasib. Yes, something else will surely work out. Have faith and patience—but take action as well!

When we reached the condominium, as expected, Nasib and Shahnaaz were fascinated with the technological aspects of Al-Bahar.

Shahnaaz announced triumphantly, "I already know how to go to the sheikh's office. I have already booked transportation to go there. Mom, why don't you come with me and we will try it out?"

Fatima and Shahnaaz went out on their first exploration of the IRN.

Nasib could hardly contain his excitement, "Dad, I feel like a kid in a candy store. There are so many things to implement. What I was doing in America is quite simple compared to the complexity of many requirements here. I could choose one of the many projects Sheikh Zahid must have. Al-Bahar reminds me of the complexities and possibilities at the Kennedy Space Center when you took us there. What is so exciting and new is that such an innovative, huge, and complex project is happening in an Islamic country."

I was encouraged by Nasib's admission that what he was doing currently was a lot simpler than the requirements of Al-Bahar. "Yes, Nasib, the Muslim world has a lot to catch up with. Remember at one time we were at the forefront of technological and social development. How could you contribute?"

He seemed to have already worked out a strategy. "I could propose to Sheikh Zahid what I believe I could do. Alternatively, I can share and deploy Sheikh Zahid's vision in any aspect of the project he would like me to execute."

Then he added emphatically, "The one thing I am sure of is that I can and I want to share in Sheikh Zahid's vision. I just hope that he is willing to give me the opportunity."

That gave me the opportunity to ask the question I was most concerned about, "But, Nasib, do you share in Sheikh Zahid's vision of a world with a peaceful, prosperous, and glorious Islam?"

He answered confidently and without hesitation, "Of course I do. Why do you ask?"

I tried to put Nasib on the spot, "How do you reconcile the use of terrorism and violence by Muslims in a peaceful world?"

He started very calmly, "Dad, you are very selective in defining terrorism and violence. It is as though only Muslims are terrorists. In reality, it is the Western and Christian world who are the initiators, instigators, and perpetrators of terrorism and violence. What are they doing in Iraq? What are they doing in Afghanistan? We are only defending ourselves against their terrorism and violence.

"We defend ourselves with the means that we have. We do not have the missiles or drones or the bombs that our enemies have. What you and the West describe as terrorist acts is a very legitimate means to fight against the enemy. We have no other means."

It seemed that Nasib had been wrestling to rationalize his beliefs and wanted to enlighten me.

"Dad, what is the difference between Kamikaze pilots and suicide bombers?"

I resisted the temptation to answer because I wanted to understand Nasib's rationalization. "Why don't you explain the difference to me?"

"Dad, there is no difference! At that time during the war, the Japanese did not have any other means to defeat the Americans. So they trained their pilots to become suicide bombers. At that time, they were considered war heroes for sacrificing their lives for their country. Today they are revered in Japan, and there is grudging admiration even by the Americans for the Kamikaze pilots.

"Similarly the Taliban and Al-Qaida do not have any other means to defend themselves and to drive out the invaders. So they have trained some of their soldiers to become suicide bombers. By millions of Muslims, they are considered *shaheeds* of today and forever for sacrificing their lives for Islam and their countries. The Americans and even some Muslims consider them to be terrorists, but I can assure you that after Islam has become a powerful force in the world, they will be admired by everybody as heroes who sacrificed their lives for their religion and countries."

I had never thought about some similarities between the Kamikaze and the modern-day suicide bombers and at the same time, I felt cornered by Nasib's narrowly framed example of similarity.

I tried to challenge him by widening the context, "Nasib, the Kamikaze pilots targeted the American navy. The suicide bombers target civilians, both Western and Muslim. Did the Kamikaze ever target American civilians?"

I was surprised by Nasib's tactical agreement before he posed more awkward arguments, "Dad, you may be right there. But let me ask you one thing. If the Americans had been invaded, and they did not have conventional military means, don't you think they would have used terrorism to defeat the Japanese?"

I answered honestly, "Nasib, that is a hypothetical scenario, but the French resistance did use terrorism as a justifiable means to achieve their end. I suppose the Americans would have done the same."

Nasib nodded with satisfaction. "Dad, I am sure they would have resorted to terrorism. Even when they had military advantage and had conventional arsenal, they used the most inhumane method against the

Japanese—they dropped atomic bombs on innocent civilians, killing and maiming hundreds and thousands of them."

I could not refute what actually happened, and it felt very strange to be put on the defensive by thoughts that challenged my worldview.

Meanwhile, Nasib continued, "The Americans committed the mother of all crimes against humanity by perpetrating mass destruction and then have the audacity of accusing Muslim countries of possessing weapons of mass destruction!"

Then he clenched his fists and banged them on the table. "There will never be peace in the world until Islam becomes powerful once again."

I was tempted to argue that throughout history, all superpowers, including Muslim invaders, have used brute force to maintain dominance. However, I chose to use the power of questioning to divert his thoughts. "Nasib, how do you believe the Islamic world can become powerful again?"

"We need to develop our own powerful offensive weapons which provide credible deterrence to our enemies. We will establish peace through power."

I was saddened by Nasib's naivety. "But, Nasib, the Islamic world does not have the technical know-how to develop powerful weapons. We will be in a catch-up mode. The Western world will take preemptive action to destroy our progress before we make real progress."

Nasib again seemed to have worked out everything. "Dad, you are too timid. Sheikh Zahid has the vision which will develop the technical know-how."

Now I became dismayed. How does Nasib keep me on the defensive and dictate the agenda? It appeared I was paying too much heed to listening to him. While practicing the good advice of listening twice as much as speaking, I had allowed the balance toward listening too much and speaking too little. What could I do to get my message across?

Once again, I tried to use the power of question. "But, Nasib, you told the sheikh that you share in his vision of a world with a peaceful, prosperous, and glorious Islam. You envision peace through power, and the sheikh envisions peace through prosperity. How do you reconcile the two?"

This time, instead of answering immediately, Nasib paused for what seemed like eternity and responded thoughtfully, "Dad, I am sure the sheikh also believes in peace through power. If he decides I do not agree with his vision, I will gladly continue with my own business venture. Why don't you clarify with him?"

For once, I felt encouraged. Regardless of our strategic differences, Nasib's offer was very fair. In fact, it was even better than that. If Zahid did end up hiring him after knowing about this strategic difference, my conscience would be clear that I did not withhold crucial information from my friend. And I thanked Allah for a small breakthrough instead of a big blowup with Nasib.

"Son, I appreciate your honesty. I will talk to the sheikh."

Tip of the Iceberg in the Desert

I updated Fatima about my conversation with Nasib.

"Jee, I am very happy that you ended on an amicable note with Nasib. This small opening could lead to a big breakthrough. I really admire your patience and perseverance."

"Thank you, my dear. For some reason this time I feel hopeful of the outcome," I said confidently.

Fatima wanted to make sure. "We have always been hopeful and confident. What is so different this time, Sheikh Jee?"

I continued confidently, "Fatima, we have continued to have faith in the principles of life. Even when we have been bitterly disappointed, we have never given up. We have learned and grown, and we have persisted. Allah is on our side. Allah wants us to succeed!"

Fatima hugged me tightly. "Jee, I agree that we will succeed this time. We will not be discouraged by any temporary setback. When are you going to speak to the sheikh? Are you going to tell the sheikh about Nasib's terrorist links or talk about generalities of renouncing violence and adopting peaceful ways?"

I smiled and replied, "Fatima, I don't really know. You are in charge this time. This is why you, not me, will be talking to Sheikh Zahid."

"Nice try, Sheikh Jee. I am the one who dishes out the medicine, and since I am in charge, I insist you are there with me. I will propose to meet him tomorrow evening. You better be there!"

"Only if you insist, Fatima, only if you insist," I replied with a grin.

Fatima was very pleased that she had booked the driverless car and that we reached the sheikh's condominium on time.

Zahid greeted us warmly, "Zafar and sister Fatima, I want to thank you both for giving me a forced break from my job. If you had not asked me to meet with you, I would still be working at the office. It has been too long since I have had a relaxed evening just chilling with friends. I hope you are enjoying your visit to Al-Bahar. Sunrises and sunsets are beautiful in Al-Bahar. Let us enjoy this sunset."

Fatima and I looked at each other. The sheikh was in a mood for a relaxing evening, and we were about to bring up a very serious topic.

At the first instant that Sheikh Zahid looked away, I looked at Fatima and moved my lips to say, "Go with the flow!"

Fatima smiled and nodded. It felt liberating to go with the flow sometimes.

But it wasn't long before Zahid himself brought about a discussion leading to serious conversations.

"Zafar, you and Fatima seem to lead a well-balanced life. My life has been taken over by Al-Bahar. I have become so task oriented that I have neglected social aspects of my life. I have become a loner. How do you maintain balance in your life?"

I smirked as I replied, "My problem is solved for me. I have the same affliction of working so hard and neglecting my social obligations. Fatima enforces the social balance in my life. Zahid, you need to get married!"

Fatima was just waiting for me to finish. "Brother Zahid, please don't burden your wife to reform you. From personal experience, I can tell you how exhausting it is. On top of that, I have to put up with mockery. What happened to gratitude?"

Being once bitten and twice shy, I retracted quickly, "Fatima, I am grateful for your constructive interventions, and, Zahid, I suggest that you reform before marriage. In fact, you need to live a balanced life whatever your marital status.

"Now let me comment on your real question as to how I maintain balance in my life. At the end of every month, I monitor if I am becoming unbalanced. There has to be balance between several of our core needs—health, spiritual, mental, and social needs.

"For example, if I note that I have been neglecting exercise during the past month, I will allocate priority to physical exercise going forward."

Zahid had been listening very intently and questioned, "So, Zafar, would you ease off on another core need to maintain balance?"

"Zahid, surprisingly the answer is yes. You may consciously cut down a little on how much time you spend at the office. From my experience, you will find that you improve both your health and accomplish more at the office even though you spend less time because you will have become more productive.

"These needs are like the four wheels of a car. They need to be balanced in order for the car to drive smooth and straight. If one wheel is unbalanced, your car will go off the road!"

Zahid nodded his head in agreement. "I like the way you dramatize to drive home the message—your car will go off the road."

I glanced at Fatima and Zahid and back at Fatima, who gave me a satisfied smile because I was practicing what she always urged me to do.

I continued with my own challenges with maintaining balance in life, "Zahid, please understand that I have to continuously struggle with balance in my life. There are some situations in life when it is necessary, indeed very beneficial for us to go into imbalance. I remember when I became the first Afghani to become an account manager in BMW that I had to spend more than eighty hours per week to grasp my new responsibility."

"Zafar, that is exactly the situation I am in. How did you manage to regain balance?" Zahid asked hopefully.

"I was fortunate to have a very good German coach. His name was Gunther. His advice was very simple. He said just be aware that you are in a temporary state of imbalance and visualize that you are feeling confident and in control. And every day ask this question: what actions can I take to regain balance?"

"Zafar, I can see from your looks that you succeeded."

I reported happily, "Yes, indeed I felt very serene, and that gave me confidence for future situations of imbalance. Believe me, maintaining balance is a continuous process.

"As you well know, the ocean of life does not remain calm for long. There are always storms brewing, and they seem to buffet us forever. But they do pass, and the ocean does become calm once again."

Zahid looked very deep in thought. I was surprised that he thought I led a balanced life. I often felt that I was out of balance more than I was in balance. It made me wonder if I was harder on myself than I should be.

Suddenly Zahid's eyes widened, and he proclaimed, "Without being consciously aware I have been asking the right question, and I believe I have already taken the necessary action. Do you want to know the progress I have made?"

Before we could answer, he continued excitedly, "I interviewed two candidates for two very important leadership positions for the very crucial next phase of Al-Bahar. I was not happy with any of the previous candidates, but these two will require very little guidance, and I predict stellar performance from them. I hope they are not frightened and accept the challenges I am offering them. After that, I will regain balance in my life."

Fatima and I were very happy in the expectation that the two candidates were Nasib and Shahnaaz but remained discreet.

Fatima diverted the conversation, "Brother Zahid, I find Al-Bahar to be a very clean, green, and peaceful city and yet there are a lot of people. What is the population of Al-Bahar?"

Zahid was pleased with the feedback. "Sister Fatima, there are about forty thousand permanent residents and about five thousand people from all parts of the world who come to study at the university and research facilities who live here temporarily. Another five thousand come to work each day and leave at the end of the day. When it is fully developed, the population will be about a million."

"I still cannot get over the fact that the traffic is so busy and yet it is so quiet! When the population grows to a million, will it still be so peaceful, clean and green?"

Zahid beamed with joy to answer this question, "Sister Fatima, what you see now has been scaled up from a population of five thousand people. The current net energy footprint of a resident of Al-Bahar is about 20 percent of the footprint of an American city. One of the cardinal rules of Al-Bahar is that there will be no further growth if the energy footprint is increased."

Then he said very confidently, "So, absolutely, the same model will work for future growth!

"The Saudi government has been very supportive and generous and has given me full freedom and authority to run the project. They donated seventeen square miles of land and a modest sum of seed money as investment. During the first five years of financial difficulties, they continued their support because they shared the vision of Al-Bahar. Of course, now Al-Bahar is financially prosperous."

Once again, I was genuinely impressed. "Zahid, I really believe Al-Bahar is a thriving, self-sustaining city in the desert. What we see is even more impressive than what we thought it would be. You have indeed converted vision into reality. This is exactly the type of leadership, innovation, and prosperity the Islamic world needs to provide. We are so proud of you!"

Zahid was very gracious but modest. "I am very honored by your praise for me, and at the same time I attribute the success of Al-Bahar to thousands of people all over the world who have been so fired up by the vision that they have made it a reality.

"What you see on the surface is the current success. What you don't see are the huge obstacles and setbacks and failures that had to be overcome. This is where all the people kept faith and persevered and worked tirelessly until we succeeded. This is their success. I am just a tool in Allah's hands in His grand scheme.

"Now Al-Bahar has taken on a life of its own, and I am immensely relieved that it will continue to flourish even if I were to die today."

Fatima and I nodded our heads in reverence. "Wow, Sheikh Zahid, what a living legacy to leave!"

Zahid smiled nervously. "I am glad you said a 'living legacy' because I intend to keep on living.

"There are always many challenges to overcome. The most urgent and dangerous threat has come about as a result of the spectacular success of Al-Bahar. Do you know what it is?"

Fatima and I were perplexed by his question. "Terrorism!" Zahid answered gravely.

"Terrorism? In Saudi Arabia?" Fatima and I asked incredulously, in unison.

"Yes, all countries are under threat, even Saudi Arabia. There are many extremist organisations all around the world. The terrorists hit any high-profile target to get publicity. The success of Al-Bahar has generated a lot of international interest, and we have received a lot of threats.

"These extremists completely reject our vision of peaceful, prosperous, and glorious Islam. They oppose cooperation with the Western world. They oppose the power we are giving to women.

"They want glory through power. They want me to use Islamic technical innovation specifically targeted to developing advanced offensive weapons, not cities like Al-Bahar."

Fatima sympathized with Zahid's predicament. "Brother Zahid, this is terrible. I would have thought all Muslims would be very proud of what you have accomplished."

Zahid responded a little sadly, "If only they knew that I too believe in the Islamic world having its own homegrown military might!"

This statement from the sheikh really intrigued me. "But, Zahid, how do you reconcile military might with your vision of peaceful, prosperous, and powerful Islam?"

Zahid straightened his shoulders and looked directly at me. "Zafar, I am very glad you asked that question. There is no contradiction between being peaceful and having military power. It is only the sequence of peace and power. Let us not be naive. We cannot let ourselves be governed by the goodwill of the mighty. We need our own power to preserve peace. So how will we get that power?

"This is my simple but guaranteed strategy. By first developing peaceful technology, we will generate the broad-based know-how and prosperity that will enable us soon afterward to develop our own military capability. We must always remain genuinely peaceful and nonthreatening. That will enable us to acquire the independent military deterrence."

Fatima was skeptical. "Brother Zahid, are you sure this itself is not a naive strategy?"

Zahid was very adamant. "On the contrary. This is the wisest and the surest strategy. Our power has to be based on deterrence, not aggression. Let me give examples that have failed and examples that have succeeded.

"Look at North Korea. Their belligerence has driven them to poverty. At best their military strength may last a few minutes in case of war. The base of their technical know-how is narrow and single dimensional.

"Look what happened to Iraq. Their aggressive behavior led to the Israelis preemptively bombing their nascent nuclear facilities. Since then they have been reliant on foreign military powers for their weaponry.

"Now let us examine the case of India. They kept a low profile and quietly became technically and industrially powerful and advanced in all areas and built their military power base. When the world knew about their nuclear capability, they were already too far advanced. They remained peaceful and nonthreatening. From a country that suffered famines, it has become an industrially advanced and a militarily strong nation—within our lifetime.

"Similarly, China suffered through famines and weaned itself from reliance on Russian technology. Now they have become industrially and militarily advanced and self-sufficient. They have the financial and technical resources to land a man on the moon. They remained assertive but not aggressive toward the current military superpowers. They used peaceful industrial might to build up their military might. Once again, a country which suffered famines, it has become an industrial and military superpower—within our lifetime."

What Zahid said made sense to us. Fatima tried to summarize his message, "Brother Zahid, so what you are saying is that by peaceful technical and industrial development of Islamic countries, we will be able to acquire the military strength—within our lifetime."

Zahid replied triumphantly, "Yes! Behind the shield of peace we will develop our industrial and military strength. Preservation of peace is based on power. Every country has the right to arm itself and defend itself. So long as we do not threaten any other country, we will become strong enough that no other country will dictate to us and manipulate us."

It struck me that Zahid's comment, "Preservation of peace is based on power" was the same as what Nasib had said to me, "Dad, I am sure the sheikh also believes in peace through power."

The crucial difference was that peace came first.

Now I felt confident to agree with Zahid. "I sincerely believe that the best strategy for the Islamic world to become powerful is through peace. I do not think there is any other strategy."

Fatima tried to break up the serious discussion that had manifested itself during an evening of supposed relaxation. "Sheikh Jee, may I propose some light conversation with Brother Zahid? After all he has all the stress of growing Al-Bahar."

Zahid started to laugh. "Zafar, it is true. Whenever you are talking to me, the conversation ends up being very serious. Sister Fatima, does that happen to you as well?"

Fatima looked at me and smiled naughtily. "It is true. My constant complaint is that he does not know when to stop solving all the problems. I have to put a forced stop on him so that we end on a good note."

I tried to protest, but Zahid spoke first, "Fatima, I request that I be allowed to end a serious topic that I started, but I promise to finish on a good note.

"I do not want you to worry about the terrorist threats to Al-Bahar. There are two kinds of terrorist threats. The Saudi authorities are fully alerted to the immediate threat of violence. It uses up huge resources of the state, but they are fully capable of protecting Al-Bahar against any terrorist attacks.

"There is perhaps a more serious but long-term terrorist threat that I am responsible to defend against. That is the threat of sabotaging the software systems of Al-Bahar. Terrorists could hack into the system and cause major accidents. I am hiring someone to eliminate the second threat—high-tech remote terrorism.

"So in either case you do not need to worry. This is the end of all serious matters for tonight.

"It is getting chilly on this beautiful moonlit starry night in the desert. Let us go inside and have dinner which should be delivered very soon."

I deflected attention toward Zahid. "So, my friend, I hear you have become a loner. Perhaps we can help fix you up with a beautiful bride. What do you think, Fatima?"

Zahid protested in vain and tried to fend off our prying questions. "I can see you two have made up your minds. Can we go back to discussing serious issues?

"Look I have ordered special camel steaks for us. Doesn't it smell so delicious?"

Fatima rubbed her hands with glee. "Brother Zahid, what can be more serious than a handsome, healthy, brilliant, and billionaire bachelor being a loner? We feel compelled to help you. Jee, would you agree?"

I joined in the gentle ribbing of Zahid, "Absolutely, Fatima. Even the best of us can get lost along the way of life. It will be a pleasure, indeed our duty, to help our friend, whether he wants us to or not."

Zahid protested again, "Look you two, I appreciate your concern. I think it is too late for me now. Besides, I am not a billionaire. I am investing all my income into growing Al-Bahar."

"Jee, did you hear that? He is a billionaire turned philanthropist. That makes it even more serious. Brother Zahid, what qualities would you want in your wife?"

Despite his protest, we could sense that Zahid was beginning to like the topic. "I don't know how I let myself be talked into discussing my private life. It is only with you two that I feel comfortable to talk about such things. I will admit that if I could turn the clock back, I would have married twenty years ago. It would have made my life complete, but I was so consumed by my vision of a self-sustaining city in the desert."

Fatima seemed to be on a mission. "Brother Zahid, if you would have married twenty years ago, that would have been the spring of your life. Ten years ago, it would have been the summer of your life. If you marry now, it would be the autumn of your life. Now is the best time for you. You do not want to get married in the winter of your life. Now tell me, what qualities would you want in your wife?"

As we started eating the tasty Arabian delicacies, Zahid slowly opened, "I am a very simple person. I would like my wife to be caring, spiritual, intelligent, and beautiful."

I started laughing out loud, "Zahid, that is four qualities you want. Do you want the four qualities in the same woman or one quality each in four women?"

Fatima joined in, "Yes, brother Zahid, you are allowed four wives! How many wives do you want?"

"I really appreciate you two laughing at my predicament. I can live with that. One wife is all that I want, but let me add one other quality— she should want to have four children!"

I replied after quietening down, "Zahid, your wish is our command. Give us time to think. Thank you for a delightful dinner of camel steak and delightful conversation, both at your expense."

We reached our condominium late that night and were pleasantly surprised that the transportation system operated around the clock every day. There was never more than five minutes wait. It was indeed a very smooth and reliable system.

We had full use of customized and private transportation but no ownership.

When we got up late the next morning, Shahnaaz and Nasib were waiting impatiently in the kitchen to share some good news with us.

They had even prepared breakfast for us. We knew what the good news was about but did not want to steal their thunder.

Shahnaaz was happier than usual. "Dad and Mom, you will be so proud of us. We prepared special Arabian brunch for you.

"Actually I prepared the brunch while all Nasib had to do was to buy the ingredients from the supermarket. You can feast on egg kebab with cinnamon and side dishes of apricots in light honey, olives, yogurt cheese, bread, and *halwa*."

Nasib remained very cheerful despite the jocular slight from Shahnaaz. "Mom and Dad, you would not believe how many things you can get from the supermarket. It is open all the time. Mom, you would be in heaven. Al-Bahar is such a lovely and functional city. I could live here forever."

Then he sneered at Shahnaaz. "Meanwhile, I would like to make a small correction. I made the *halwa*, just like Dad showed me. It will be the tastiest of all the dishes, Shahnaaz."

I was very happy to see the antics of Shahnaaz and Nasib. "It is so refreshing to see that you are still the same little squabbling children. It is always good to keep some childish innocence even when we grow up."

Fatima was even more impatient to hear whatever good news Shahnaaz and Nasib had to share. "Children, this brunch is heavenly. Now tell us the good news you want to share."

Shahnaaz started excitedly, "You will never guess! I have been offered the position of ambassador of sales and marketing for the city of Al-Bahar. I will be reporting to Sheikh Zahid. I never imagined I would be offered such a position at this stage of my life. I am so happy, so happy!" And she burst out crying.

Fatima and I rushed to hug her and could not help crying ourselves. We never expected this kind of early success for Shahnaaz but thanked Allah for giving us this vicarious experience.

After she had stopped sobbing with happiness, I consoled her, "Shahnaaz, we are very proud of you. We know you will succeed in your new post."

Her next response was much unexpected, "But, Mom and Dad, I am afraid this post is too big for me. I am not sure if I can do the job!"

Fatima and I nodded at each other knowingly. Everybody has to overcome doubts and fears.

Fatima shared her own experience, "Shahnaaz, I too was afraid of success at one time. But no more! You should go for it! I hope you have accepted the offer."

Shahnaaz continued doubtfully, "You are really confusing me, Mom. I am afraid of failure, not success. I am afraid of failing at my new job!"

Nasib cut in impatiently, "Mom and Dad, please don't waste time analyzing and explaining to her the difference between being afraid of success and being afraid of failure. There is no difference!

"Shahnaaz, I have gone through with you all the advantages and disadvantages of this job. Even you agree that the advantages outweigh the disadvantages by far.

"Even after agreeing with me you are hesitant. For someone with a lot of attitude and even more intelligence, you are being very stupid. Now cut it out and accept a most generous offer to work as the ambassador of sales and marketing for the city of Al-Bahar. After that I want to share my good news."

After failing previously with rational explanations, I could see that if I connected with Shahnaaz's emotions, she would be convinced to accept the offer.

I cleared my throat and visualized succeeding in convincing her, "Shahnaaz, you are the one who has to make a choice which could take you to heights you never thought you could reach. Imagine you are hosting a conference where hundreds of dignitaries have come to see the spectacular success of Al-Bahar. You are wearing the hijab and presenting the modern face of Islam to the world. You are actively contributing to glorify Islam. The audience is giving you standing ovations, and at the end, you are being interviewed by the world press.

"Now you have a choice to make. Does that experience excite you, or does that frighten you?" And then I remained silent.

It did not take her long to jump up excitedly with her arms flailing in the air. "Of course it excites me. I am going to accept Sheikh Zahid's offer right now!"

Amid all the happy commotion, Fatima gave an approving glance. I had put into practice Fatima's suggestion of connecting by adding emotion to reason. I could read her lips. "Well done!" she said.

Then Fatima turned to Nasib. "And what good news do you have to share with us?"

Nasib started methodically, "I have already accepted the sheikh's offer. Despite being one of the most brilliant minds, he is a very simple and a humble human being. I am so impressed with his vision that I have already decided to suspend my operations in the United States.

"Because of him, I want to use my talents to promote Islam. I have negotiated a very generous compensation package."

Shahnaaz pinched his cheek. "Nasib, my brother, you are such a geek! Why don't you just tell them what lofty position you have accepted? Otherwise I will."

Nasib finally announced, "You are now talking to the person responsible for safeguarding the guaranteed success of Al-Bahar. I am the new vice president of information technology security, reporting directly to Sheikh Zahid!"

Nasib, Fatima, and Shahnaaz started jumping up and down with glee while I joined in awkwardly.

Fatima hugged him tightly. "Nasib, we are so proud of you. Jee, did you ever expect he would be offered such an important and responsible position?"

I hid my reservations well. "This might be unexpected at such a young age, but Nasib, you are very capable and we are very proud of you."

Meanwhile my mind was racing in a different direction. *What was Sheikh Zahid thinking of when he offered this position to Nasib? Was he trying to turn a poacher into a gamekeeper?*

I recovered my composure. "Nasib and Shahnaaz, we feel very proud that the sheikh has such a high level of confidence in your abilities. I am sure that he has made his decisions based on your abilities and not because of my friendship with him. Nevertheless, your mother and I would like to see him this evening to thank him for offering you such high-profile posts."

By now, Fatima had become very conversant and enjoyed getting around Al-Bahar.

I had calmed down after digesting that Nasib was going to be working for protecting Al-Bahar against IT security threats. After all, Sheikh Zahid had just told us about his fear of high-tech terrorism.

We were alone in the car, so I shared my apprehension with Fatima. "Do you think they even run security checks on the people who work in Al-Bahar?"

"Jee, for such a sophisticated experimental city, I am sure they do. However, since Nasib and Shahnaaz have been interviewed directly by the sheikh, the security check on them may have been unwittingly superficial."

I stayed in silent thought, but as usual, Fatima knew what I was thinking. "Jee, why don't you share your apprehension with the sheikh? I know we have not shared our thoughts with anyone else except Jaffar, but I believe it is right and justifiable to let him know."

I sighed and agreed, "I am relieved that we both agree on this one. Just for once, I would have liked everything to work out happily. Why couldn't the sheikh offer Nasib the position of VP of programs management?"

Before we could discuss any further, we had already reached the sheikh's office. He greeted us warmly and asked jokingly, "What can I do for the proud parents? I hope Nasib and Shahnaaz have not changed their minds and sent you to justify their decisions."

I replied a little nervously, "Zahid, on the contrary. We are very thankful that you have great faith in them to offer them positions which may be beyond their current capabilities."

The sheikh smiled broadly. "It seems you are more nervous than your children. They have all the pressure to succeed, not you.

"Allow me to elaborate. If I may say so, I have a pretty good record for judgment of human character. I hire the best talent, and I pay extremely well for the pressure I put on my people. They will either succeed spectacularly or fail miserably. It is true that I always give them challenges which are constantly beyond their current abilities.

"We have established a very good team atmosphere. Even lone star geniuses soon realize that they can achieve more success through sharing knowledge than by hoarding knowledge. Teamwork also provides a lot of moral support during periods of hardship. I honestly believe the success of Al-Bahar is based on cooperative teamwork.

"Everybody gets all the technical training and personal coaching. All they have to do is put in tons of effort. Not everybody does, and I have had some people who failed miserably. But I set up everybody for success. They fall many times, they get up, and they push themselves and grow to succeed. The vision and goals are so compelling that they actually enjoy the stumbling journey toward success."

Fatima showed her motherly concern for Nasib and Shahnaaz's future. "But, brother Zahid, you do believe Nasib and Shahnaaz will succeed, don't you?"

At this, Zahid burst out laughing. "Sister Fatima, I really do not know for sure. If they put in the effort, they will succeed for sure. You can better answer the question you are asking me. Will they put in the effort?"

Fatima straightened her posture and replied, "Of course they will succeed. They have always put in the effort, and they have always shown a lot of perseverance."

Meanwhile, I had been formulating how I would inform Zahid about my apprehension about Nasib's involvement with terrorism. I had run out of time and just spoke what came to my mind. "Zahid, what kind of security checks do you do before you hire someone to work in Al-Bahar?"

Zahid replied casually, "These checks are done by the Saudi government. The offer is conditional on passing security checks. Normally they are done before they are offered employment. I have discretionary power to start their three-month orientation before the checks are complete.

"But you do not need to worry. I am sure Shahnaaz and Nasib will have no problem. The three-month period of orientation is in a segregated part of Al-Bahar as an additional security measure before they start their employment. Remember, they also get an intensive course in Arabic during that time, and they have to pass that.

"I am sure Shahnaaz will learn Arabic very quickly. I am impressed that Nasib already speaks it quite well. So there is no need to worry, especially about Nasib."

I realized that I would have to be more specific about Nasib, so I decided to just be blunt and say what needed to be said. "Zahid, I would like to point out that the reason why Nasib speaks Arabic is because he has been to Afghanistan a few times and made friends with people from Saudi Arabia who studied with him at the madrassas.

"We only know one of his friends from his stay in Afghanistan. His name is Jaffar, and he knows you. I am sure you know him. His company makes the advanced solar panels which you have invented. His wives Tahira and Sajjda were trained at your research facility to manufacture the solar panels. They told us that you have also visited their factory and that you were very impressed.

"Zahid, even though we have brought up our children to be peaceful Muslims, they can be influenced by some extremely angry extremists. I feel it is my duty to let you know about Nasib's possible connections with people who subsequently may have committed terrorist acts. I am letting you know that to protect you, Al-Bahar, Nasib, and Fatima and me."

Zahid lowered his head and kept silent for a long time. He spoke slowly, "Zafar, it must have taken a lot of courage to tell me this. I can only imagine the heavy burden you and Fatima must have been carrying all this time."

Fatima burst out crying as I tried to console her. After quietening down a little, she pleaded, sobbing intermittently, "I don't want any harm to come to Nasib. My son is a good boy. Brother Zahid, I want my son to be safe. He really is a very caring person. He will never do any harm to anyone."

Zahid continued thoughtfully, "Sister Fatima and Zafar, I bet you have been thinking all this time that you are the only people in this world with this problem. Of course I do not want to trivialize your situation, but I have had to deal with several similar cases.

"There are thousands of very angry young Muslims, and there are twice as many anguished Muslim parents. But in my experience, once their anger is channelled toward construction, they completely turn away from destruction.

"I can assure you that this is not the first case where we have hired someone who has had religious training at madrassas or military training at clandestine training camps in Afghanistan. So far all of them who got security clearance from the Saudi authorities have worked out extremely well."

Fatima remained unmoved, so Zahid continued, "I can understand that you are just concerned about your son. Let me propose the worst-case scenario which I hope will be satisfactory for you. Would you like to hear it?"

For once, Fatima showed a glint of hope. "Yes, brother Zahid. We have faith in you."

"So here is what I propose. We will remain completely detached from the outcome. I will inform him that he can only start his three-month orientation once he has security clearance. Nasib has to go to back to America in any case to wind down his business. If he does not get security clearance, he stays in America and does not get tangled here. This is the worst-case scenario. It will be up to him if he wants to risk winding down his business before he gets the security clearance.

"The best-case scenario is that he gets security clearance and starts his job in Al-Bahar.

"In either case, we will all have done our due diligence and be morally absolved of any responsibility in case anything bad happens in the future."

It took some time for me to digest what Zahid had proposed before I responded, "Fatima, I do not know how you feel, but I feel very relieved. We were always anguished by deferring whether we should tell or what we should tell and to whom we should tell about Nasib's training in Afghanistan.

"By Nasib being offered the job in Al-Bahar, the decision has been made for us. It is a huge burden lifted from our shoulders. Let the authorities do their job, and we will live with whatever the outcome."

By now Fatima had composed herself and saw the sense in what Zahid and I had said. "Jee, I too feel very relieved. I am sure Nasib will get security clearance and everything will be fine."

Zahid was quick to lighten the atmosphere, "Zafar and Sister Fatima, I am glad you believe everything will be fine. So please relax and leave security concerns to the authorities.

"I would also like to take this opportunity to thank you for visiting Al-Bahar because I will be flying out to Los Angeles tomorrow morning to attend the International Convention on Sustainable Development.

I am the keynote speaker and will be sharing the innovations of Al-Bahar. Since tomorrow is your last day in Al-Bahar, enjoy it.

"We shall meet again, *Inshallah*."

Zahid and I shook hands and embraced each other in a bear hug. "Zahid, we are so proud of you. This is the kind of publicity Islam needs and deserves."

Fatima choked and blurted, "Brother Zahid, these are tears of happiness. We are very proud of you. We shall meet again, *Inshallah*." And then made us all burst out with laughter. "Next time with your wife!"

When we reached our condominium late that night, Shahnaaz and Nasib were still awake and talking excitedly.

Fatima and I were pleasantly surprised by Nasib's request. "Can we have a family meeting tomorrow morning? Shahnaaz and I would like to share the report on Al-Bahar that Sheikh Zahid requested and our future plans?"

The next morning, Fatima and I were surprised at how much Shahnaaz and Nasib relished cooking all of a sudden. We sat down in one of the many beautiful green parks dotted around Al-Bahar to share our experiences.

Fatima started first, "I know how to get around Al-Bahar. It is very easy. It is a very well-planned city. I don't know all the technical innovations, but I did not feel I had to change anything for the worse.

"I don't know how to describe it, but I just feel so much at ease here. If living like this is also sustainable, then Al-Bahar is succeeding very well."

Shahnaaz commented next, "I find everything is very clean and tidy. Comparing that with all the other places we have been, I would be afraid to drop litter here.

"I did not notice before, but almost all the women wear the abaya. Very few wear the full-veiled niqab to cover their face with just their eyes showing. I know there is a large percentage of non-Muslim women in Al-Bahar, and they are not required to wear the abaya. All that is required of them is to dress modestly. So I can only conclude that they wear the abaya voluntarily and feel comfortable wearing it.

"I just loved browsing in all the fashion shops for women. I can certainly say that devout need not mean drab. What beautiful combinations of elegance and modesty!

"However, I do find it a little too quiet. I am sure that once the novelty of newness wears off, I will find Al-Bahar boring. No discos!"

She concluded a little sadly, "I suppose I will have to invent other excitement."

I gave my assessment of Al-Bahar, "I was a bit preoccupied with other things to pay detailed attention, but I agree with Fatima's experience of Al-Bahar.

"I did notice all the various international gardens. I particularly enjoyed strolling around the rose garden with different kinds and colors of roses blooming and the Japanese garden in the middle of the desert!

"Of course I enjoyed praying in some of the mosques in the city.

"I found Al-Bahar to be very busy but strangely quiet and peaceful. I would love to live here."

Nasib started in an animated way, "I think all of you have described just the tip of the iceberg in the desert. There is so much more to marvel at below the surface.

"Do you realize that for some of the results you see how many things have to function correctly and in unison? What you are experiencing is simplicity on the far side of complexity of Al-Bahar."

Shahnaaz interrupted him, this time gently for once, "Excuse me, Nasib, but I do not understand what you mean about simplicity and the far side of complexity."

Fatima and I did not know either but were glad that Shahnaaz had the courage to ask instead of pretend like us that we knew.

Nasib was kind and generous in explaining, "You probably did not even think about where the water used in Al-Bahar came from. It is very pure and tastes better than the typical bottled water. You just turned on the tap and drank it or showered with it. This is simplicity.

"I have done some research on the water supply of Al-Bahar. It is pumped from deep under the stony desert. Why it is so pure is that it is rainfall accumulated from centuries ago. However, there is a finite supply. "So the water is purified and recycled in Al-Bahar. At the moment, almost 70 percent is recycled. Compare that to any other modern city where the water is just consumed and almost none is recycled.

"The energy used to purify the water is from solar and wind power. So the whole water supply of Al-Bahar is self-sustaining!

"But the purification system is based on extremely complex technology. The system has been developed by the scientists in Al-Bahar and is the most revolutionary and advanced system in the world and is internationally patented. Some large cities around the world have already signed contracts with Al-Bahar to transfer the technology and to provide advice to implement the self-sustaining water supply.

"This is the far side of self-sustaining complexity which gives you the simplicity to just turn the tap and enjoy safe and clean water without the fear of it ever running out."

I was very impressed and said what everybody thought. "This is a matter of great pride for Muslims all over the world. Here we are making great advances in yet another field by universities and industries in an Islamic country. What is even more encouraging is that this is just the beginning."

Nasib nodded his head with great satisfaction. "I have only investigated the water supply sustainability, but everywhere I look, there is much more to discover than what can be seen on the surface.

"I can't wait to start. I am very passionate to contribute to the advancement of the Islamic world. This is why I say Al-Bahar is just the tip of the self-sustaining iceberg in the desert!"

Fatima added another observation, "Nasib has been looking at sophistication. Let me share with you one small thing done well. You may recall the concept of human speed bump to slow down technology to give it a human touch. Well, I think this small thing is a very big thing. I am sure there must be many more small things."

Nasib seemed impatient to share his plans to start his new assignment. "Yes, Mom. As I said before you have just seen the tip of the iceberg. Now who is interested to know my plan?"

He continued very enthusiastically, knowing what the answer would be, "Well, Shahnaaz and I leave for New York tomorrow. I am going to let the bank know that I propose to terminate my contract with them in three months.

"I will make sure that I leave on very good terms. I have some very good and capable employees who are quite capable to continue on their own. I believe the bank will be quite pleased with the continuity.

"After that I will use all my mental, physical, and financial resources to promote Islam."

His next statement really alarmed me. "My first priority is to help my friend Rashid who I met during the hajj to set up a charity to help the families of the mujahedeen who have been murdered by the Americans and their traitorous Afghani allies."

The whole meeting suddenly took on a very serious tone. Fatima questioned nervously, "But, Nasib, how can you be sure that the money you donate will be used for a good cause?"

Nasib retorted tersely, "Helping the families of the mujahedeen martyrs is always a good cause. How can you and Dad be sure that the charities you are funding are using the funds properly?"

Fatima and I glanced at each other and signalled with our eyes not to answer.

I spoke about our plans, "Nasib, our causes are dear to us. We have changed our plans slightly. Fatima will be joining me for my trip to Kabul one day after your departure to New York. I want to check on the progress made with the charity my friends Muhsin and Mahnoor are running, and Fatima wants to meet her childhood friend Wazeera who is running a girls' school in a remote village near Jalalabad."

Fortunately for us Shahnaaz made the atmosphere brighter by grinning. "It seems I am the only one who is not supporting any charities, but you also know that charity begins at home. How about being charitable to me? I am a poor, jobless student looking for employment. Oops, forget it!

"Well, I have very little to prepare physically when I return to New York, but I will prepare myself mentally for the new and exciting position as the ambassador of sales and marketing for Al-Bahar. I have the added responsibility of representing the modern Muslim woman. I am looking forward to the pressure and the prestige!"

I was relieved that we ended our family meeting amicably.

We spent the rest of the day strolling around Al-Bahar. I was shocked when Fatima started packing at night.

"Fatima, my dear, when did you do all this shopping? I think we are going to need another suitcase!"

She replied sheepishly, "Sheikh Jee, when I asked you to come shopping with me this evening, you declined. You should have come with me. Al-Bahar has huge shopping centers. I could not resist buying gifts to give to our relatives and friends in Afghanistan."

Then she started laughing. "Sheikh Jee, since you were not there to stop me, it's your fault. Meanwhile, I was proactive and bought an extra suitcase. Could you pass it to me please?"

I shook my head as I passed the big new suitcase. "Fatima, it is always a question of balance. You have to balance generosity with common sense. Individually everything looks reasonable, but when you put it all together, it becomes too much."

She continued packing nonchalantly. "Jee, everything was balanced and reasonable until I started buying gifts for your family and friends."

Then she conceded smilingly, "But my wise Sheikh Jee, I do understand, and next time I will look at everything together as well as individually. This way I will not go overboard buying too many gifts. And there are some of the same gifts we could buy in Kabul and help the Afghani economy."

I brought up the subject of Nasib wanting to contribute to a charity of his choice. "Fatima, what do you think of Nasib wishing to contribute to the charity for helping families of mujahedeen killed in action?"

Her forehead wrinkled as she replied, "I am not happy about it, but once your loyalties and sympathies are with the mujahedeen, it is only natural that you would want to help their families.

"We definitely do not support the mujahedeen, but we cannot deny that there are millions of people who sincerely sympathize with their cause. They are soldiers just as much as the American, NATO, and Afghan army soldiers. The only difference is that they are not listed in their army, but everybody knows them, including their supporters and their enemies. This is not a conventional war, but a war nonetheless."

I continued to listen intently to some explanations I had never considered before.

"Jee, I know it is jarring to think this way, but what is the difference between an Afghani soldier using arms at his disposal to kill the mujahedeen soldiers and a mujahedeen soldier killing Afghani soldiers using arms at his disposal?"

I rubbed my forehead hard as I tried to answer her question and came to the same conclusion as Nasib. "Fatima, I know the only difference is the arms at their disposal. The only effective weapons the mujahedeen have at their disposal are the roadside bombs and the suicide bombs. So they use these weapons and tactics, and we call them terrorists.

"The only thing I am convinced of is that the motives and tactics of the mujahedeen are totally wrong and counterproductive to Islam, and that is why I am working so hard to find wiser ways to succeed."

Then I relaxed and confidently proclaimed my firm conviction. "Wisdom has a far better chance of success than violence. Fatima, we will succeed with wisdom."

Fatima spoke, feeling relieved, "Jee, we have had a wonderful stay in Al-Bahar, and there are so many good things happening here. Let us be energized by that than torment ourselves with things totally beyond our control."

I hugged her tightly. "Fatima, I love you for focusing on the positive. Yes, let us be energized by the vision of Al-Bahar. There is indeed so much under the tip of the sustainable iceberg in the desert!"

NOSTALGIC RETURN TO AFGHANISTAN

"There they are, Fatima, my friend Muhsin and his wife Mahnoor, still looking young. It is so good to be back in Afghanistan for the first time since we had to flee twenty-seven years ago," I said excitedly as we came out from customs.

Muhsin and I greeted each other like long-lost brothers. "Muhsin, I am extremely glad to see you and Mahnoor. Let me introduce you to Fatima."

Meanwhile, even though they had never known each other before, Fatima and Mahnoor had already hugged each other and started crying as though they had been reunited after years of separation. I was bemused and impressed at how naturally and spontaneously the women connected with each other.

After Fatima and Mahnoor had composed themselves, Muhsin addressed us very respectfully, "Brother Umeed and sister Fatima, we are much honored to host your stay in Afghanistan. We insist that you stay with us throughout your visit in Kabul. Mahnoor and I will do everything to make your stay safe and comfortable. Our driver is ready to take you to our humble home. Let us proceed."

As we walked toward the car, I turned to Muhsin to finally introduce Fatima. "Muhsin, this is my dear wife Fatima. We have now been married thirty-one years, and Allah has blessed us with two beautiful children, our son Nasib and daughter Shahnaaz.

"Fatima, this is my dear friend who I always talk about. Do you remember the terrorist bomb which exploded in Kabul's main bus station a year before our house was firebombed? We met in the city hospital when I went to visit my uncle who had been injured by the terrorist bomb. Muhsin had come to visit his parents who had been severely injured in the same bomb blast. My uncle survived, but unfortunately, Muhsin's parents both died a few days later. We have always kept in touch with each and have a lot to catch up on."

It was a cool and bright afternoon. The hustle and bustle of Kabul was a stark contrast to the peace and order of Al-Bahar. Even after twenty-seven years, the sights and smells were comfortably familiar.

One thing that had changed for the worse was the traffic and the resulting pollution.

The car turned out to be a beat-up van without any windows. We all sat in the back on hard wooden benches facing each other— Muhsin and me on one bench and Fatima and Mahnoor on the other. Instinctively, Fatima and I tried to reach to put on our safety belts. There were none!

Very soon, after we had set off, our driver sounded his horn and braked hard to avoid hitting a donkey pulling a cart. Fatima almost fell onto the floor of the van and looked shocked. Muhsin tried to calm her down. "Sister Fatima, please don't worry. Our driver Ehsan is very experienced. He sharpened his driving skills in Karachi."

Fatima was not impressed, so Mahnoor put in the soothing words. "Muhsin Jee, please tell Ehsan to drive more carefully. Sister Fatima, we know you have come to Kabul after twenty-seven years, and you are not used to the chaotic traffic. Please rest assured you will get used to the order underneath the chaos."

She squeezed Fatima's hand and smiled. "You will be safe in Afghanistan. Allah will keep you safe!"

That connection with Fatima's emotions relaxed her, and she spoke after composing herself, "I have full confidence that we will be safe with you and Brother Muhsin."

After spending more time stuck in the traffic than moving, the van turned onto a dusty unpaved road. The potholes and what seemed like reckless speed of the van combined to make our heads almost hit the roof of the car a number of times.

I could sense that Muhsin and Mahnoor were feeling embarrassed that Fatima and I were being subjected to totally unexpected and jarring experiences. After all, Muhsin had insisted that we stay with them while we were in Kabul.

In return, Fatima and I were being too polite to complain. After all, what could we do? But even more to the point, what could Muhsin and Mahnoor do?

As they welcomed us to their home very warmly, we could see that it was very small with a small kitchen on one end of what was their sitting room. There was another adjoining room which was supposedly their bedroom.

One thing that pleasantly struck us was that it was very clean, tidy, and sparse. What a contrast with the dusty, dirty, and cluttered road outside.

Their genuine hospitality made us overlook the many shortcomings of our comfort, at least temporarily. While Fatima started helping Mahnoor with preparing tea and showing family photographs of our hajj, Muhsin started updating me with the progress made on the orphanage I was funding.

When the women joined us, Muhsin started explaining the security situation in Kabul, "Brother Umeed and sister Fatima, by following a few safety instructions, you will be safe and secure. I do not want to alarm you, but it is a very different Kabul since you left twenty-seven years ago.

"It was dangerous then, but you knew all the warring groups. You knew who your enemies were. It is much more complex now. You have the various Taliban groups, Al-Qaida groups, drug smugglers, warlords, and gangsters. Alliances shift unpredictably. And of course, you have the Americans, British, Russians, Pakistanis, and many other foreign countries backing proxy factions to maintain their interests.

"Storm clouds gather suddenly on a clear day and rain death and destruction on targeted victims as well as innocent bystanders. And sometimes innocent bystanders are the targeted victims."

Fatima's eyes widened with fear. "How do people live their life under this ever-present danger?"

Muhsin replied casually, "Unfortunately, Afghans have become used to living with violence. They go about doing their everyday routines like you do in America—waking up, going to work, school, playing, shopping, and sleeping.

"You can call it fatalistic acceptance, but everybody realizes that they could be victims of terrorist attacks anytime. We all have to die one way or the other. We thank Allah for every day that we are alive and continue making the best of our lives."

I interjected politely to change the direction of the conversation, "So, Muhsin, please tell us what we need to do so that we can keep on living and do the many good things we plan to do."

Muhsin smiled at my impatience. "Brother Umeed and sister Fatima, I apologize for dwelling on doom and gloom.

"All you have to do is to dress as the locals do and stay with us! I know you have many relatives and friends. It will be safer for them to meet you at our house. That is all!"

I was very surprised at the simplicity of his requirements for our safety. "Blend in and don't wander alone. Our friends and relatives will meet us at your home. We can definitely do that. Is that all?"

Mahnoor replied happily, "Yes, that is all. I have some dresses ready for both of you. They are used dresses, but I have cleaned them. I am sure they will fit you reasonably well. I believe they will be more comfortable than what you are wearing now.

"You are in very good hands. Now please relax and let us enjoy eating special dishes I have prepared for you. I just guessed that you will find the piping hot lamb kebabs, Kabuli rice pulao followed by Shir-Berenj rice pudding very delicious on a cold, clear night."

The food was indeed very delicious. "Mahnoor and Muhsin, you do not know how nostalgic this is for us. We thank you for the delightful conversation and the Afghan delights served with Afghan hospitality."

While the women were cleaning up, Muhsin called me aside discreetly, "Brother Umeed, let me tell you what measures we have implemented to preserve the safety of the orphanage and all the people who work there.

"Our mission is to keep a low profile, remain neutral, and deliver high-impact aid with care and honesty.

"Keeping a low profile is the key. Of course, we are very devout Muslims by nature, and because the orphanage is run by the local Afghanis, we have not attracted the attention of the extremists.

"Then there are some elementary precautions we take. As you can see, the van has no windows so nobody knows what or who is inside. You may have realized that it is neither heated nor air-conditioned and looks quite old. This discomfort is a small price to pay for us to fulfil our purpose undisturbed."

I had to interrupt Muhsin because I was genuinely impressed with his wise strategy, "Muhsin, you are just confirming why I have so much faith in you and Mahnoor and fund the orphanage with the knowledge that every cent is spent honestly. Please continue."

"Brother Umeed, thank you for your trust and your continued financial contributions. When we go to the orphanage tomorrow, you will see the same strategy deployed. We have kept the outside as it was—old and dilapidated. All the improvements have been on the inside. Once inside I hope you will see that it is very organized, clean, tidy, and cheerful."

I smiled and hugged him tightly. "Muhsin, you just described your house! Without seeing the orphanage, I can tell you that I will see what you are describing."

After an exhausting day, Fatima and I finally got ready to go to bed. Fatima rubbed her hands and tried to warm them with her breath.

"Jee, I had forgotten how cold it can get here at night. Where is the heater?"

I started to laugh. "Fatima, there are two heaters in the room. You will sleep very comfortably." Then I pointed to myself and the blanket on the bed.

Fatima pursed her lips trying hard not to laugh. "Sheikh Jee, just get into bed. I am too tired."

As we cuddled, I could not resist teasing her, "Fatima, if you had to choose just one heater, which one would you choose?"

This time she burst out laughing and cupped her lips lest Muhsin and Mahnoor heard us.

Then she pulled the blanket from me. "Sheikh Jee, you sleep in the cold. And if you cause any more commotion, you will have to sleep on the floor!"

I continued my antics and pretended to be shivering uncontrollably until Fatima relented, hissing and laughing at the same time. "Jee, you are lucky that you had deposited a lot of goodwill in your bank account. Be very careful now because you have very little left."

In the morning, we were woken by the melodious chanting emanating from the minaret. We were surprised that it was a real muezzin calling the faithful to the dawn prayer.

We walked quietly to the mosque with Muhsin and Mahnoor on a cold and crisp morning. It felt very peaceful, and I felt so nostalgic that tears started flowing down my cheeks. It felt so good to be back in Afghanistan, to be home.

After returning to the house, Muhsin started preparing for the day at the orphanage while Mahnoor prepared a special breakfast for us. Fatima and I went to the small courtyard at the back of their house and sat in the sun to soak up some warmth.

We were feeling very relaxed after the morning prayers. Fatima started the conversation, "Jee, this morning I was going to ask you if from today onward we should stay at a hotel. I thank Allah that we could stay at a five-star hotel in Kabul for the duration of our visit without thinking about the expenses. But I am not sure anymore."

To confirm my suspicion, I asked Fatima, "Why do you believe we should stay at the hotel?"

Fatima replied readily, "Jee, I have become spoiled by the creature comforts of America. We used to live in Afghanistan oblivious of the filth and chaos of the surroundings. I know it is our country, but it is very hard to get used to this, especially if we have the choice to live in the cocooned comfort of a five-star hotel in Kabul."

I empathized with her, "Look, Fatima, I am even more of a creature of comfort than you are. I find everything very unhygienic here. The open sewers stink, and I felt like throwing up a few times. I am tempted to stay at the hotel myself, but why aren't you sure anymore?"

Fatima answered in a hushed voice, "What if they feel offended? After all, this is their way of life!"

"But the real reason is that Muhsin and Mahnoor are very hospitable. They are so simple and serene. I don't know how to explain, but I feel very comfortable here."

I rubbed my confused forehead. "Fatima, you just said that you are a creature of comfort, and yet you say you feel comfortable in their filthy neighborhood."

Fatima started to explain, "Jee, can you smell the sweet *roht* that Mahnoor is preparing? Can you smell the aroma of the *qaymac* chai wafting around us? In between the malodours of the neighborhood, there are delicate smells which soothe my senses.

"The simplest things we experience here make me very nostalgic. We cannot experience them anywhere else. This is where we grew up. It is our country, our people.

"But most of all it is the loving hospitality and simplicity of Mahnoor and Muhsin that I believe overcompensates for the lack of physical comfort.

"I may encounter some jarring event that could change my mind, but for now I would feel comfortable living with them."

I offered my opinion, "Fatima, I think I am even queasier than you when it comes to hygiene. I am not sure if I could get used to living with them. The stink from the public toilets we have to use almost made me vomit.

"When we were living in Kabul, our house was sanitary and clean, and we had a private toilet, but this is really a huge contrast.

"You are right that Muhsin and Mahnoor are very good hosts and do everything in their control to make us feel at home.

"They have no influence on the sanitation in Kabul, the chaos of the traffic, the noise, the pollution, and the sudden interruption of water and electricity.

"However they are extremely good at what they can control. Their home is clean and tidy and hygienic. As soon as you enter through their door, you enter a peaceful oasis of tranquility.

"To tell you the truth, my motivation to stay with them is to find out firsthand how Afghanis live.

"Do you remember one politician who lived in a cardboard box on the rough streets of New York? He wanted to experience what it was like for the homeless people so that he could serve them better. He got elected. I admired him and always wondered how I would fare living in poverty."

Fatima looked stunned. "That is a very good challenge. I remember my grandmother always framed something unpleasant that she wanted us to do in the form of a challenge. Jee, I agree that we should stay with Mahnoor and Muhsin while we are in Kabul."

I straightened my shoulders. "Your grandmother was very wise. Since experiencing the life of poor Afghanis has now become a challenge, I am in for the exciting challenge!"

Fatima still looked a little troubled. "Jee, there is one thing I feel uncomfortable with. How do we compensate Muhsin and Mahnoor for the extra expense they are incurring because we will be staying with them?"

I smiled and answered, "I have thought about that, and I have two suggestions. We know that they will not ask for any compensation and will not accept any direct compensation. This is how Afghan hospitality works.

"However, we will find indirect ways to pay them. To donate money to the orphanage is one way, but to pay them is going to be a challenge. We will have to be creative."

Fatima's responded excitedly, "Why don't you get the van repaired? Get the engine tuned, install new tires and new brakes, get the heating repaired, put in padded seats, and get the suspension changed. This will all be for our comfort of course!"

I was impressed, "Fatima, this is an excellent idea. You solved this challenge with creativity. And with that, you have created synergy. Do you want to know how?

"We will find out how much it would cost to stay in the best hotel in Kabul. Then we will donate all the money we save by staying with Muhsin and Mahnoor to the orphanage. You may not realize it, but the luxury hotels in Kabul are more expensive than comparable five-star hotels in New York."

Fatima was very complimentary. "Sheikh Jee, that is very synergistic. We can meet our challenge of living like the poor people of Kabul and benefit the orphanage at the same time."

And then I saw her cheeky smile. "Jee, don't you think that Muhsin and Mahnoor may need some privacy? I suggest we spend two nights a week at the hotel. There is no Internet or phone in their house. You will be able to monitor our rental properties and all the administrative stuff that you do. Mostly it is to give some privacy to Muhsin and Mahnoor, of course."

I pinched her cheeks and nodded my head. "That is very thoughtful of you, Fatima. Of course, Muhsin and Mahnoor need some privacy!"

"Oh, there is one other little benefit of your suggestion. We will ask all our friends and relatives to meet us in the hotel. It is alright for us to stay with Muhsin and Mahnoor, but I would not want to impose on them to entertain our friends and relatives as well.

"This will also address Muhsin's security concerns for us. Since all the foreigners stay there, it will be very safe for them and us."

Feeling very pleased with our brainstorming, we followed the sweet aromas of Mahnoor's cooking. All of us sat down to relish the hot and delicious Afghan breakfast on a cold and crisp morning before leaving to see the orphanage for the very first time.

On the way to the orphanage, Muhsin asked Mahnoor to tell us how the idea of the orphanage became reality.

Mahnoor started sadly, "We were married one month after Muhsin's parents died. He was very saddened by the plight of a three-year-old boy at the same hospital who suffered severe head injuries and a girl who had severe eye injuries. The terrorists had packed nails in the bomb for maximum damage. Both her eyes had nails in them. They were found beside each other, and later he learned that they were twins. Nobody came to claim them.

"It was impossible to identify the victims from thousands of body parts. The authorities could not identify the parents of the children. Muhsin thought that like him and his parents, the children's parents had come from some poor, remote village to earn a meager living and had no family in Kabul.

"With the little money he earned by driving a truck, he paid for their medical expenses. The girl died two weeks later, and the boy remained in a coma.

"The day after our wedding, Muhsin took me to the hospital to see the boy. Miraculously, the boy had gained consciousness. It broke our hearts when he started crying out for his parents and his sister, especially his sister. Where is my sister Noor? He would ask.

"How terribly ironic! Her parents must have named her Noor because they thought she was the light of their life. And the terrorists extinguished that light and life forever."

Fatima consoled Mahnoor as she continued while crying, "We promised that day that we will care for him until someone came to claim him, but no one came to claim him!

"We named him Zebadiyah which as you know means Allah's gift in Arabic and raised him as our son. He just completed his medical degree in England and is specializing in caring for mentally handicapped children. He wants to come back to Afghanistan and help us with the orphanage. He is such a good boy, our Zebadiyah. He is our eternal inspiration for establishing the orphanage!"

By this time we were all crying. I spoke after clearing my throat, "Mahnoor and Muhsin, you two are the perfect example of selfless caring. May Allah always give you the energy to continue your good deeds. Fatima and I are blessed to be a small part of your contribution to rebuild our beautiful but war-torn country."

Muhsin wiped his eyes and continued in a choking voice, "It is with generous donations from people like you that we are able to carry on.

You are one of the biggest donors, and you have used your good name to persuade others to donate from America, Australia, Germany, and other European countries.

"We started raising Zebadiyah in our home. Word soon spread about the tragic story of Zebadiyah and of our good deed. People in the neighborhood started donating small sums of money to help us raise him. "I continued to work as a truck driver, and Mahnoor started to work sewing clothes for the affluent Afghani women. We kept all the donations for Zebadiyah's education. There were no schools in our remote villages, so Mahnoor and I never had formal schooling. We are both uneducated, but we vowed that Zebadiyah would get the best education.

"Unfortunately, as you know there are terrorist attacks in Afghanistan all the time. Two years after we started caring for Zebadiyah, the doctor who had cared for him sent a message asking us to see him in the hospital.

"He told us that there were four children whose parents or guardians could not be identified. They had survived the bombing but were badly maimed. Three little boys, perhaps two years old, had to have their arms amputated, and there was one five-year-old girl who had her foot amputated. He wanted to know if we were willing to care for any of them."

By this time Mahnoor had recovered enough to speak, "When I looked at the five-year-old girl, I immediately thought of the sister Zebadiyah had lost. I immediately told the doctor we would care for her.

"One of the three boys in the same room started to cry, and I instinctively went to pick him up."

Then Muhsin took over the story, "My heart told me that we would take the three boys with us as well. So without consulting with Mahnoor, I told the doctor that we would care for all of them!

"The doctor was very shocked and advised us to think again and come back the following day. He reminded us that these were disabled children who would require very specialized and expensive care and wondered how we would be able to afford caring for all of them.

"The following day we reconsidered whether we were being rational undertaking such a challenge. Mahnoor, why don't you tell them why we reached the decision to bring all four children home?"

"It will be my pleasure," Mahnoor said happily. "Rationally, it did not make any sense, but we knew in our hearts that Allah would help us to mobilize others to help us. We would both have to stop working and would have no income. We did not know *how* we would succeed, but we knew *why* we had to succeed!"

Fatima was very moved with Mahnoor and Muhsin's passion. "You two amaze us with your faith in your success. I am sure you had to overcome many obstacles to succeed."

Mahnoor replied confidently, "We face obstacles every day, and we overcome obstacles every day. We have made many mistakes, but we have always learned from them.

"If I look back, Allah has always provided just a little bit more help than the obstacles required. Of course we had to persevere to overcome the obstacles."

Muhsin continued, "The following day when we went to see the doctor, he told us that he already knew our decision. So he offered to come to see all the children once a week to monitor their progress free of charge. This is my contribution to your noble effort he said.

"Since then he has persuaded other doctors and technicians to provide free orthotics for the orphanage.

"The first day we brought the girl and the three boys home, Zebadiyah was extremely happy and instantly bonded with the girl who he named Noor after his sister he loved so much.

"Now we had four disabled children to care for. We had no income and did not know how we would manage."

Mahnoor took over the explanation, "But we knew Allah would help us. When the word spread that we were caring for four disabled children in our tiny little home, people that we did not even know started to help us, both financially and providing care for our children. One landlord offered us a room in his building.

"From that room and five children, we grew to run an orphanage you are about to see."

The van stopped outside what seemed to be a dilapidated building. There was no name or number on the building. Mahnoor and Muhsin led the way into the orphanage. We were overwhelmed by the scene inside the orphanage.

The children, who could, came running to greet Muhsin and Mahnoor. The others greeted them from where they were. We had never seen so much love and happiness in one place!

Muhsin proclaimed proudly, "Here you are, brother Umeed and sister Fatima, at the Zebadiyah Foundation you have been supporting for the last fifteen years. What do you think?"

Once again, tears started flowing down Fatima's and my cheeks. Fatima blurted out, "This is wonderful. It is even better than I had imagined. It is such a joy to see bright shining eyes and such happy faces. Mahnoor, how many children do you have?"

Mahnoor blushed at the unintended question, so Muhsin smiled and answered for her, "Sister Fatima, we have had more than a thousand children in the last thirty years. They have all grown up and left except for the one hundred and fifty-one currently housed in compound and the twenty-five who are living here permanently."

Then Mahnoor answered cheerfully, "We tried to have our own children for ten years after our marriage when I found out that I could not have any children, but we are very grateful for all the children Allah has given to us."

As most of the children left to walk to school, the driver and some older children helped the disabled ones into the van.

Muhsin and Mahnoor took us on a tour of the building. We could see that it was extremely well managed. There was a large playground in the center with a soccer field, a large library, a large kitchen, a medical room, and four small gardens scattered around the complex. The children were housed in dormitories around the four sides of the field. There were separate rooms for boys and girls. Everything was clean, tidy, and well-organized.

Fatima and I were amazed. "Mahnoor and Muhsin, what is you secret for running the foundation so smoothly?" I asked curiously.

Muhsin answered after a long pause, "Love and discipline."

Then he expanded, "Love provides the emotional support everybody needs, and discipline provides the physical needs."

Mahnoor chipped in, "We learned that from Zebadiyah and Noor. They helped so much to care for their three disabled brothers. Perhaps it was the force of our circumstances, but fortunately, they quickly became disciplined and would do the chores we assigned to them. This freed us to do many other tasks.

"So we have a few rules that each child is required to follow. Each child is paired with one or two younger siblings, and they care for their mundane needs. They start showing pride in their responsibility.

"This frees us to provide the specialized care that the more disabled children need.

"We allocate chores like cleaning, cooking, and washing. It is surprising that the children volunteer before we even ask and do them responsibly.

"Even after they leave, they come back to help us and they always donate whatever they can once they start earning money.

"This is the model we follow throughout—be self-reliant for the majority of our needs and only get help for specialized needs like physical and mental medical care.

"We have found that being mostly self-reliant makes people help us even more for the things we cannot do ourselves."

"Can you give us an example of when people helped you with things you could not do yourselves?" I asked.

Muhsin replied eagerly, "Brother Umeed, as you know the neighborhood still does not have a reliable electricity supply. We wanted a generator installed for the orphanage. As soon as people became aware of this, they started donating to buy a generator. Some people who worked for the electricity board volunteered their services to install the generator for free. I don't know how to explain it, but everything just happened spontaneously."

I nodded my head and responded, "Muhsin and Mahnoor, if I may say so, this is the result of your sincerity and honesty."

Muhsin was happy to acknowledge, "It is true that we have full accountability of our funds we collect and spend. The mullah of our neighborhood mosque is one of the most respected people, and we have asked him to monitor the accounts of the Zebadiyah Foundation.

"He also comes to teach the Koran to all the disabled children who cannot go to the mosque.

"As you have probably noticed yourself, Mahnoor and I live a very simple life. Whatever money we have, we invest in the foundation.

"So we have earned the trust of the people, and they donate freely, knowing that every cent will be spent wisely. To tell you the truth, we have never had to ask for money. It just flows to us and through us."

Fatima smiled and agreed, "This is why Umeed Jee and I are very happy and honored to help the foundation."

Fatima and I spent the rest of the day observing how the orphanage was run and how the children interacted with each other.

In the evening, I carried two cups of chai from the communal kitchen for Fatima and me. Fatima gave her comments on her experiences, "Jee, there is so much love and care here. Every child feels important and worthwhile. Some of the children are severely disabled, but they are treated with dignity and compassion by other children and adult volunteers."

I concurred with her, "Fatima, I was talking with some of the older children and was very impressed with how deeply they care for their younger siblings. They are very disciplined indeed. But I wonder how Muhsin and Mahnoor deal with difficult children."

Just then Mahnoor and Muhsin came by so I asked them.

Mahnoor replied thoughtfully, "There are always thorns among the roses. The thorns prick us painfully. It is predictable and possible to care for physical disabilities. However, it is extremely exasperating and exhausting caring for some very difficult children who are mentally disturbed. Usually these children are both mentally and physically traumatized. These are the results of terrorism.

"But they are Allah's children just like everyone else. When we look at them that way, we accept the challenge and opportunity Allah gives us to increase our wisdom and patience.

"It is still extremely difficult, but we manage. Difficult does not mean impossible. We do not pick and choose for whom we will care. We care for everybody. It is very fulfilling.

"We know when we have reached the limit of our capabilities, and then we pay for specialized medical care in the hospital."

Fatima rushed to hug Mahnoor. "Wow! You and Muhsin are an inspiration for all of us!"

Muhsin smiled and continued, "What keeps us going is the scent of the roses. We cannot even remember how many of our children have become doctors, engineers, and professionals. Some of them have become renowned authors, musicians, poets, and artists.

"Noor went to Saudi Arabia to become an orthopaedic doctor. She got married and moved to Kandahar and is running the main hospital there. Can you imagine the multiplication of benefits throughout the country?

"Zebadiyah finishes his specialization in mental care from the most prestigious hospital in England and will come back to Kabul next year to help us in the most critical need of the orphanage. We have talked to him often about how much both of you support us. One day, *Inshallah*, he will have the honor of meeting you.

"When we started, we did not know how much we would accomplish. We must admit that we never thought we would progress so far. At that time we did not have any goals. We were just working hard and honestly every day.

"Now the Zebadiyah Foundation is so strong that we can visualize it continually growing. It has taken on an unstoppable momentum of its own. We can visualize Zebadiyah universities, Zebadiyah hospitals, and Zebadiyah schools in many Afghan cities. They will be the perfect answer to the terrorists. They will show the true face of Islam."

I looked up at the sky in amazement and thanked Allah. After wiping tears of joy, I composed myself. "You two are just amazing. We can indeed visualize your vision. We are fortunate to be a small part of the present and the continuing success."

Muhsin replied modestly, "We are mere puppets executing Allah's commands. He gives us the energy and perseverance to continue."

Fatima had one more question for them, "Muhsin and Mahnoor, do you ever feel anger towards the terrorists for the great suffering they cause to your children?"

Muhsin responded quietly, "Initially we got extremely angry. Now we just do our duty of caring for the children. We forgive the terrorists."

Fatima asked incredulously, "You forgive them?"

Muhsin started to explain, "Yes, sister Fatima, we forgive them! You see we need all the energy to do what we have to do. Anger consumes a lot of energy. We do not want to waste any energy.

"We let the authorities take care of the security situation. We just do our job silently and diligently.

"The biggest satisfaction we have is that terrorists can never destroy our spirit. We have unshakable faith in our vision. We could die tomorrow and the foundation will continue to flourish.

"Meanwhile the terrorists are becoming more and more isolated and more and more desperate. They have lost all the forced goodwill they used to count on. They find it increasingly difficult to recruit people who share their view of Islam because so few do.

"Don't get me wrong. They are still able to carry out isolated attacks. That does not mean they are winning."

"We just know that good always triumphs over evil, and this simple belief keeps us going."

Again I was extremely impressed with Muhsin and Mahnoor's prediction. "We totally agree with the universal belief that good always triumphs over evil. This is why the Zebadiyah Foundation is succeeding now and will flourish in the future."

Fatima smiled and added, "And on that cheerful note, I suggest we eat the tasty dinner prepared by some of the older children."

Each day at the orphanage passed quickly, and we were constantly amazed at the seemingly effortless way everything functioned. We were privileged to actually see in practice what is supposed to happen in theory.

At the end of the first week, Muhsin and Mahnoor dropped us at the luxury hotel where we had booked ourselves for two days.

Fatima and I finally got the privacy we missed and the opportunity to reflect on our stay at the orphanage. We kept the first day all to ourselves, and as Muhsin had suggested, we were going to phone our friends and relatives to visit us at the hotel on the second day of our stay.

We were jarred by the contrast between the immaculate hotel grounds and the messy streets of Kabul.

As we sat down for afternoon tea and scones as a change from Afghani fare, Fatima drew close to me and asked curiously, "Jee, how can two simple people with no formal education have the vision and wisdom to accomplish so much?"

"Fatima, I think they have kept things very simple. They practice love and discipline. They believe love provides the emotional support everybody needs, and discipline provides the physical needs.

"They could have practiced faith and perseverance and accomplished just as much. The success is determined by 'practice.' I believe practicing any one positive characteristic improves all of the other positive characteristics. The key is to take action, to practice.

"As far as formal education is concerned, I believe it is an enabler but never a limiter. They do recognize that education can enable them to succeed faster, but instead of spending time and effort to educate themselves, they leverage the ability of others with education. That is why they focus so much on their children's education."

Fatima nodded her head in agreement. "I can see what you mean about keeping things simple and practicing. I used to spend a lot of time getting educated about dieting and exercising, but I failed to practice. So I changed programs. Any program would have benefitted me if I had practiced it, if I had taken action."

Then she finished triumphantly, "It is actually very simple. Just eat healthy food and exercise regularly. I can say that now because I am actually succeeding by taking action!"

I was very happy with her personal example. "Fatima, I am very proud of you. As you always say, let us end on a positive note."

Then I added humorously, "Fatima, why don't you check all our messages and e-mails and arrange for some of our relatives and friends to meet us tomorrow while I pay for all the shopping you have done?"

She burst out laughing. "Sheikh Jee, please be very careful. I can spend faster than you can pay!"

Later that evening, she came back looking very excited. "Jee, what a coincidence! I got a call from my childhood friend Wazeera. She is the one who was running a girls' school in a remote village. Her husband was murdered by the Taliban to force her to shut down the school. She persevered fearlessly. Now her students are ending up doing extremely well.

"She is flying back from Jeddah tomorrow with one of them. Her name is Nabiha, and she has become the preeminent doctor in Jeddah's biggest hospital.

"I know we were planning to go and see Wazeera at her village school, but I asked them to see us in the hotel tomorrow."

I was happy to share in her excitement, "Fatima, I am looking forward to meeting Wazeera and her protégé, Nabiha. I am sure we will be able to find some time to meet with them in between seeing our relatives."

Fatima cleared her throat, "Sheikh Jee, I am sure we will be able to meet with them because I decided to invite our relatives and friends next time we stay at the hotel.

"Wazeera and Nabiha are the only people we will meet tomorrow. I just feel very strongly that we need to allocate a completely free time slot for them. I hope you understand."

I pondered for a long time before answering, "Fatima, initially I was upset because it is also very important for us to meet our friends and relatives as we had planned, but I understand that sometimes our feelings guide us to change our plans. We may not be able to explain in words, but I have gradually learned to follow my feelings. This is very different from being indecisive and changing our plans. On the contrary, these feelings are very strong and decisive. Fatima, we will follow your feelings."

After the anticipated hugging and sobbing between Fatima and Wazeera, they finally started to talk coherently.

Wazeera came across as being gentle but very strong-willed.

She was extremely proud to introduce Nabiha. "Sister Fatima and brother Umeed, when I look at my students doing so well, it makes all my sacrifices seem worthwhile. Nabiha is one of the best doctors at the largest hospital at Jeddah and is teaching other doctors. Allah has blessed her with intelligence and beauty."

Nabiha was indeed very graceful and delicately beautiful. She smiled and responded shyly to her glowing introduction, "Auntie Wazeera always brags about her students. I am what I am today because of Auntie Wazeera's bravery and love for her students. The only way we could repay her efforts was by studying and succeeding."

Wazeera patted her gently and added, "She is also modest. But she cannot hide her talents. My only complaint about her is that she has been concentrating so hard on her career that she has neglected marriage. She is so capable that men are wary of marrying her. Muslim men, they are so insecure!"

Nabiha smiled shyly and protested, "Auntie Fatima and Uncle Umeed, I hope that you can persuade Auntie Wazeera to stop pestering me about marriage."

Fatima's eyes suddenly lit up as she questioned Nabiha. "What if a tall, dark, and handsome man who was caring and secure wanted to marry you?"

Nabiha started to laugh and pleaded, "Uncle Umeed, please save me from these two women who are forcing me into marriage."

Fatima looked at me smugly, knowing my response, "Fatima and sister Wazeera, I insist that you stop pestering Nabiha.

"But, Nabiha, what if you did meet someone who is tall, dark, and handsome and caring and very secure and you liked him. If it was truly your decision, would you marry him?"

Nabiha replied thoughtfully, "If he was caring, that would be enough."

Fatima jumped in immediately, "I agree that it must be your decision. So if you permit me, I can arrange for you to meet a very caring man, who is a billionaire philanthropist. He often comes to Jeddah on business. Your Uncle Jee can arrange for him to meet you at our son's friend's house."

Wazeera's curiosity was piqued. "Who is this billionaire philanthropist?"

I replied proudly, "He is a visionary. You may have heard of Al-Bahar, the self-sustaining city in the Arabian Desert. That city is his vision becoming a reality. His name is Sheikh Zahid."

Nabiha's eyes widened, and her jaw dropped. "The Sheikh Zahid! Of course I have heard of him. I fear that I am not worthy of him. No, I will not meet him."

Wazeera looked at Nabiha with piercing eyes. "Nabiha, I have always taught my students to be confident and fearless. I believe once he meets you, he will pray to Allah that you agree to marry him. Then it will be your choice."

Again, Nabiha replied thoughtfully, "Auntie Wazeera, it is true that you have taught us to be fearless, yet sometimes I still doubt my own capabilities."

Then she stood erect and proclaimed, "I am worthy. I will meet Sheikh Zahid and decide if we are compatible. It will be my choice."

Wazeera and Fatima rushed to hug her as I witnessed confidence triumph over doubt.

After Wazeera and Nabiha had left, Fatima hugged me. "Jee, I hope Sheikh Zahid and Nabiha like each other. Do you think they will marry?"

I replied gently, "Fatima, we really have to be detached from the outcome. Let us not be more anxious than them."

As we were about to retire for the night, Fatima came looking very sombre and handed me the phone. "Jee, you have to listen to this message."

I took a deep breath as I listened to my cousin's message. "Fatima, I need to fly back to New York. My aunt Raashida is very sick and may not live for long. She is asking for me. I am her favorite nephew and you know she is my favorite aunt. She is so pious and so gentle. She is the only surviving elder from our family. I do not know how to explain it, but I really need to see her. I know we have not seen any of our family and friends, and we really want to see them. They may be disappointed that I chose to leave to see my aunt. It is always difficult to choose between two good things. In this case I really need to see my aunt. I hope you understand."

Fatima held my hand gently and replied sympathetically, "Jee, I understand. You do not have to explain. I will try to book the first flight back to New York. Let us pray to Allah that we are able to see her."

The following day, Muhsin and Mahnoor were disappointed that we were going to leave suddenly.

As expected, Muhsin started with deep gratitude. "Brother Umeed and sister Fatima, you two have pulled two surprises for which we are very thankful."

Mahnoor continued, "Thank you for the new van you bought for the orphanage. I had been pestering Muhsin Jee here to buy another van or at least get the old van repaired. Buying a new van was out of the question, but he even refused to spend money on getting the old one heated and air-conditioned!

"Now thanks to you, the orphanage has a new van, and the old one has been fully repaired, and the seats are safe and comfortable for the children."

Then she turned to Muhsin pointedly, "Why did we struggle for so long with a beat-up old van?"

Muhsin owned up readily, "I was afraid to appear ostentatious. This is a poor neighborhood, and we are running a charity. I did not want anybody to accuse us of being spendthrift with donated money.

"Mind you we could have fitted the van with comfortable seats and have the heating and air-conditioning repaired many years ago. Mahnoor, I apologize for not listening to you earlier."

Mahnoor laughed and turned to Fatima. "Muhsin Jee lost his way during the day but came home before just before sundown. So he was not lost. I think we should forgive him. What do you think, Fatima?"

Fatima burst out laughing as she looked at me. "Mahnoor, Sheikh Umeed Jee here still comes home just before sundown sometimes, and I forgive him. I think we should forgive brother Muhsin even though from personal experience with Sheikh Jee it will not be the last time."

I looked at Muhsin and commented smilingly, "Muhsin, let us thank Allah that we have such understanding wives who have never lost their way."

Just before saying our farewells, I addressed Muhsin, "I would like to share something which I learned during my stay in Germany. Initially I was saving each deutschmark so that I could send it to Fatima. I started to confuse need with luxury which led to self-denial, but I soon realized that self-denial is no virtue. It leads to misery.

"In fact I learned that spending wisely on needs expands your ability to earn more and give more. Once I started to spend on needs, it enabled me to earn more. I bought a car, and that saved me travel time which I used to work overtime and send more money home. This type of spending is actually investment in our growth."

Then Fatima owned up sheepishly, "I used to confuse need with luxury as well. In my case if I wanted to spend money on luxury, I called it a need. It used to exasperate Sheikh Jee. But now I am able to exercise self-discipline and have a good balance between self-denial and indulgence."

It was getting late, so we bid our emotional farewells.

Muhsin addressed us, "Sheikh Jee and Fatima, we are extremely thankful for your support to our orphanage. It will enable us to spend more, actually invest more of your contributions to help the children even more."

Mahnoor hugged Fatima tearfully. "It is because of people like you that we never have to worry about money. This allows us and encourages us to fulfill our mission in life to help the children of Afghanistan. Next time you visit us, you will see even more progress made by the Zebadiyah Foundation."

I turned toward them with tears streaming down my cheeks. "Muhsin and Mahnoor, we are extremely proud of you and are humbled by the selfless contribution you are making to humanity. You are putting into practice the values of Islam and portraying the true face of Islam.

"Fatima and I are looking forward to seeing you again. *Inshalla.*!"

Muhsin and Mahnoor replied chokingly, "We look forward to seeing you soon. *Inshallah!*"

BACK TO THE USA

Aboard the flight back to New York, Fatima and I had quiet time to reflect on the events and progress made during the hajj, the visit to Al-Bahar, and the visit to the Zebadiyah Foundation.

Fatima held my hand and started softly, "Jee, we are truly blessed. Just look around us. Here we are, sitting in the first class of the biggest jumbo jet in the world after spending three most eventful months of our lives.

"I never thought Allah would give us such an opulent lifestyle after we had to flee Afghanistan literally with just the clothes on our backs."

I took a deep breath and replied appreciatively, "Indeed, Fatima, we are truly blessed. I thank Allah for giving us the wisdom to convert misfortune to fortune.

"We could have become despondent and given up many times. Allah gave us the resilience to carry on. I am not tempting fate, but we grew the most during the most difficult periods of our lives and succeeded the most as a direct result of overcoming our obstacles.

"Our enemies wished to destroy us. They must be extremely disappointed. We not only survived, but we thrived. Perhaps we should thank our enemies for spectacular success!"

Fatima squeezed my hand tightly and spoke with clenched teeth, "Jee, let us not tempt fate. Hardships come unannounced. We have already had enough difficulties to last our lifetime. We do not need any more, thank you. Let us just savor the fruits of our success."

I nodded my head slowly. "Of course, Fatima, we deserve what we worked so hard for. Why don't you recount what we learned and accomplished during the last three months?"

Fatima sat up excitedly. "There are so many accomplishments we can be very proud of. The biggest one was to perform our Hajj. I hope I am not being arrogant but I don't think I learned anything new. I relearned many things I knew already, but more importantly, I restarted practicing what I had stopped."

She knew the next question I would ask so she added voluntarily, "Let me give you some examples, Sheikh Jee."

As we started to eat the delightful halal meal served by our friendly hostess, Fatima continued, "There are some things I have restarted to practice more consciously. Shahnaaz taught me to be more patient, and Nasib taught me to be more compassionate.

"I added another practice myself, and that is to be less judgemental of others.

"During the hajj, I learned that hajj is just a catalyst for making improvements. We do not need to wait for hajj.

"And let me credit you with really understanding for once that fear is for our protection and not for our paralysis.

"Another concept I have started to practice is that we should compare in order to motivate and improve, not to gloat or punish.

"At the moment I do not remember any more examples, but I feel good whenever I put into practice any improvement. Sheikh Jee, it is your turn now."

"Fatima, you have reinforced some improvements I need to put into practice."

As the hostess came to serve us fruit cocktails for desert, l licked my lips and smiled at Fatima.

"Let us savor the fruit of our efforts. During the hajj, I learned that some situations have their own rules and rhythms, and it is best to accept that and just go with the flow. I am getting better at discerning when to influence the outcome and when to let go.

"There was one concept that was new for me. Do you remember Shahnaaz asking why Allah gives so much to so few, and so little to so many? Well, Nasib explained that rather than spending the effort on some unanswerable question, it is better to ask another empowering question like 'What can I do to alleviate this situation?' So I have started asking empowering questions.

"I have also learned to listen to my heart and feelings. This is why I decided to open up to Jaffar when he offered to help influence Nasib.

"Fatima, you already talked about not judging. Well, I do not spend energy to condemn or reform the terrorists. Instead I have become even more determined in my peaceful way to truly help the cause of Islam and benefit personally in the process.

"And the biggest lesson I learned is that we are being constantly tested by fear and doubts, but since I know that, I am not exhausted by the effort required to face another new fear that rears its ugly head. Instead, I feel encouraged because this will be another fear I will be able to overcome like I have overcome others before that."

Fatima seemed very impressed. "Sheikh Jee, I am very pleased that we are motivating each other."

I took a deep breath and whispered, "Fatima, there is one gnawing fear that I would like to share with you. I am still extremely worried about Nasib. His extreme sympathy with Rashid is very disturbing."

Fatima replied emphatically, "Jee, I am just as confused and worried. If only we did not have this worry, our life would be perfect. Instead of seeing some encouraging signs, I see very discouraging developments. Even when he appears calm and rational, I do not know what is brewing in his mind."

Then she added disappointedly, "The hope we had of Jaffar being able to influence him toward peace has been dashed. There is no other hope on the horizon."

I sat up erect in my seat and spoke confidently, "In life nothing ever lines up straight, but life with its unresolved contradictions and crookedness carries on. We can focus on happiness or misery."

As Fatima ate the last tasty spoonful of the fruit cocktail, she replied softly, "Let us be grateful to Allah, focus on the happiness, and go with the bumpy flow. If you don't mind, we will talk about our experiences in Al-Bahar and in Kabul later.

"I just want to enjoy the luxury and serenity of flying in the most advanced jumbo jet."

It felt very good to land in New York. We were pleasantly surprised to be greeted by an American immigration officer wearing the hijab.

Fatima commented excitedly, "Jee, is it just me or is it true that many more women have started to wear the hijab in America?"

"Fatima, it is very encouraging indeed, but it is not only in America, and it is not only confined to women. Even in Europe and Canada, more and more Muslims are showing their pride confidently and openly.

"What is even more encouraging is that Muslims have become actively involved in mainstream politics and representing the interests of their local communities."

"It was unthinkable even a decade ago that Muslims would get voted into parliaments in various countries. Many countries in Europe have elected Muslim members of parliament, including some women.

"There are Muslim members of parliament in Canada, Australia, and New Zealand, and there are even Muslim congressmen in the United States Congress."

Fatima looked surprised. "Jee, do you think a predominantly non-Muslim country could elect a Muslim head of state?"

I thought deeply and nodded. "Nowadays, it makes news when a Muslim is elected to a prominent position, but we can soon look forward to a time when it will be quite common.

"After that stage, it will be newsworthy when a Muslim becomes a prime minister or a president. I do not know if it will happen, but then again, very unlikely events came to pass. Who would have thought that Nelson Mandela would become president of South Africa?

"We have many challenges to overcome. Of course the biggest challenge is overcoming the damage to Islam being inflicted by the terrorists. Unfortunately, at the moment, most of the world links Islam and Muslims with terrorism."

Fatima protested painfully, "But this is completely wrong! Islam is a religion of peace!"

"Fatima, of course that is true. The challenge to the vast majority of the peaceful Muslims is to convey the truth about Islam.

"Peaceful engagement at every level with the rest of the world is the right path. And we are on the right path."

As soon as we exited the customs lobby, we were happy to see Shahnaaz waiting for us.

She ran to hug us tightly. "Hello, Haddy and Hummy, I really missed you! There was nobody to spoil me."

As we sat in the car on our way to the hospital to see my aunt Raashida, Shahnaaz broke what to her was very good news. "Well, you only have one week to spoil me because both Nasib and I have got security clearance, and we are off to Al-Bahar!"

Fatima and I looked at each other both questioning what kind of security checks had been done on Nasib.

Fatima was quick to cover our apprehension. "Shahnaaz, we are extremely happy for you and Nasib. We were just a little surprised that both of you got security clearance so quickly."

Shahnaaz continued blissfully unaware, "The Saudi authorities did not even need to do any security check. Haddy here is the well-known imam of peace, and on top of that, we have been personally selected by Sheikh Zahid to work in Al-Bahar. Why would anybody want to do security checks on Nasib and me?"

Even though I had been suppressing it, the conflict in my mind came out into the open. I was secretly wishing that there would be enough intelligence on Nasib to deny him security clearance, and at the same time I really wanted him to get the job in Al-Bahar because he would be in an environment that would harness his huge potential for good.

I recovered in time to maintain Shahnaaz's naivety. "Shahnaaz, they have to go through the formality of checking everybody's background. In the vast majority of the cases, it really is a formality. The challenge all security organizations face is to catch that one in a million applicants who is a security threat."

I did not mention the other challenges that all security organizations face, namely petty jealousies about sharing information and incompetence even in the face of grave threat.

Shahnaaz sighed and continued, "I suppose you are right. Still, I get extremely frustrated when I am always singled out for extra attention just because I wear the hijab. It is as though they assume I am carrying a bomb. One of these days they are going to let a determined suicide bomber slip by while they misguidedly concentrate on frisking millions of law-abiding citizens."

Fatima immediately hissed her admonishment, "Shahnaaz, please don't tempt fate. We should be grateful for the sincere effort the security organizations make to keep us safe. Undergoing extra security because you wear the hijab is a small sacrifice for greater good. After all, I wear the hijab and get extra attention as well."

When we reached Aunt Raashida's bedside, we were saddened to see her immobilized with a breathing tube down her throat. She was in deep sleep due to sedation.

My cousin and his wife were happy to see us come to provide moral support to their mother and to them. My aunt was breathing very shallowly.

Since my cousin and his wife had been taking turns to be near Aunt Raashida, I offered to give them some rest by staying overnight with her. I asked Fatima and Shahnaaz to go home as well.

I spent the night in prayer and silent reflection of her life and imminent death. She never smoked in her life and lived a very healthy life until a few months ago, and yet she was dying of lung cancer!

I held her hand and remembered her as the person who cared for everybody very deeply, especially me, and taught me to read the Koran. Like all the women of her generation, she had no formal education. For girls in her village, there were no schools, yet she was extremely intelligent and wise. I never knew how she gained so much knowledge. If she were born today, she would easily become a university professor.

After a while, I fell asleep only to be woken up by the nurse. I got up to see Aunt Raashida. Her eyes were open, and she was momentarily conscious and alert.

As soon as she saw me, she smiled. I squeezed her hand gently and nodded. She squeezed my hand and smiled again as tears of happiness started flowing down her cheeks. She had obviously recognized me.

I kissed her hand and started to cry so loudly that the nurse had to ask me to be quiet lest other patients got disturbed.

I composed myself, wiped my eyes to look presentable for her, and started to smile back at her. She tried to speak, but I put a finger on my lips and told her to just smile. It seemed we were talking in smiles with each other for a long time, but after just a few minutes, she fell asleep.

I reminisced about how strong and energetic she had been all her life.

She had more stamina than a marathoner.

I remembered her beautiful face and sparkling eyes. Now it was all wrinkled, and her eyes were sunken into the sockets. She did not have enough strength to lift her finger. She was just skin and bones, and she was suffering.

"Aunt Raashida never smoked in her life, but why did she get lung cancer? Why does Allah make good people suffer?" I questioned.

Immediately I remembered not to get sucked into a whirlpool of unanswerable questions. It is best to accept the will of Allah and live the best life that we can.

To quieten my mind, I went out for a long walk in the night. It felt very peaceful until my cell phone rang. I recognized the trembling voice of Ehsan, Muhsin and Mahnoor's driver.

Muhsin and Mahnoor had been killed in a double suicide bombing near the hotel we had stayed at!

I was stunned and incredulous for a moment. Then I felt outraged. Why Muhsin and Mahnoor? They were such peaceful and pious Muslims murdered by the enemies of Islam. I started to weep inconsolably, but in New York everybody is too afraid to ask why or to help.

Then strangely I felt very calm. It was the will of Allah that they died, I told myself. They had contributed so much and transformed so many lives. I knew their death would not be in vain. I remembered what Muhsin had said during our visit at the orphanage. "We could die tomorrow and the foundation will continue to flourish."

I knew that somehow their vision would indeed continue to flourish, perhaps even more than before. When I reached the hospital ward, my thoughts went back to when Muhsin and Mahnoor parted at the hotel and told us, "We look forward to seeing you soon, *Inshallah!*" I started to weep inconsolably again.

The nurse came toward me, put her hand gently on my shoulder, and announced sympathetically, "Sir, I am very sorry to inform you that your aunt died shortly after you went out for your walk."

She led me to the waiting room and stayed with me until I composed myself. Some people have such a peaceful aura about them. She was one of them.

I did not tell her about the murder of my dear friends Muhsin and Mahnoor. I was sad about Aunt Raashida's death, but she had led a very good and full life. I felt that her death was a relief from her suffering.

But Muhsin and Mahnoor! I started to weep again.

It was dawn when Fatima and my cousin and his wife came to the hospital.

Aunt Raashida's death was a very sombre time in our lives. At the same time, I thanked Allah that I was able to pay my respects to her before she died.

When we reached home, I burst out loudly, "Fatima, they have murdered our dear Muhsin and Mahnoor!"

Fatima was just as incredulous. "Jee, please tell me that it is not true! Allah, it can't be true!"

We hugged each other, our bodies heaving uncontrollably. "Fatima, I wish it was not true, but it was Ehsan, their driver, who told me exactly what happened.

"After we went to the airport, they got stuck in a traffic jam near the hotel. They heard a huge explosion about hundred meters away near the police station. A suicide bomber had driven his explosive-laden truck into the police station compound. At least fifty people were killed and hundreds more maimed. Later on it became clear that the suicide bomber was targeting two American soldiers helping to patrol the police station. They were both killed.

"Muhsin and Mahnoor immediately jumped out of their van and rushed toward the police station to help. Ehsan tried to stop them, but they just ran to help.

"They started to help some severely injured people near the epicenter of the explosion. Ehsan saw another man rushing to help.

"As he neared them, there was another huge explosion. It was another suicide bomber following up to cause more destruction on the people who rushed to help.

"Muhsin and Mahnoor sacrificed their lives helping others!"

Fatima lashed out angrily at the faceless terrorists, "Jee, I wish that the terrorists should burn in hell!"

We were expecting to bask in the glow of some of the most enjoyable and enriching experiences of our lives. Instead, gloom had descended over our home.

In the past we were dismayed by just reading the news of acts of terrorism, but now we were experiencing firsthand the terrible loss and sadness of the victims of terrorist acts.

All our friends, Muslim and non-Muslim, were extremely sympathetic. Shahnaaz was very supportive and encouraging.

Meanwhile, Nasib was completely at a loss as to what to say to us and how to respond. It seemed that what we were experiencing was too close to be explained or justified by him. The awkwardness between Nasib and both of us was very uncomfortable. He just avoided us.

From that time onward, there was an unannounced recognition that there would be no discussion about terrorism between Nasib and us.

Slowly the shock and sadness of Mahnoor and Muhsin's death started to subside.

A day before Nasib and Shahnaaz were to leave for Al-Bahar, Fatima started cheerfully, "Jee, it may seem strange to say, but I am beginning to feel at peace now. I am not angry anymore."

I smiled back and observed, "Where there is peace there can be no anger. I am at peace as well.

"The real reason is that the terrorists may have killed some people, but they have strengthened the resolve of peaceful majority of the population.

"I really do believe that Mahnoor and Muhsin's legacy will flourish even more after their death. This deep satisfaction has replaced my seething anger."

Fatima agreed but questioned hesitatingly, "Do you think we could ever forgive the terrorists, whoever they are?"

I responded after thinking carefully, "Fatima, absence of anger does not mean forgiveness. At the moment I do not know if we could forgive the perpetrators.

"But we can take encouragement from other terrible examples. After the end of apartheid in South Africa, the government set up the Truth and Reconciliation Commission and it has been generally successful.

"After all, the terrorists are our brothers, however misguided they may be. We do not know what desperation drives the suicide bombers to commit such evil deeds. They may have been victims of gross injustice themselves. The real culprits are the people who control them.

"At one time they may give their testimony and request amnesty. Today it seems that time will never come, but I believe it will come. Then we will be ready to forgive. Remember, forgiving each other, even forgiving one's enemies is one of the most important teachings of Islam."

Fatima sighed, "But, Sheikh Jee, I know that it would be very difficult for me to forgive."

I empathized with her, "Fatima, if we think this is difficult, then not forgiving will be even more painful. The alternative is revenge. Fighting fire with fire leaves only ashes. We need to break this cycle of revenge and violence. We need to heal each other, not burn each other.

"The wise path is the path of forgiveness. It is a long and an arduous path, but let us start walking. It leads to healing and peace."

Fatima nodded her head sadly. "It is going to be a slow walk requiring great effort. The victims of terrorism are severely hurt."

Then she stood erect and announced confidently, "But you are right, especially because the rewards for the effort are peace and prosperity."

I felt encouraged by Fatima's response. "Fatima, our individual hopes, aspirations, and visualizations join together to become global hopes, aspirations, and visualizations. So it is our duty to predetermine the outcome of peace and prosperity of Islam."

Fatima looked confused. "What do you mean by predetermining the outcome?"

I took a deep breath and started to explain, "Very often we do not know the results of our efforts. There are many possible outcomes, including failure. However, if we visualize the outcome, we end up aligning enough factors positively which predetermines the outcome as we visualized it.

"There are always many factors to thwart our desires. But with our visualization, we can convert enough maybe's to positive certainties and achieve the desired outcome.

"Fatima, it is a very hopeful and an exciting way to live."

Fatima's eyes widened with surprise. "Jee, in my experience I ended up being disillusioned when I visualized success and failed. So now I have started to expect failure and become very happy when I succeed."

I shook my head strongly. "Fatima, my dear, we always have a choice in the way we think. Remember, life is lived on probabilities, not certainties.

"It is not certain that every time you visualize an outcome you will achieve it, but your negative visualizations become reality much more often than your positive visualizations. My suggestion is that if you visualize a positive outcome and fail, chose to learn the valuable lesson from it and try again.

"But please do not choose to visualize a negative outcome just to become happy if it fails. You will end up converting enough maybes into definite nos. Most of the time you will end up aligning enough negative factors to make the negative outcome become the unpleasant reality.

"We need to choose a thought process which significantly increases our chances of success. So what thought process would significantly increase your chance of achieving the outcome you truly desire?"

Fatima nodded her head and broke into a broad smile. "Sheikh Jee, I must say you are very artful in getting your message across by asking me to answer a question. Of course from now on I will increase the probability of success and always visualize a positive outcome, and if it fails, learn the lesson and try again."

I felt pleased that she had understood my message and hugged her, but as usual, she had another question for me, "But, Jee, I think this kind of visualization only works for personally desired outcomes. What you are talking about is visualizing peace and prosperity of Islam. Do you really believe this is in our control?"

I answered passionately, "Absolutely! There are many factors at play here. You have already seen what great strides are being made in Al-Bahar and the breakthrough progress being made by the Zebadiyah Foundation. These are just two instances of great progress being made that we personally know about. Do you think these are the only instances?"

Fatima was quick to reply, "Of course not. My friend Wazeera has planted many seeds of progress. We only met Nabiha.

"Then there is Jaffar and his wives, Tahira and Sajjda running a state-of-the art high-tech company.

"Come to think of it, we have done extremely well professionally and financially.'

"And just look at how accomplished Nasib and Shahnaaz are."

Then she became even more animated. "All our relatives and friends are doing extremely well no matter if they are living in the United States, Europe, or Afghanistan. This is wonderful!"

I continued passionately, "We have been mesmerized into focusing at the destruction and chaos in the Muslim world, but underneath the chaos, progress is sprouting vigorously, and it is only matter of time before progress overcomes chaos.

"Fatima, there is another major factor helping us, and that is terrorism!"

Fatima was shocked. "Sheikh Jee, that is ridiculous. How can terrorism be helping us?"

I hastened to explain, "Fatima, it is a help of the most perverse and unwelcome kind. The vast majority of Muslims all over the world are disgusted by the terrorists' actions and are applying themselves toward peaceful progress.

"They have lost any sympathy they may have had at one time. Now they impose their will through force and fear.

"They are slowly becoming more isolated and they have difficulty to recruit new would-be terrorists. Even within their ranks, there is complete disillusionment with violent tactics. Even their most dedicated recruits are deserting them."

Fatima still looked perplexed. "Jee, so do you think that the terrorists are going to just wither away and leave us in peace?"

I took a deep breath and replied, "The terrorists are becoming so desperate that they will end up committing such a heinous and cowardly act that even their diehard sympathizers will be disgusted. We don't know what that incident will be and when it will happen, but it will unleash such raw emotions that they will not be able to hide and survive. They will bring their own permanent downfall.

"Fatima, this was never their intention, but they have already served their purpose. In trying to attack their Western and Christian enemies, they have woken the Muslim world into action. They have exposed structural and political weaknesses in many Muslim countries that have stunted their progress. Many of these countries had been ruled by dictatorships where there was no freedom of expression.

"Of course there was some progress made, but it is very hard to know how much more progress would have been made if there was true freedom. However, we just know that dictatorships of any kind are disastrous for everybody except for the elite in power.

"The natural resources of these countries were mostly squandered by corruption and meaningless military buildup with very few benefits trickling down to the masses.

"One by one these dictatorships have been thrown out, and people have seized their rights and freedom."

Then I raised my hands in triumph. "We have a clean slate to start. Now progress will be based on freedom and not suppression. This is why these countries will make more sustained progress in the next ten years as well as making up for the losses of the last fifty years."

Fatima commented hopefully, "Jee, I am convinced that progress based on freedom will be solid and lasting. I just wish it actually happens."

I wanted to drive the point home, "Wishing is not enough! Fatima, how do we convert wish into reality?"

Fatima beamed her reply, "I can see you are very confident and convinced of the future of the Islamic world. To answer your question, it is through personal action. Hope confirms the outcome we will achieve, but we have to put in the effort."

I thumped my fist on the table. "Yes! Each Muslim making a personal vow to progress peacefully and purposefully will bring us back to glory. Every individual effort, no matter how small or how big, will add up coherently and put Islam back into power in our lifetime. The world will be a better and peaceful place."

Fatima's forehead wrinkled. "Sheikh Jee, are you sure this can happenin our lifetime?"

I took a deep breath and replied, "Fatima, I am sure Islam can be back in power and influence within our lifetime. There have been some totally new events that at one time no one thought could happen in their lifetimes—independence of past colonies like India, end of apartheid, and start of majority rule in South Africa, the Berlin wall coming down to name just a few.

"In the case of Islam, it will be nothing new. We will merely be reclaiming the power and influence we once had!"

Once again I became animated, "Imagine that Islam has reclaimed its rightful place in the world. The world has become a better and more peaceful place for all mankind. How would we feel?" Then I became completely silent.

It did not take Fatima long to reply enthusiastically, "Sheikh Jee, I would feel extremely proud and happy. I will put in all the effort required to make it possible. I guess that up to now, it never occurred to me that we could succeed. The way you put it, reclaiming our rightful place is definitely possible. I am convinced that Islam will reclaim its rightful place in the world."

I felt encouraged and continued, "Fatima, you are right that Muslims have to put in the effort. We are talking about power and influence in the world, not dominance of the world. This is the key to peace.

"The status quo is very good for the Western and Christian world but miserable for us. This is why we have to make the effort and take action."

Fatima had one reservation. "Jee, I believe what you believe is true, but there may be some who think you are being naive. How would you reply to them?"

I smiled and replied, "If they have a better solution, we will follow them. Otherwise we will follow our strategy. They will end up adopting our strategy.

"At the moment many Muslims are just beginning to feel in their hearts that they can get back in power.

"It is very encouraging to know that we already have a critical mass of people who actually believe in that. Very soon the majority will climb on board the train to glory.

"Look at the progression of China toward becoming a superpower. "And you are right that there are some Muslims and especially majority of non-Muslims who think we are all terrorists and destined to remain poor and mediocre.

"Are we going to let them decide our future, or are we going to create our own future?"

Fatima replied immediately, "Of course we need to create our own future."

I became very passionate and emotional. "Fatima, it does not matter if some believe we are naive.

"On the contrary, we are sophisticated and alert and confident. We will seize our future. Nobody can stop us. We will create our future. We just need to believe. Islam will be glorious once again!"

Fatima put her arms around me and hugged me tightly. "Nothing can stop us now. I am convinced of our future."

Then she started to grin. "Jee, I have made a very delicious dessert for you. Please stay here, and I will bring you a bowl full. I think you will really enjoy the quiet break. This dessert really sticks to your teeth."

We replaced the despair and sadness of Muhsin and Mahnoor's death with hope and happiness for the future. This is what they would have wished.

Soon the day came for Shahnaaz and Nasib to start their new and exciting careers. We dropped them off at the airport feeling sad knowing that we would be seeing them a lot less often.

Nasib had never been very communicative to begin with, but now he became even more laconic and distant but remained polite. It became very difficult to know what he was thinking. Fatima and I just wished that Shahnaaz would keep dialogue open with him.

Shahnaaz on the other hand became even more ebullient. We were thankful that at least one of our children would give us the pleasure of reporting her successes.

The peaks of the excitement of our hajj, visiting Al-Bahar and the Zebadiyah Foundation in Kabul and the valley of despair at the passing away of Muhsin and Mahnoor gave way to passing more reflective days. We started to face the challenges of our promises of self-improvement easily made in a state of high emotion charged with adrenaline.

An Unexpected Fall

"Jee, it really bothers me that the children have stopped phoning us!" Fatima complained angrily.

I took a deep breath before explaining, "My dear, Shahnaaz phoned two weeks ago. I am sure she will phone soon. As you well know, they have been extremely busy. They are responsible and grown-up adults. I don't think you need to worry."

Fatima stared at me and hissed, "Sheikh Jee, nothing seems to bother you! Shahnaaz used to phone every day at first and then she became too busy to phone me.

"Meanwhile your son has phoned me once since he went to Al-Bahar. Then he sent an e-mail saying that he is very busy and will contact me soon. That was a year ago. You have not done anything about that. Doesn't that bother you?"

I bit my tongue and replied calmly, "Fatima, Nasib is your son as much as my son. I am worried that Nasib has become very silent. I have not been able to do anything about that, but neither have you.

"If it is any consolation, we know through Shahnaaz that he has settled down in Al-Bahar and is doing extremely well."

Fatima kept on pouting. "He will only realize how much he neglected me after I die. I bet you he will be too busy to come to my funeral!"

Just then the phone rang, and when she read the number, she pounced on it. Her pouting transformed to purring. It was Shahnaaz!

Fatima talked to her for an hour and then cheerfully handed me the phone. "See, she cares about me."

As usual, Shahnaaz brightened up our home even when she was not present. "Hello, my handsome Haddy. Please go into another room. I want to share some very good news with you."

Then she continued excitedly but in a hushed voice, "Haddy, I am in love. I am very happy, but I am also very nervous. He really loves me very much, in fact, he worships me, but I am not sure if I should marry him."

I was surprised at the transformation from her usual strident and feminist self to being smitten with love. However, I reassured her happily, "Shahnaaz, this is wonderful news. You say he worships you, but how deeply do you love him?"

She cooed her answer, "Dad, I love him to eternity. I cannot sleep at night. I am always thinking about him. I am hopelessly in love. I think I am losing control of myself. I have never felt like this before. That is why I am so confused and scared. Will it last?"

I started to laugh, "Shahnaaz, I am happy to say that I lost control of myself when I married your mother, but we have survived and thrived together. If you both love each other, everything will work out. So don't worry if you are swept by the current of love. Go with the flow!"

Shahnaaz agreed with relief, "Haddy, you are the best. I just needed that reassurance from you."

I still did not know who she wanted to marry. "Shahnaaz, who is this lucky knight marrying my precious princess?"

She replied excitedly, "Wait till you see him. He is a very warm and charming person, and very supportive of my career and delights in my success.

"He is extremely smart. He was born and raised in Tulsa, Oklahoma. He has a doctorate from the California Institute of Technology, and is presently doing research on the next generation of solar cells at Al-Bahar University."

Then she added humorously, "But he is not a nerd like Nasib."

Everything sounded perfect, but I felt that she was withholding some crucial information. "Shahnaaz, what is his name?"

She took a deep breath and answered quickly, "Dad, his name is Christopher Harris, and he is tall, blonde, and handsome."

I swallowed my breath. A thousand thoughts whizzed in my mind. The imam's daughter marrying a white American Christian! What will my Afghani and Muslim friends say? Fatima would be distraught.

I had always preached that all humans are equal and that love overcomes everything, but I was facing the reality of my own daughter marrying a Christian.

Sometimes I had wondered how I would react if my son or daughter wanted to marry a non-Muslim. I had always justified to myself that I would be able to cross that bridge if ever I had to and give my blessing if my children truly loved a non-Muslim. But I was now facing a real, not a hypothetical scenario.

But this was different. Fatima and I had always told our children to make their own choices. Of course we always visualized very elaborate Muslim weddings for both our children with hundreds of our relatives and friends celebrating the grand occasions.

We would rent a few floors of a luxury hotel where all our friends would stay. We would fly in some famous Afghani singers for entertaining the guests. After all money would not be an issue for us.

We always imagined Shahnaaz marrying a Muslim boy from Afghanistan. He would be as handsome as Shahnaaz is beautiful and would love her and cherish her. He would be well educated and be either a doctor or an engineer graduated from a European or an American university.

But as we had always told her, she had made her own choice. Now my daughter was telling me who she loved and wished to marry. It was up to me whether I give my blessing to her marriage or reason with her not to marry a non-Muslim.

I was at the bridge!

After what seemed like an eternity, I made my decision that I had to live according to what I preached. All human beings are equal in the eyes of Allah and that love overcomes everything.

I decided to give my blessing immediately and promised myself that over time I would be able to happily accept my daughter marrying a non-Muslim.

I cleared my throat and spoke chokingly, "Shahnaaz, my precious daughter, I wish you and Christopher everlasting happiness in your married life. May your love for each other be stronger than any challenges you may face in your life. I respect and trust your decision to marry him."

I could hear Shahnaaz crying with happiness, "Dad, I love you! Your blessing means the world to me. Chris will be so happy. Wait till you meet him; you will be extremely impressed with him. Even Nasib is very impressed with him."

Then she burst out laughing, "Haddy, I hope you forgive me for withholding some crucial information from you. Chris is a Muslim!"

I bellowed with relief and happiness. "What! Christopher Harris is a Muslim?"

Shahnaaz elaborated with excitement, "Yes, Haddy, he converted to Islam five years ago. He was at the hajj the same time as we were. He is a very devout Muslim. In fact, he is more observant than I am.

"Dad, you will love him. He is six foot five inches tall, plays basketball, and is a fitness instructor. He is a very health-conscious vegetarian. I met him in our Arabic class in Al-Bahar. I am also glad that Nasib and Chris get on well together."

I thanked Allah that Shahnaaz and I had such a close relationship that she sought my advice even though she had pretty well made up her mind. It reminded me of the time I asked for my father's approval after making my decision to change my family name from Khan to my poetic name Umeed. My father was perceptive enough to give the answer I wanted.

I started to feel very excited about Shahnaaz marrying Christopher but wanted a little more information about him. "Shahnaaz, has Christopher shared his decision with his family?"

"Of course, Dad. We talked to his parents on videophone. They are extremely happy now."

The word *now* raised my antenna. "What do you mean 'now'?"

Shahnaaz explained patiently, "Chris's parents were very upset when he converted to Islam five years ago. According to Chris, his parents are WASPs. I never knew the meaning of that, but I am sure you know what it stands for."

I offered my answer, "Unfortunately your mother and I know from firsthand experience that it stands for White Anglo-Saxon Protestant. There are bigots in all religions, including Islam."

Shahnaaz continued, "Chris's parents were born in Tulsa, Oklahoma. They are very deeply involved with their church. You can just imagine the heartache they suffered when Chris converted to Islam without telling them—as if they would have approved.

"Over time they started to accept the fact and grudgingly respected Chris's decision. When they found out that Chris wanted to marry an almond-brown, hijab-wearing Afghani Muslim girl, they were upset all over again."

I breathed a deep sigh and interrupted, "Shahnaaz, I can understand his parents' disappointment. Your mother and I would have been very disappointed if you were to marry a non-Muslim. It is very difficult to break out of the mold of our upbringing and emotions. We humans have created the divisions by religion instead of accepting and embracing that Allah created all human beings as equals.

"However, I am relieved that I accepted, albeit disappointedly, your decision to marry a Christian because at one time you had not told me that Chris is a Muslim. I really thought he was a Christian."

Shahnaaz continued, "Dad, I am very proud of you that you would have accepted my decision to marry a Christian. I am equally proud of Chris's parents. They have summoned the courage and wisdom to break out of their mold of upbringing and emotions to accept me. In fact, his father said I am a fine human being and that they are honored to accept me as their daughter-in-law, damning the consequences of their friends' reactions. Dad, they really love me." And then she started to cry.

After she quieted down, I spoke softly, "Shahnaaz, I am extremely happy for you and Chris. Yours will be a dream wedding and I will spare no expense. It will be the most lavish wedding in the Afghani community of New York. Why don't you share the good news with your mother?"

Shahnaaz laughed out loud. "I am afraid to tell her. You were calm, but she will become hysterical thinking I am marrying a Christian. Don't tell her that Chris Harris is Muslim until after she has gone ballistic."

I tried to be stern with Shahnaaz but as usual failed. "Shahnaaz, that is being mean. I won't do that to your mother. I will let her know that Chris is Muslim from the start."

Then her laughter became even louder. "My poor Haddy, you are so innocent! I added the mean bit so that you could have the satisfaction of saying no to one thing and agree to do the one thing I really wanted you to do. So please tell Mom and clear the coast for me. I will phone her tomorrow."

I smiled and shook my head at her street-smart antics, as I walked tall to break the good news to Fatima. She was ecstatic.

I rubbed my hands with glee as I looked forward to their wedding. "Fatima, this will be the happiest and the most lavish wedding in the Afghani community. I am just waiting for Shahnaaz and Chris to set the wedding date. Just imagine our beautiful princess marrying her prince charming. I will rent the best hotel, the best caterer, and fly in the best musicians from Afghanistan."

To my surprise, Fatima replied in a subdued voice, "Sheikh Jee, you seem to be more excited than Shahnaaz. There are many details to be worked out before you put your plans into action. Please be patient and remember, it is her wedding. We need to find out what she wants."

I realized my motivation for a lavish wedding and retracted quickly, "Fatima, you are right. I wanted to use Shahnaaz's wedding as a statement to show off to everybody as to how well we have done financially and in raising our family. I was letting my ego take charge. However, now we will do everything in consultation with Shahnaaz and Chris. Even if we have a lavish wedding, we will remain humble."

The following day turned out to be very momentous. For the first time, Fatima and I saw Chris on videophone. We were delighted to meet him. He was indeed tall, blonde, and handsome. Even while sitting beside Shahnaaz, he appeared a foot taller, but they looked very beautiful together. Their faces glowed with happiness. He was very pleasant and polite.

I started with the obvious question, "Chris, we are very honored to have you as part of our family. We are happy to know that Shahnaaz and you love each other very deeply and want to get married. But, Chris, we do have one question. What made you convert to Islam?

Chris replied calmly, "Mr. and Mrs. Umeed, you are entitled to ask many questions. You have such a loving, talented, and beautiful daughter. You need all the reassurance that she is marrying someone worthy of her. I just hope you believe I am that lucky man. All I know is that I will love her and cherish her for the rest of my life."

Fatima squeezed my hand and became overjoyed and emotional listening to Chris's reply.

I was very moved by the sincerity and wisdom of his response. "Chris, love and respect for each other are the only requirements in a relationship. Everything else works out by itself. I can feel it in my heart how deeply you love and respect each other. I don't have any more questions. May Allah bless you with happiness forever."

Fatima continued after wiping her eyes, "Chris, we believe you will care for our Shahnaaz. Once again, if I may ask, what made you convert to Islam?"

Chris cleared his throat and started, "Growing up in a very religious family in Tulsa, my sister and I were expected to be very observant and go to church regularly. I was an altar boy when I was growing up. We had no other reference point, and Christianity was the one and only religion to follow.

"I was happy and content being a Protestant. However, I started to notice a big disconnect between what we were required to follow and what a lot of members of the congregation practiced. A lot of them were arrogant, racist bigots. Islam was regarded as a religion of sword and coercion in which women had no rights. The western and American media and public opinion became extremely hostile to Islam since the Iranians held American hostages.

We listened intently as he continued, "And when the terrible 9/11 terrorist attack happened, things became even worse. All Muslims were viewed as being terrorists.

"Meanwhile, I had made a lot of Muslim friends in the university, and my personal experience was totally the opposite. Muslims were very peaceful, hardworking people trying to live a decent life.

"I became very curious about Islamic history. I talked to some Americans who had converted to Islam. They were genuinely very impressed with the true message of Islam. I felt I had to counter the totally wrong image of Islam in the Western Christian world. The more I thought about it, the more I felt I should convert to Islam.

"So it was the attraction of Islam after studying about it that I decided to convert. I particularly liked the discipline of praying five times a day. This discipline helps in all facets of your life. Fasting during the month of Ramadan makes one realize firsthand the plight of the poor and makes one humble and generous to those less fortunate.

"Please remember, I respect Christianity. There is nothing wrong with Christianity if it is practiced the way it is supposed to be. To tell you the truth, all religions will make humans better humans.

"However, I am happy to become more human while following Islam."

We were very impressed with Chris's answer. Fatima commented softly, "Chris, you are a very enlightened human being. If you are a good Muslim, you truly respect all religions."

Then she asked excitedly, "I have one other very important question. When do you two want to get married?"

Shahnaaz replied equally excitedly, "Mom and Dad, you wouldn't believe it, but we have already set a date. It is exactly two weeks from now!"

Fatima jumped out of her chair. "Jee, isn't that wonderful? We will have the most opulent wedding for Shahnaaz and Chris."

It seemed I was the only one who was pensive instead of ecstatic. "But, Shahnaaz, I will need more time to make all the arrangements. Arranging hotel bookings, inviting our friends, families, and musicians from Afghanistan. You know we always planned these exciting events for both your and Nasib's weddings."

I was taken aback when Shahnaaz answered uncharacteristically seriously, "Dad, I understand all your dreams for our wedding, but Chris and I have discussed, and we agreed that we want a simple wedding. A very simple religious wedding."

Chris added his suggestion, "Mr. and Mrs. Umeed, we did sincerely take your wishes into consideration. We are faced with a choice of wedding, which is going to consume a huge amount of time and energy from all of us and additional expense from you. Shahnaaz told me you contribute to some very noble charities in Afghanistan. If you were to save that money on one event, you could help thousands of others. We are not saying what you should do with your money, but you may want to consider that."

There was a long and uncomfortable silence until Fatima pinched my hand and prodded me, "Sheikh Jee, the children bring up a good point, don't you think so?"

I was still in a daze seeing my opportunity of flaunting my wealth disappearing. I shook my head and replied, "Of course you bring up a very good point." And then I added with a forced smile, "We will do as you wish. It is your wedding after all."

Fatima showed her displeasure at my lack of enthusiasm by pinching me harder this time and commented, "Shahnaaz and Chris, we are very happy to comply with your wishes for a very simple wedding. Sheikh Jee has all the resources to make all the arrangements after he has overcome his personal disappointment of not having the most lavish wedding."

Shahnaaz tried to lighten the mood and questioned, "Dad, do you remember how much you laughed when we saw the movie *My Big Fat Greek Wedding*?"

Suddenly we all started laughing. "Yes, Shahnaaz, we laughed because the girl's relatives outnumbered the guy's relatives hundred to one."

Then she turned to Chris. "My dad's version of *My Big Fat Afghani Wedding* would have my relatives outnumber your relatives a thousand to one."

All this humor made it easy for me to overcome my reluctance and confessed happily, "To be honest, Chris and Shahnaaz make a very good point. It is not easy for parents to accept that their children have come up with a suggestion that is wiser than the parents' suggestion. I must admit that I let my selfish wish for a lavish wedding blind me from doing the right thing.

"Fatima and I will have to hear a lot of unkind comments and gossip from our relatives because our daughter got married in a hasty and exceedingly simple wedding.

Then I proclaimed by raising my hands, "But as Mr. Harris said, we will deal with them—damn the consequences."

So we agreed with an exceedingly simple wedding in two weeks' time where there would be Shahnaaz and Chris, Mr. and Mrs. Harris, Mr. and Mrs. Umeed, and the imam to conduct the ceremony. Fatima and I were very excited as we counted the days to our daughter's wedding.

Shahnaaz and Chris flew in from Riyadh together three days before the wedding, but Chris then flew on to Tulsa. We were overjoyed to have our daughter back for a short but momentous visit.

The day before the wedding, I went to pick up Fatima after the Muslim Women's Association meeting at the mosque. There had been freezing rain, and I phoned ahead to tell Fatima to stay in the mosque as I would bring her winter boots. As I drove into the mosque, I saw a woman lying still at the bottom of the stairs. People had gathered around her in hushed silence.

I went in to see what help I could provide, but to my horror, I discovered it was Fatima. She was completely still!

The ambulance rushed her to the hospital. The doctor said she had hurt her back, but he was more worried by severe injury to the back of her head. They gave her medicine to reduce the swelling. She was unconscious but breathing. The next twenty-four hours would be crucial they said.

I prayed and cried and stayed by her bedside all night. Shahnaaz rushed to see Fatima and tried to be very brave most of the time, but in between sobbed uncontrollably. And the wedding was the following day. Meanwhile, Mr. and Mrs. Harris and Chris had flown in from Tulsa and checked into their hotel.

As Shahnaaz and I were deciding to call the Harris family to inform them about Fatima's accident and to cancel the wedding, Fatima gained consciousness. The doctor was very surprised and informed us that Fatima was out of danger, but the recovery would be long.

Shahnaaz became very emotional to see her mother lying helpless. "Dad, I want to postpone the wedding. I will tell Chris. I was going to chair my first conference next week on the sustainable city in Australia. Chris and I were going there as husband and wife. After the conference, we were going to celebrate our honeymoon." Then she started sobbing. "I pray to Allah, postponing our wedding and honeymoon is nothing. I just want my mother to be okay."

A few hours later, Fatima stirred. Shahnaaz and I were holding her hands. To our great surprise, she squeezed our hands ever so gently and opened her eyes. We both cried with relief at this hopeful sign.

Shahnaaz spoke to her, "Mother, do you know who I am?"

She blinked her eyelids. I asked gently, "Fatima, do you know who I am?"

She opened her eyes and whispered, "Jee." After remaining stoic for so long, I started to sob with happiness. Thanks to Allah my loving wife was going to be OK. Meanwhile, Shahnaaz ran to call the nurse. She advised us to give Fatima some more rest. We thanked Allah and waited for more encouraging responses from Fatima.

After a few more hours, Fatima woke up and for the first time tried to speak, but I told her to just answer yes or no to our questions.

Shahnaaz wanted to ask her first, "Mother, do you know I was going to get married tomorrow?"

Fatima nodded.

Then I asked her, "Fatima, you are going to be well soon. We all want you to be at the Shahnaaz's wedding. Is it OK if we postpone the wedding?"

Fatima shook her head.

Shahnaaz asked her again, "Mom, are you sure you want Chris and me to get married tomorrow?" This time Fatima smiled faintly and nodded.

Shahnaaz squeezed her hand gently. "We will respect your wish, Mom."

The following day, Chris and Shahnaaz got married. Mr. and Mrs. Harris were among the warmest and loving people I had met in my life. The wedding was simple but spiritually profound. We missed Fatima's presence at the wedding but were happy to comply with her wishes.

When Chris and Shahnaaz and Mr. and Mrs. Harris went to visit Fatima, she was feeling much better. Even though she could not say much, her gentle smile made her face glow with happiness.

Shahnaaz and Chris went to see Fatima regularly. Once, Shahnaaz asked Fatima about their departure, "Mom, Chris and I are going to fly back to Al-Bahar and then to Australia for my first conference followed by our honeymoon there. I am going to cancel our plans to go back until you come home. Is this OK?"

This time instead of nodding yes or no, Fatima spoke slowly but clearly, "No! You go on your honeymoon." Chris and Shahnaaz looked at each other, confused.

I confirmed Fatima's wish, "Shahnaaz and Chris, I think you should do as Fatima says. Please come back as soon as you are able to, after your honeymoon. Your mother does not want you to miss your first conference either."

Then I turned to Fatima and held her hand. "Fatima, I love you and will take good care of you. I know that circumstances have not allowed us the time to discuss what to do with the money Shahnaaz and Chris asked us to save for charity.

"I have come to a decision. I know roughly how much money we would have spent on the wedding. We will donate half of that to our charities. It will come to about a quarter of a million dollars. Fatima, are you happy about that?"

Fatima nodded her head firmly twice. Then I turned to Chris and Shahnaaz. "And the second half is your wedding gift from your mother and me. Fatima, are you happy with that?"

Fatima smiled and nodded her head firmly several times.

Shahnaaz and Chris hugged me and thanked me and then held Fatima's hands and kissed them.

Chris turned to me and spoke, "Dad, Shahnaaz has already told me that we should not refuse a gift. We promise we will make very good use of your gift. Thank you for your generosity."

It felt very good that he addressed me as dad. "There is one small instruction Fatima and I would request you to follow. Fly first-class to your honeymoon and stay in the honeymoon suite in the best hotel in Australia. Fatima, does this make you happy?"

Of course Fatima nodded her head in agreement.

One chapter ended in our life. Our daughter started her married life as Fatima and I started on the long road to recovery after an unexpected and life-changing fall.

The Long Journey to Recovery

"Allah! What did I do to deserve this fate?" I heard Fatima wailing loudly while I was preparing her favorite cinnamon waffles and tea to take to her bedside.

I felt extremely sorry for her predicament but decided to let her vent her anger and disappointment.

It had been a month since she had been discharged from the hospital. Her neck injury was healing slowly, but her back was severely damaged. She could not move her legs and sometimes suffered excruciatingly painful back spasms.

When I brought the tray to her bed, she put on a brave face and smiled. "Jee, the waffles smell so nice. I could smell them from here while you were making them. And you made me Lady Earl Grey tea! This was never my idea of tea in bed, but thank you, Jee."

I smiled back, "Anything for you, Fatima. But I don't think I will be able to keep that up. You better start walking soon."

Fatima sighed sadly, "Jee, I visualize, every day getting up and going for a long enjoyable walk with you, but it's been more than a month and instead of getting better I am feeling worse."

I paused and held her hand and looked directly into her eyes. "Fatima, visualization definitely helps. Please be patient—progress is never linear. In so many other instances, we had to take two steps backward before moving just one step forward, but then went on to progress, sometimes by leaps and bounds.

"I admire you for the bravery you have shown so far. It is only natural that you will feel disheartened sometimes. It may take time, but I know you will recover."

Fatima felt very encouraged. "Jee, thank you for lifting my spirit. Can I share with you what upsets me the most?"

I knew this would take a long time, and I had a very important appointment with my bank manager, but I decided that this chat with Fatima was more important.

"Fatima, I have all the time for you," I told her as I pulled my chair nearer.

She took a deep breath and started, "Jee, I blame myself for my situation. You had phoned me that it was extremely slippery and that I should wear the boots you were bringing for me, but I was so excited to prepare for Shahnaaz's wedding. I thought I would just be careful going down the few steps. The one moment of impatience resulted in missing my daughter's wedding."

She continued while staring out of the window, "I was looking forward to travelling with you. After hajj I had planned to spend more time volunteering and getting more involved in the community. Instead I am bedridden, and I have become a burden on you and on society. This is what upsets me the most. I have no one to blame but myself."

I turned her head toward me and looked into her eyes and started gently, "Fatima, there are situations where there is no blame. This was an accident. Please do not blame yourself. As far as being a burden is concerned, nobody likes to be dependent. I know that you are very tough, and it is only a matter of time before you will be up and about. In the meantime, please accept all the help I give you. If I got injured, would you do the same for me?"

She replied immediately, "Of course I would, but I never imagined I would be the one being dependent on you."

She instinctively tried to get up but couldn't, but still proclaimed quietly, "This is the will of Allah! I will not blame myself. Some greater good will come out of my accident. I don't know what it is, but I will discover it."

I was moved by Fatima's fortitude. "Fatima, you are a great inspiration. I am not sure if I would be able to accept the will of Allah if I had suffered the accident. I also know that you would reframe my adversity as an opportunity for some new breakthrough."

From that moment, I knew Fatima would be all right. Slowly but surely, Fatima's spinal mobility increased, and she was able to sit up for a few minutes at a time.

One day when I came home, I saw her weeping loudly with her fists in her eyes.

I rushed with great concern. "Fatima, my dear, what is the matter?"

After some more crying, she blurted, "It has been almost a year since my accident, and today I received another e-mail from him. I sacrificed so much for him. He hasn't even phoned me! Your son is so inconsiderate. An e-mail!"

Before I could respond, she continued angrily, "Shahnaaz and Chris have come to see me twice. Don't tell me your son is busier than them."

I tried to calm her down, "Fatima, I agree with you that he should show more care. He is good in every other way. Even when he left, he was very aloof and distant. He may be fighting his own battles. He may be too busy."

Fatima hissed at my feeble explanation, "Don't tell me he is busier than Shahnaaz and Chris. He just doesn't care about me. When I die, I don't want him to come to my funeral!"

It was time for me to reframe her thinking. "Fatima, my dear, I really understand you're hurt. If it is any consolation, he has not contacted me at all. If I had been in an accident, I bet you he would not have e-mailed me at all. He would just e-mail you to find out how I was doing.

"He is our son. Why don't we put our minds together and get him to be more communicative?"

She was still angry. "We have tried that so many times before. I am fed up. He is your son. You can try again."

I smirked, "Fatima, if he is not your son, then it should not upset you if he does not care about you. But I can definitely get my son to call you via videophone. Would you like that?"

She pouted her reply, "Yes, of course I would like my son to call me."

I started to laugh. "Fatima, I am happy to establish a three-way call between your son, my son, and you."

She called me to her bedside and hugged me. "Jee, you won't understand a mother's heart, but thank you for your help."

Nasib countered my invitation to the video call to be one day later. I was relieved that he actually responded. Of course Fatima was excited for the next two days. I wondered if Nasib would have postponed the call by two days, Fatima's anticipation and excitement would have lasted for three days instead of two.

On the day of the call, Fatima told me that she heard on the news that one of the most prominent Muslim clerics in the Helmand province had been assassinated. "Jee, this is terrible. I can understand the terrorists targeting the coalition forces, the Afghani government, the army, and the police."

"But why do the terrorists target the Muslim clerics?" she asked in an exasperated tone.

I replied with equal exasperation, "Fatima, they are ruthless murderers. They are hell-bent to destroy anyone who opposes their view. This cleric was courageous enough to talk to any faction that wanted to renounce violence. He was working hard to establish pacts of peace among the various factions and with government.

"Fatima, that they murder courageous clerics who openly promote peace is a good sign."

Fatima questioned with a pained look, "Sheikh Jee, this is a terrible new development. What do you mean it is a good sign?"

"Look, Fatima, these clerics have no bodyguards. Their only shield is their moral authority. It is a sign of desperation on the part of the terrorists that they have to murder defenseless clerics who promote peace. We are now facing last-gasp terrorism."

"Jee, I pray to Allah that your prediction is correct," Fatima commented hopefully.

I replied confidently, "Fatima, it is not my prediction—it is the process of peace that prevails inexorably. But there is one concern gnawing at me."

"Jee, go ahead, I am listening," Fatima replied intently.

"You know I always said that we should keep communications and dialogue open, even when we don't agree with someone. In the past, we would discuss any terrorist incident with Nasib, and he would challenge us with any news of Western killings of innocent civilians. We always talked. Now there is dead silence. I don't know what is going on in Nasib's mind. This vacuum of silence is being filled with deep apprehension in my mind."

Fatima spoke after a long silence, "Jee, now that you bring it up, it is uncomfortably true. I am sorry I can't help you. I am preoccupied with my own plans for dealing with my disability.

Then she spoke dismissively, "Sheikh Jee, I suggest you fill the vacuum of your mind with some new excitement in your life."

Her comment stung me painfully and left a lasting impression.

At the appointment time, Fatima sat near the phone and pounced on it as soon as it rang. "Nasib, it is so good to hear from you. I am very annoyed. You haven't called since my injury. What took you so long?"

Nasib smiled and replied, "Hello, Mom. Hello, Dad. Mom, I hope you are recovering well. You look well. I did e-mail you a few times, but I know I should have called. I am really sorry, I have been extremely busy. Things have turned out very differently in Al-Bahar."

As usual, he looked very presentable and fit. I was surprised that he had shaved his beard.

For what seemed like more than an hour, Fatima hogged the conversation with Nasib. He was very patient and polite with motherly guilt trips and admonishments. It made me laugh how she still treated him like a little boy, and he meekly accepted it.

I could never get away treating Nasib like a little boy.

At one time I had to interrupt Fatima to speak with Nasib. "Nasib, what do you mean by things are working out very differently than what you expected in Al-Bahar?"

He answered very calmly, "Dad, I don't work for Sheikh Zahid anymore."

I was deeply disappointed, "But you were his vice president for security in Al-Bahar. What happened?"

For once he elaborated his explanation, "Dad, he is a man of vision. I share his vision but not his style. I find him to be very condescending, and he finds me to be very stubborn and arrogant, and I agreed with that. So I resigned."

Fatima asked in a panicked voice, "You resigned! But you still live in Al-Bahar, don't you?"

Nasib smiled. "Yes, I resigned. I took your advice. Even though the sheikh and I don't like each other, we need each other. He knows that I am the best person for the security program in Al-Bahar, so I have established my own company and have signed a contract with Sheikh Zahid's company. The sheikh has asked his program director to interface with my company. I must admit that the sheikh is very wise. He does not let personalities prevent progress. Meanwhile, I am very happy being an employer and not an employee. I will make a lot more money."

I admired Nasib's self-confidence but was disappointed that I would not be able to count on the sheikh to discreetly steer Nasib toward peace, and more importantly to sense if he was involved in any nefarious terrorist activities.

Fatima was too eager to congratulate him, "Nasib, we are very proud of you. We know you will do an excellent job.

"You see, Jee, that is why my son was too busy to phone. He was setting up his own business."

I simply nodded my head. It was so easy for Fatima to reclaim him as her son for any good deeds and to justify his faults.

I was very alarmed by Nasib's next comment. "Well, actually, Mom, I was in Afghanistan for the last month."

I could not help but question him, "Nasib, last week Shahnaaz and Chris phoned, and they didn't tell us that you had gone to Afghanistan. What were you doing there?"

Nasib replied politely but in an irritated voice, "Chris is a very nice guy, and Shahnaaz is my dear sister, but they are very happily married now and living their own life. I want to live my own life. I don't want to report to them or you as to what I do with my life.

"Dad, since you asked, just this time I will tell you what I was doing in Afghanistan. I went to see my friend Aziz. In the future, please respect my privacy, and I will respect yours."

Even Fatima was taken aback by Nasib's demeanor but tried to end on a good note, "Nasib, we understand. We just need to know that you are doing well. Here is my suggestion. Why don't you program a recurring appointment on your cell phone to call us once a month?"

Nasib spoke as he typed into his cell phone, "Mom and Dad, I will be happy to call once a month. How is that for action? I also need to know that both of you are doing well. I will call you a month from today."

After the call ended, I could not hide my deep apprehension. "Fatima, this is definitely not good news. I was hoping that while working with Sheikh Zahid, Nasib would benefit from his peaceful influence. I do not like at all that Nasib went to Afghanistan to meet his friend Aziz. Do you know who he is?"

Fatima was similarly apprehensive. "I know that Nasib helped Aziz to kill Jahanbaksh, the bandit turned mujahedeen. I don't want Nasib to get hurt."

My apprehension turned into deep worry. "Fatima, Nasib is very stubborn, but he is also naive. He could get kidnapped or killed. Now we will not know anything about his activities. Once again there is a very uncomfortable vacuum of information."

Fatima sighed and agreed with me, "Jee, I am very worried as well. But what can we do?"

We both paused for a moment and then spoke in unison, "We will fill the vacuum with massive action."

For once we really understood that we cannot change others, only ourselves. We cannot change the events, but we can determine how we react to them.

It took us a lifetime to progress from superficial understanding to the deep understanding that we can only change ourselves.

From that day onward, we became extremely busy. We started to put into practice many things we had learned during hajj.

During the next ten years, we had many setbacks but used them as stepping-stones to climb upward.

Fatima found out that she would never be able to walk again. She suffered from chronic pain in her spine. Instead of being angry and despondent, she graciously accepted Allah's will and accomplished much more than what she had planned on accomplishing as an able-bodied person.

She replaced her initial modest and mediocre plans with even more exciting and challenging plans.

She started a chat program on the local Afghani radio station answering questions from new immigrants ranging from health and education to dealing with culture shock and integration into a new country.

She started giving personal tutoring lessons in Pashto and Farsi to Afghani children via videophone.

The demand was so great that she could not keep up. Instead of limiting the benefits because of her personal time and abilities, she trained some other parents to teach the children.

Every challenge required learning brand-new skills and leveraging her abilities through others. As soon as she reached one plateau, she worked hard to reach the next plateau of achievement. There was no single mountaintop to reach. She has steadily reached heights that would have frightened her initially.

Some of the children who learned Pashto or Farsi became tutors for other children who had challenges with maths, English, and sciences. She called this 123Tutoring to ensure it is personalized and that there are no more than three children to one tutor.

This embryonic idea led her to establish a not-for-profit organization, which she named Striving Toward Excellence. The idea quickly led to others teaching other Afghani languages and then Arabic.

To test out and improve the methods, she learned Arabic. This became a perfect marriage of videophone technology and preservation of mother tongues of scattered minorities in many countries.

She invited her friend Wazeera to visit her for a month, and together they set up a student exchange program between the students from Afghanistan and students from the United States. The synergy they have created has led to many unexpected breakthroughs.

Each senior student is required to volunteer five hours per week mentoring a junior student. This exchange benefits both the Afghani children and the American- Afghani children.

The confidence they gain from mentoring and being mentored has helped the children excel academically and socially. Several of these students have received the American Citizenship Award. They attributed their success to the mentoring program established by Fatima.

An independent study by one of the most prestigious American university has found that American-Afghani students are among the top performing graduates.

The mentoring programs have done so well that they are being used as models by other communities as well as in other countries.

In between, she has had some extremely discouraging setbacks. Her success aroused many hostilities and jealousies. Instead of being thanked for her efforts, she has been kicked in the teeth by some of the very people she was helping. Instead of giving up, she thanked Allah for making her stronger, and her burning desires to contribute anyway made her persevere.

I believe her when Fatima says that were it not for being so busy with her contributions, she would be in so much physical pain.

Because of her selfless service and dedication, Fatima has been interviewed on radio and television programs from many countries. She has become internationally known as the founder of Striving Towards Excellence organization and innovator of the 123Tutoring concept. For once it is so refreshing to earn good publicity about the Muslim community around the world.

Since Fatima has always worn the hijab, she has become the face of the modern, progressive, and proud Muslim woman.

What started off as contribution to the Afghani and the Muslim community soon started to benefit the mainstream American community. Her organization Striving Toward Excellence is now popularly referred to as Stexcel, and 123Tutoring has become a registered trademark of Stexcel. Her efforts have gained her great respect, and she has won many international awards. The award she cherishes the most is the Presidential Citizens Medal, being the first American-Afghani woman to win such an award.

She continues to inspire thousands of others by her exemplary life of contribution.

My life took on a very different but an even more fulfilling course than what I had charted for myself. Instead of leading a relaxing, retired life, I became even busier than before. It is as though I gained second wind and renewed energy.

Fatima's student exchange program required heavy financing. I started with paying the expenses for five Afghani students to come to the United States and five American students to go to Afghanistan in the first year.

The program was so successful and beneficial that we felt we should expand the program. So I started to think about generating more income to fund Fatima's Stexcel program.

I built up on the limited experience I had with buying, renovating, and renting apartment buildings. Over the years I was able to buy some buildings at bargain prices, and after renovation, they became very desirable to live in. I was then able to sell them for a handsome profit.

I had been too busy working before to even realize this was possible. I failed with some projects and suffered losses but learned the lessons in hurry. These lessons have now enabled me to buy and sell apartment buildings into a repeatable formula.

Initially most of the profits were invested in growing the Stexcel organization, but in just five years, the not-for-profit organization started to break even and did not require more funding.

I progressed from being a millionaire to a multimillionaire, facing the delightful problem of how to donate my wealth in the most useful way.

While continuing my donations to the Zebadiyah Foundation, I also started to donate to the local charities such as women's shelters and food banks. Islam teaches us to help all humanity.

I remembered my father explaining to me the difference between passive help and active help. He taught us to give both kinds of help. Donating money to the charities was passive help. I had to think of ways to provide active help.

I decided to reinstate the blood drive our mosque used to organize.

Over time, the blood drive had stopped through lack of participation.

We mobilized the congregation to pledge to give regular donations without being reminded as a very symbolic way to promote Islam. The "Pledge to Save Lives" program generated its own momentum, and even people from the rest of the American community have pledged to donate regularly.

Additionally, I started spending more time and energy expanding the role of our local mosque and became actively involved with the interfaith understanding forum.

This provided the Muslim community a much-needed platform to counter the negative image of Islam. The mosque nominated me to be their spokesman.

Soon I found myself speaking to school boards and community groups about Islam. The feedback we received was extremely positive. Overwhelmingly, the feedback was that the ordinary Americans in the audience had completely changed their view of Muslims.

The image most people held of Muslims is that they are all extremists and terrorists. They were honest enough to admit that their image was wrong. It was based on what they saw on television and what they read in the newspapers.

It was very encouraging to know that they now recognized Muslims as peaceful citizens just like themselves. We felt there was a lot of work to do, but we were on the right path to portray the truth of Islam being a religion of peace.

I thanked Allah for giving me the opportunity to promote peace among the different religions.

It also put the heavy weight of responsibility on my shoulders. I soon realized that my public speaking skills as a mullah were not suitable for conveying the true message of Islam to non-Muslims.

So I took some courses in public speaking. The benefits were dramatic. I really felt I connected with the new and diverse audiences.

The interfaith forum brought us in contact with other community leaders from the churches, synagogues, and Buddhist, Hindu, and Sikh temples.

I was invited to speak at their places of worship. I proposed that all of us send participants to blood donations organized by the mosques, churches, temples, and synagogues.

For a very small minority of the extremists in the mosque, this was too much, and they became very hostile toward me, but the silent majority of the congregation welcomed opening dialogue with other religions. I was assured by other members of the forum that they had similar experiences with the extremist members of their churches, temples, and synagogues.

For my efforts, I received many death threats, but that made me even more determined. I took that as a sign that I was doing the right thing. It reminded me of my grandmother telling us that whenever you have an opportunity to do good in life, stick your neck out. You will fear that people will chop it off, but Allah will protect you and put a garland of flowers around it.

And so it happened. The first time I was asked to make a speech at the church, I joked with the priest that I would cross the bridge of hope to meet with them. Our mosque was on one side of the river, and the church was the other side. We all started to refer to it as Hope Bridge. Once they found out that *umeed* means hope, I felt very honored when they requested the local authorities to rename the bridge as Umeed Bridge to appreciate my courage to continue my peace efforts despite the death threats I kept on receiving.

Over the years, I made many good friends from many other religions and communities, and they nominated me for the Presidential Citizens Medal for promoting peace and harmony among various religions.

We thanked Allah the day I received the award, being the first husband and wife to have received it.

Meanwhile, Shahnaaz and Chris continued to do extremely well. Shahnaaz continued to travel the world organizing conferences and promoting the self-sustaining model of the city of Al-Bahar. She has been featured in all the major international magazines and been interviewed on international radio and television. We cannot keep track of where she would appear next. One day, when we were shopping we saw her face on the cover of *TIME* magazine!

She has become the face of the young hijab-wearing, confident, modern, and progressive Muslim woman and has become a role model for other women. She has the biggest following in the Muslim world in social media.

Chris has become one of the chief research scientists at Al-Bahar University and has registered many international patents and published several papers. The revenue generated by the royalty from the patents enables the university to fund further research.

He has been instrumental in making Al-Bahar University one of the leading materials research facilities in the world.

The biggest pleasure Fatima and I get is to follow the progress of our granddaughter Faiza and our grandson Jalaal.

They bring the purest joy to us. They really are miracles unfolding in the most delightful ways, captivating us with their brilliance and innocence. We never knew the joy of being grandparents until we became grandparents.

We have only seen them once, four years ago, and our only wish is that they lived near us so that we could physically be with them.

As far as Nasib is concerned, unfortunately there has been minimal one-sided communication. Fatima sends him an occasional e-mail, and he sometimes replies.

Meanwhile, our life carried on with the course set by our purposes, mostly unaffected by Nasib's unknown course.

It had been nine years since we came back from hajj. We went through very traumatic passages and managed to reach heights we had never thought possible. And our fortieth wedding anniversary was coming up on June 5, 2020. I decided to take action before Fatima started to drop not-so-subtle hints.

PAST PROGRESS AND FUTURE HOPE

Fatima held my hand as I wheeled her to the viewing deck of our luxury cruise ship. "Jee, this is so wonderful. We cannot thank Allah enough for what we have."

I pulled a deck chair and sat beside her admiring the sunset. "Indeed, Fatima. We are floating in the laps of luxury. This is one of the most luxurious cruise liners, and we have the best suite on the ship with a private butler to attend to our every need. You always wished to go on a transatlantic cruise.

"And your wish is my command. So here we are, taking a luxury cruise on our fortieth wedding anniversary! We will reach Southampton in one week, spend a week sightseeing in England, and get back to New York during the third week."

Fatima squeezed my hand tighter. "Sheikh Jee, I am very impressed. Thank you for being so caring. With my chronic back pain, a cruise is the best type of vacation for me.

"But it does bother me that I have prevented you from doing the activities that you enjoy. I apologize for tying you down. Do you forgive me?"

I lifted her chin so that I could look directly into her eyes. "Fatima, the minor adjustments I had to make in my life are insignificant compared to the pain you have endured. I know you would do the same for me if I had been injured. So please do not apologize. Instead be grateful to Allah for the accomplishments you have made despite being injured."

At this she started to cry, "Jee, I love you! I must admit that sometimes I blamed Allah. I am only human, but of course I am grateful to Him. I have so much more to be thankful for. You, for example! Were it not for your support and encouragement, I would not have achieved what I have been able to achieve."

I was very moved by her appreciation of my support. "Fatima, I love you too. We have been married for forty years, and I can truly say that I would not have achieved as much as I have without your support. I believe that we have had a happy marriage because we communicated our hopes and fears and complaints to each other and worked things out.

"There have been a few stormy days in our marriage, but we knew that they would pass and that our love would shine through."

Her crying turned to laughter. "Sheikh Jee, before I get drawn into a whirlpool of analysis with you, let us just embrace each other lovingly and enjoy this present moment."

I was only too happy to oblige. "Of course, Fatima. We are on our honeymoon. Let us extend this present moment until we get up in the morning."

It had become a habit for us to get up early in the morning. The gentle sound of the waves and the bright moonlight beckoned us to go to the balcony of our suite and see the sunrise.

On the day of our fortieth wedding anniversary, we both did our *subh* prayer and then sat quietly breathing in the fresh sea breeze. We gazed at the deep blue sea below as the sun warmed our faces and we enjoyed another present moment.

Fatima gently broke the silence, "Jee, this is so romantic. Thank you for arranging this cruise. We both needed this to spoil each other, relax, and recharge our batteries."

Just then my cell phone rang. As an exception, I had left it on in anticipation of a call from Shahnaaz or possibly even from Nasib.

It was a call from Chris and Shahnaaz and their children. I turned on the video link.

Fatima and I were thrilled to hear their congratulations in unison and in Arabic!

Our granddaughter Faiza had just turned five and looked beautiful as ever, and our four-year-old grandson Jalaal looked as handsome as ever.

"Jee, this is the best start to our anniversary. I am still as starry-eyed today as I was in 1980 when we got married, but now I am beginning to feel hungry. What delicacies are you going to cook for me?"

I smirked and replied, "Fatima, if you don't mind, I need to relax as well, so I will not be able to cook for you. We will just go to the restaurant and enjoy a gourmet breakfast by the sea."

As soon as I said that, the waiter knocked on our door and brought in the breakfast I had ordered for us the previous night.

Fatima exclaimed with delight, "I did not even realize I have been missing this for a long time! Jee, this is what Nasib and Shahnaaz cooked for us in Al-Bahar. How on earth did you arrange this Arabian breakfast—egg kebab with cinnamon and side dishes of apricots in light honey, olives, yogurt cheese, bread, and *halwa*?"

I replied smugly, "Fatima, first of all, we are at sea, not on earth. Secondly, there is a chef on this ship from Saudi Arabia. We will be served halal food on this cruise."

As we sat down at the table of our balcony overlooking the sea, Fatima commented happily, "Jee, you have truly outdone yourself. I guess I will just have to get used to being spoiled by you, won't I?"

I replied cheekily, "Fatima, nothing in this universe is free. You have to work hard for what you get in life. And you have worked extremely hard.

"Fatima, you deserve all this. And I will spoil you just short of you becoming spoiled."

As we were savoring our Arabian breakfast, Fatima asked curiously, "Jee, is it just my imagination, or is it true that there are a lot of Muslims on this cruise?"

I finished enjoying an apricot before answering, "Fatima, it is true indeed. At one time it was rare to see Muslims from any part of the world to be taking luxury cruises. This time as you are noticing, you hear many people speaking Arabic. I heard some speak Urdu. And some women are very elegantly dressed wearing the hijab, just like you.

"I was reading the names of the officers of the ship and noticed quite a few Muslim names. The captain of the ship is Capt. Rabiah Bayoumi, and I hope you do not have to see her, but the doctor on board is Dr. Hunra Mubarak."

Fatima continued, "Jee, that makes me feel very proud although I am surprised to see Muslims being accepted and doing so well—"

I could not help interrupting her, "Fatima, please do not be surprised, expect that and just feel proud.

"What you are seeing is just the beginning. Muslims all over the world have become fed up of being powerless and are continuing to work even harder to make progress in every field.

"It is like the end of winter and beginning of spring. The trees look lifeless, but underneath, the sap is flowing. Then the buds start to appear. Soon the flowers start to bloom, and leaves start to unfold. Before you know it the whole forest springs to life. I believe we are at a stage where flowers are starting to bloom."

Fatima nodded her head in agreement. "Sheikh Jee, you paint a very hopeful picture."

I became more emphatic, "Fatima, this is not mere hope. It is based on natural law. There are going to be many setbacks. A frost could kill the budding flowers on some trees, but the forest will still flourish. There could be violent thunderstorms, but the forest will still flourish. There could be droughts, but the forest will still flourish afterward.

"We need to have faith, work hard, and persevere. We are bound to succeed. And nobody will be able to stop that."

Fatima seemed a little more convinced. "To tell you the truth, I do notice more tangible signs of progress. There was a wave of emigration from Afghanistan about the same time as we had to flee. I don't know about other immigrants from other countries, but here in America the Afghan community has done extremely well. Looking at the parents like us, they have done very well. Many of them hold very good, high-paying corporate jobs or have started their own flourishing businesses. Even the ones who were uneducated have ended up doing very well. They have opened up their own businesses, invested in properties, and have become very affluent indeed."

Then she became enthusiastic. "But I am most impressed by their children. With very few exceptions, each one of them has been a straight arrow hitting the bull's eye. The parents invested time and effort in their children and instilled Islamic values in them. No wonder the children have done extremely well."

I smiled with great satisfaction. "Fatima, this is both remarkable and true. But this is a small fraction of the progress. Do you know what is even more remarkable?"

Fatima's eyes lit up. "No. But I am eager to know."

I started with a question, "Fatima, how are the children of your relatives in Afghanistan doing?"

Fatima smiled broadly. "Sheikh Jee, they have done very well. They are extremely resourceful. They are very well educated, and they have turned adversity into advantage. Their resourcefulness has transformed Afghanistan from a poor country to a developing country. Foreign countries are now only too eager to invest in Afghanistan."

I concurred with her, "Fatima, these are very significant signs of progress. But now look at the progress made by some of the other predominantly Muslim countries.

"Look at Bangladesh. Look at Egypt. At one time they were very poor but have become very strong economically, and the prospects are even better."

But Fatima relapsed into doubtfulness. "Sheikh Jee, I would love to agree with your assessment of bright future prospects, but there is so much turmoil in the Muslim world. Several Muslim countries are going through major upheavals. Dictators who had ruled ruthlessly for decades have been deposed, but there is still turmoil."

I took a deep breath before responding, "Fatima, I agree with you. Deposing dictators was a very good and necessary step. People can be repressed for only so long. It is only natural that their anger finally explodes like a volcano. It may not seem so, but believe me this is very good!

"It is also natural to expect that things will improve immediately afterward. But decades of mismanagement, corruption, and wasting trillions of dollars on misguided militarization will take some time to reverse before tangible progress is made.

"This is where we need to have faith. We have to make progress amid turmoil. If we wait before turmoil ends, we will never progress. *Now* is always the best time. Remember we can make excuses, or we can make progress.

"There are enough positive signs for us to be encouraged. We need to use any and every positive sign and build up on that."

Then I remembered to use emotion to connect with her. "My dear Fatima, how much turmoil have we had in our life? How much have we progressed?" I looked into her eyes and stayed silent.

She shook her head in sadness. "We have had more turmoil in one lifetime to last many lifetimes. I wasn't even born when my father was killed by the Taliban for speaking out against the forced closure of the girls' school in our village.

"I remember my brave and beautiful mother. When I was nine, they shot her in the head because she was teaching girls in our home because the school had been closed. Oh, how I miss her."

I had to console Fatima before she could continue, "My aunt and uncle took me to their village which was much safer. They were very poor themselves and had seven children. I am eternally grateful to them for lovingly raising me as their daughter.

"Jee, I don't know how to explain it, but the traumatic childhood experiences made me very determined. I grew up in a hurry and studied extremely hard and helped my aunt and uncle to raise my younger cousins. I was very clever and helped with their homework.

"Of course they ended up being very successful and so did their children. I really wanted to meet them all in Afghanistan, but as you know we had to cut our visit short."

Then she came closer to me and held my hand. "Jee, life was very good after I married you. I thank Allah for you.

"And then there was the trauma of leaving our home and fleeing to Pakistan. Now that was turmoil!

"We could have been killed many times. I did not know if you were dead or alive. All I knew was that I had to keep Nasib and Shahnaaz safe.

"Life in the refugee camp was crowded and filthy, but at least, we were safe. I still do not know where I got the strength and determination from, but I knew I would survive. In fact, I remember visualizing every day that we would reunite and thrive."

We both looked at the blue ocean from our luxury suite and then at each other.

I smiled and observed, "Fatima, by your own accounts it seems to me that you came out stronger after every adversity. You could have justifiably given up many times."

She smiled back and continued, "Sheikh Jee, I don't want to be stronger anymore. That forced strength is enough for me.

"But you are right. I could have given up many times. It is my faith in Islam that made me persevere. I thanked Allah even for my difficulties and knew that he would give me the strength to overcome. Every time I felt like giving up, I visualized us being reunited, and that gave me the strength to continue. It was as simple as that. Do you think that is a simplistic belief?"

I shook my head. "On the contrary, Fatima, visualizing is very effective. We would all do well to do the simple things in life, but actually do them.

"When you are doing one simple thing in life, it is solving many complicated things in life, without you being aware of it. This is the beauty of simplicity."

I had one important question for her, "Fatima, I am curious to know one thing. Of all the people like us who had to flee and take refuge in the camps, how many gave up in the turmoil?"

Fatima was not expecting this question. "Jee, I was always too focused on my own life to notice. Of course, some of them did give up, but not many. Now that you ask me, most of the ones I became friends with ended up doing very well."

Then she sat up straight. "Sheikh Jee, you are right! We succeeded in the midst of turmoil. I do believe that the very hopeful picture you paint is based on natural law. It is not mere hope!"

I felt very pleased by her acknowledgment. "How have you succeeded, Fatima?"

She pulled my hand and rubbed it gently. "We succeeded together, Sheikh Jee. Of course, I continued to have many challenges that I had to overcome in America.

"It took me a long time to get used to being stared at. To be honest with you, I still have not gotten used to it. However, it is a choice that I made, so I do not complain or blame people for staring.

"Most people stare out of curiosity, but some stare out of hostility. It is very difficult not to be affected by someone driving by and gesturing and sounding the car horn in mockery.

"After any terrorist incident in the news, I notice very angry stares, and the horns blare angrily as well, but as I said, it is a choice I have made and live by it. I do become frustrated, but overall, I have become stronger and more assertive because of other peoples' ignorance, stupidity, and hostility.

"My response was to start doing things which help to improve the image of Muslims generally and Muslim women in particular who wear the hijab.

"This is why I started volunteering at the local food bank. I really believe that wearing the hijab puts added responsibility on me. I always work harder than others, and I always make sure that my conduct is polite but assertive.

"The good news is that more and more women are wearing the hijab. We are the ambassadors of Islam. The mainstream population is getting used to us, mostly in a neutral or positive way."

I raised my finger to make an important observation. "Fatima, it seems to me that you used adversity to improve yourself."

She nodded her head strongly. "Yes! I am convinced that this added pressure has made me a better and a stronger person. Maybe I should thank those ignorant, stupid, and hostile jerks!"

I agreed with Fatima, "Good people encourage you to become a better person. Bad people force you to become a better person."

Fatima continued with turmoil in her life, "Thank you, Jee. I can tell you that I have grown more through facing ignorant jerks than through encouragement of good people.

"One other turmoil I felt very bitter about was the injury to my back. There were many silent battles I fought in my mind when I almost gave up. The physical pain was excruciating. I felt that my life was over."

Her eyes welled up with tears.

"But you encouraged me and motivated me to carry on. You are the one who reminded me of the courage of the orphans at the Zebadiyah Foundation so horribly maimed and disabled, yet they still carried on. You lifted me from the gloom and ignited my passion to contribute even more despite my pain and disability. And I want to thank you."

I wiped the big teardrops running down her cheeks. "Fatima, I was the one who was cheering you on, but you were the one running the marathon with a broken back. You have been a true inspiration.

"You may not realize it, but you have already answered the question I asked before as to how you have succeeded."

Fatima burst out crying again, but this time with tears of joy. "Jee, I promise to Allah that next time I will do great even if I did not have a broken back.

"The truth is that if I had not broken my back, I would have been just good, but now I am great."

We embraced each other tightly. Just then there was an emergency announcement on board the ship for all the passengers to remain calm and to go to their rooms and stay there until further notice.

The first thing that came to our minds was that there must be a terrorist threat to the ship.

All the activity on the ship came to a standstill, including the ship itself. It seemed each minute took an hour to pass. I reasoned that the crew being professional and competent would be able to handle any emergency well.

Meanwhile, Fatima was visibly nervous but putting on a brave face. I was more worried about her in case we had to abandon ship.

The crew became very scarce and could not answer any question as to what the emergency was. The vacuum of information was being filled with unease.

The next announcement came after a couple of hours. All the passengers were asked to calmly proceed to the preassigned assembly points.

I wheeled Fatima to the assembly point. There was a strange calmness on the ship borne out of anxiety as all the passengers huddled together. By this time passengers started talking to each other quietly and encouraging each other that everything would turn out well.

After what seemed a long wait came the first informative announcement. The federal security organization had received intelligence that a bomb had been planted on board our luxury liner. The crew had made safe the preassigned assembly points and were now systematically searching the ship for any suspicious package. We were asked to remain calm and stay in place until further notice.

Suddenly there was a lot of commotion a few feet from where we were. An elderly lady was having a heart attack!

Everybody was very impressed with how quickly the doctor came and stabilized the patient, and the paramedics wheeled her away.

We were surprised that she was wearing the hijab. Fatima and I assumed it was Dr. Hunra Mubarak.

After another hour came the announcement that everything was safe. Everybody started to applaud out of relief and to thank the crew for handling the situation professionally and calmly.

After I wheeled Fatima back to our suite, she shared her thoughts about the terrorist threat with me. "Jee, I am very relieved that this was just a terrorist threat. But what I am really pleased about is that I did not sense any stares. After all I was the only visible Muslim among the passengers in our group."

I started answering slowly, "Fatima, this is a very good sign of progress for Muslims. But first of all, why should we assume that it was a threat coming from Muslim terrorists?

"However, I do agree that it is very encouraging sign that people do not automatically assign terrorism to Muslims. We have made a lot progress to change the totally wrong perception of Muslims in the Western media and public opinion. We have earned that through all the peaceful progress we have made.

"I took the opportunity last night to make a list of our accomplishments since our hajj. This list is not for bragging about, but for thanking Allah for helping us with our accomplishments and to encourage us to continue. Would you like me to share them with you?"

Fatima was happy to reply, "Jee, yes, please. I think I am too hard on myself to acknowledge and enjoy what I have achieved. I even feel guilty about our affluence."

I started enthusiastically, "Fatima, let me start with you. You started slowly with the chat show on the local Afghani radio show. You followed that with giving personal tutoring lessons in Pashto and Farsi to Afghani children via videophone. You leveraged your efforts by training others.

"Whenever you reached one plateau, you became creative as to how you would scale the next height. So you established the Striving Toward Excellence organization and launched the 123Tutoring program. Now the Stexcel organization and the 123Tutoring programs are internationally acclaimed.

"Then you created synergy by harnessing the talents of your friend Wazeera to set up a tutoring and mentoring program. You wanted to set up the student exchange program but were limited by finances. Then you were helped by the advantage of adversity."

She interrupted me, "Jee, what do you mean by the advantage of adversity?"

I explained patiently, "Allah rewards anyone who is working hard while overcoming adversity by giving them a break. In this case, the help came through me as I started to expand my real estate business, but it would have come one way or another.

"Fatima, you accomplished all that while being physically disabled. The help you elicited came through admiration and not through pity. Please remember that."

Fatima closed her eyes and smiled. "Thank you for explaining. Sometimes I felt people were helping me out of pity because I was disabled, but the way you put it, they were admiring my efforts!"

I continued listing her accomplishments. "Yes, Fatima, they helped you out of admiration, but you also overcame many setbacks and resentments caused by your success. Some people who you thought were your friends became very hostile as you received recognition.

"So it is only fitting that you received the American Citizenship Award.

"But in my opinion, your most precious achievement has been that since you have always worn the hijab, you become the face of the modern, progressive, and proud Muslim woman. You are an inspiration. Fatima, I love you!"

Fatima started to cry with happiness as I held her tightly. After recovering, she said softly, "I thank Allah for enabling me to overcome my adversity and accomplish so much. Before my injury, I had planned to settle for cozy mediocrity. I gladly accept the fruits of my efforts. I thank Allah for my adversity."

Then she asked me, "Jee, what did you accomplish since our hajj?"

Before answering her question, I realized that both of us had unconsciously forgotten to acknowledge the mother of all adversities that had shaped our lives. "Fatima, it is perhaps the best news that we have not even mentioned the adversity we are still facing—that our own son is a terrorist!

"He has not spoken with us for more than ten years. It is always you who sends him e-mails at Eid or on his birthday, and you get the briefest reply possible. On our ruby anniversary, we did not even get an e-mail let alone a phone call, but this time we did not even notice!

"All we know is that he is alive. We have no idea what is going on in his mind and what he is up to.

"I believe we launched many improvement actions to overcompensate for the actual and potential activities of Nasib. Instead of worrying about things we cannot change, we have used that uncertainty to take actions that have improved us personally and to portray the true face of Islam."

Fatima's eyes widened with this realization. "Jee, I honestly believe we have found our purpose in life by overcoming obstacles in our lives."

I concurred, "Yes, Fatima, as for what I have accomplished since hajj, I am thankful to Allah that I did not have to cross the bridge of physical adversity."

Fatima responded a little crossly, "Sheikh Umeed Jee, I am too hard on myself, and you are too modest about yourself. You crossed the bridge of hope. They named the Umeed Bridge after you!"

I started to laugh. "Fatima, I will be brief but generous about my accomplishments.

"The achievement I am most thankful for is to bring about understanding between Islam and other religions. It is an ongoing effort, and it is an honor indeed to be recognized for my efforts toward peace between religions.

"I am also grateful that I have always used my financial success for my philanthropic contributions in advance of our desires.

"Fatima, let us enjoy guilt-free indulgence. Let us thank Allah because we have earned our luxuries."

We were enjoying the cruise immensely. Fatima felt very mobile and comfortable. We made many delightful friendships with people from many different countries. And we found it very convenient to pray because there was a dedicated room for Muslims to pray on board the ship. That is where we met many other Muslims, including Capt. Rabiah Bayoumi and Dr. Hunra Mubarak.

One evening, when we were watching the sunset from our suite, Fatima shared her pleasant observation, "I feel very proud to see Captain Bayoumi and Dr. Mubarak. Doesn't it make you feel proud to see Muslims doing so well?"

I was happy to concur, "Yes, Fatima. We are beginning to see many tangible signs of progress. And did you know that the cruise ship is owned by an Egyptian company?"

Fatima was incredulous. "No, I didn't, but I am very surprised and impressed. I suppose that is why they have an Egyptian captain and doctor and many other Muslim-sounding crew members."

I continued while smiling, "Fatima, we will soon not be surprised. I was talking to Captain Bayoumi this afternoon while you were resting, and he told me that he and Dr. Mubarak have been working on the ship for ten years and the Egyptian company bought this luxury ship just five years ago."

Fatima's eyes lit up as she responded, "Jee, we should replace surprise with expectation! That is what my dear aunt who raised me used to say to my uncle whenever I did something good.

"That reminds me of another thing. How is the Zebadiyah Foundation is doing?"

I smiled back and replied, "Fatima, what do you expect? I have always had great expectations. The foundation laid by Muhsin and Mahnoor is so strong that I expect it to continue to do well.

"I often remember the words Muhsin said the last time when you and I met them. 'We could die tomorrow and the foundation will continue to flourish.' I still believe in him.

"Fatima, to tell you the truth, you and I have been too busy with our own projects to monitor the progress and activities of the Zebadiyah Foundation lately.

"Of course I am generally aware of the progress. I know that they have set up some skills training schools and that some of the orphans have become extremely successful entrepreneurs in Afghanistan,

Europe, Australia, and America. They are continuing to grow and fund the organization.

"The progress has become self-sustaining. I believe Muhsin and Mahnoor's son Zebadiyah came back from England to run the foundation. Yes, I have great expectations."

Fatima commented thoughtfully, "Jee, I suppose you are right. I remember the surprise with which the world greeted the establishment of the self-sustaining city of Al-Bahar. Now we have cities modeled on Al-Bahar being established in Pakistan, India, United States, and Australia. All the expertise was developed in Saudi Arabia. It is still a matter of great pride for the Muslim world, but even better news is that it is not a surprise anymore."

I agreed emphatically, "Fatima, what started off as single spikes of spectacular progress have become frequent clusters. The progress is now broad based. The Muslim world is leapfrogging to be among the innovators.

"We are collaborators, but we are also becoming leaders. This is a requirement to shape the future of the world.

"Fatima, even leadership has become self-sustaining. Do you remember when Sheikh Zahid retired?"

Fatima grinned with satisfaction and replied, "He retired three years after my match-making effort. It gives me great satisfaction that Sheikh Zahid and Nabiha got married three years after our hajj and have a beautiful eight-year-old daughter, Afroze."

I complimented her, "Yes, Fatima, you can feel very proud of another good deed. Sheikh Zahid's idea of successful leadership is that it should not depend on any one individual. He now has the satisfaction that Al-Bahar continues to grow and succeed even when he is not leading. Of course, he is available to provide advice when asked. To be honest we have a lot of hard work ahead of us, but we are well on the way to progress and prosperity. Let us be proud and encouraged by that. Remember the first steps are even more important than the last steps."

Fatima squeezed my hand gently. "Jee, I must admit that despite all the signs of progress in the Muslim world, I still pay more attention to negative news about us. But no more!

"It is much more exciting to be buoyed by hopefulness than to be anchored by hopelessness.

"Now I am feeling hungry. Can we go to our suite and have dinner?"

I replied cheerfully, "Of course, my dear. Today I took the liberty of ordering halal camel meat. We will have a romantic candlelit dinner. I hope you will enjoy that. After that I suggest you get a good rest because tomorrow we dock in Southampton and take a train to London."

Fatima started to grin broadly. "Sheikh Jee, you seem to have become more romantic with age."

I tried to push my luck, "Fatima, to tell you the truth I have always been this romantic. Is it possible that you only started noticing it now?"

Fatima replied with piercing looks and stern silence. I had to salvage all my hard-earned effort, "Or, Fatima, it is very possible that I have rekindled the flame of romance. But this time I will not let it die because of inattention."

Fatima relented and commented mischievously, "Sheikh Jee, you are very smooth. If you were a cat, you just saved yourself one life."

The following day was very busy. The train ride from Southampton to London was very comfortable. I had booked a first-class train ticket to London.

I had visited London thirty-five years ago while I was living in Germany. I stayed for one week with my cousin who had settled in England and had good memories. It was Fatima's first time visiting England and she was very excited.

I had booked a luxury suite in one of the best hotels in London and a private limousine to take a tour of the landmarks in and around London the following day.

Fatima was very complimentary with her first impressions of England after sightseeing. "Jee, I just love England. It seems strange to see cars driving on the left side of the road, but everything seems very organized and functioning smoothly.

"I was surprised to find out that our limousine chauffer was a Muslim Indian from Mumbai. I was expecting to see a white Englishman."

I was relieved that as the host and organizer of our fortieth wedding anniversary, Fatima was mostly approving of my choices. "Fatima, we got a very good opportunity of brushing up on our Urdu language skills. And we got a sense of how Muslim immigrants are adjusting to life in Britain.

"If you are up to more sightseeing, I can phone the same chauffer to pick us up from the hotel tomorrow."

But Fatima had other ideas. "Jee, I appreciate your considerations of my comfort, but I would like to see London more as a local resident rather than a tourist. I would like to visit the neighborhoods where Muslims and other immigrants live. I would like to travel by the underground train. It may be a bit more effort for you to help me with my wheelchair. We will also find how friendly London is for handicapped people."

After each day we discussed our observations. Fatima remarked, "Jee, I have never seen so many women wearing the hijab or the full veil. In fact, I do not recall anyone wearing the full veil in public in the United States."

"Fatima, Britain has become much more multicultural since I visited thirty-five years ago. As you saw there are whole neighborhoods which are populated by visible minorities. At one time they were all white—now there is complete inversion of population mix in these neighborhoods.

"The number of religious places in a country gives a very good indication of the population mix and the level of tolerance in a country.

"We have seen more mosques, synagogues, and temples than we could count.

"As we observed when we visited three different mosques, they are very well-attended. The Muslims seem to be thriving well in Britain."

Fatima concurred conditionally, "I have also heard of race riots in Britain and some mosques being vandalized and racist attacks against Muslims."

I paused and replied, "Fatima, this is all true. There are racists and bigots in every country and every religion. To put things in perspective, what do you think would happen if the present racial and religious mix of neighborhoods in Kabul were to be displaced by people of different races and religions?"

Fatima replied honestly, "Jee, there would be racist attacks, and the places of worship of other religions would be attacked. I mean even now Sunnis and Shias bomb each other's mosques."

I continued with my observations, "Yes, Fatima. What it means is that we have to continually fight racism and bigotry, but if we look objectively, the Western countries are making a decent effort to allow freedom of religion and enforce minority rights.

"Of course there are still many injustices, so we have to be continually assertive. It is through assertiveness that Muslims have the right to wear the hijab and the veiled niqab in public places. And there are Muslims and other minorities in very prominent places and doing extremely well. Of course they have earned the success and prominence.

"We have to be continually vigilant to protect our rights, but to be honest, Fatima, Muslims enjoy equal or more rights in most Western countries than they would in their own countries. We need to appreciate this freedom."

Fatima was a little perplexed by my comment. "Jee, what makes you reach that conclusion?"

I replied promptly, "A Muslim woman in Egypt or Turkey cannot attend university wearing the veiled niqab, which covers the full face. In Britain and United States, she would be able to."

Fatima persisted in her questioning, "But, Jee, is it not true that there is a law that she would not be able to attend university wearing a niqab in France?"

I replied thoughtfully, "Yes, it is true, Fatima. In fact, if she was wearing the hijab, she would not even be able to attend school, but neither could a Christian wearing a cross, a Jew wearing a Star of David, or a Sikh wearing a turban. So this law is not aimed at Muslims but against all religions. As I said before, we need to be assertive and vigilant at all times. Perhaps we should join forces with other religions to keep on fighting peacefully against this unjust law."

Fatima seemed a bit more convinced. "Jee, I agree that we need to be more assertive and vigilant. This way we can preserve our own identity and still be integrated into the mainstream society of any country we live in."

"Precisely, Fatima. We need to be integrated, not assimilated."

I added another dimension, "We need to be assertive, not aggressive. Aggression will backfire on our progress."

As usual, Fatima had another question, "Jee, if we were to visit other European countries, would we see women wearing the hijab or the niqab like we see in England?"

"Fatima, different European countries have different laws regarding the wearing of the niqab, which covers the full face, but generally it is not allowed.

"There is no restriction on wearing the hijab which just covers the hair, and the face is fully visible.

"However, like I said before, in some Muslim countries such as Turkey, the laws are more restrictive than in most European countries.

"Fatima, in Europe wearing the niqab in public places just fans the flames of Islamophobia. There are very, very few women who wear the niqab, but the image and the association with Islamic fundamentalism persist. It just seems that a lot of women wear the niqab. The niqab acts as a red flag, enraging the bull of Islamophobia.

"Mind you, even if there was no law banning the wearing of the niqab, very few women would want to wear it."

Fatima reiterated her own strong views. "Jee, there is a very fundamental difference between wearing the hijab and wearing the niqab. The niqab is physically restrictive because it covers your whole face. The hijab preserves modesty without any physical restrictions.

"There is no requirement in the Koran to wear the niqab or the hijab. The fundamental requirement is to dress modestly."

"But the fundamentalists have turned centuries-old social customs into religious requirements and continue to use them to suppress women."

"Fatima, I agree with you, but this is a very divisive issue in the Muslim as well as the non-Muslim world. I believe we need to be consciously inactive on this issue. Let us consciously decide to let things take their own course."

Fatima replied with a sigh of relief, "Jee, I am very happy with your suggestion. We won't worry that we need to be worried about this issue. We have a lot more constructive things on which to spend our energy."

The week in England passed very quickly, and soon it was time for us to depart.

As we boarded our cruise ship, Fatima was a little disappointed to leave. "Jee, I would have loved to live in England. You told me that it is always rainy and damp in England, but the weather has been so beautifully warm and sunny. Why didn't you settle in England?"

I looked into her eyes and smiled. "Fatima, you are looking at England through the eyes of a tourist. I agree it is a very pleasant and free country, but the week I was here thirty-five years ago, it was damp and miserable. We have been very lucky with the weather this week.

"To answer your question, my decision as to where to settle was made by circumstances. The quickest way to work and stay legally in any European country for me at that time was in Germany, and I had some friends who were already there.

"Later on I decided to move to the United States because of greater opportunities there and because you would not have to learn another new language."

Then I spoke earnestly, "I agree that we would have done very well in England or Germany, but I believe in doing the best wherever we are and however we are and not think about what could have been or what would have been."

Fatima was a little startled. "Sheikh Jee, I didn't mean to complain. I am very happy to be living in America."

Then she added half seriously, "I think you should buy some residential property in England so that we can live here part of the year. Go global, Sheikh Jee!"

Now I was startled. "Fatima, it never occurred to me to buy real estate outside of the United States. If you had said that a few years ago, I would have considered it. We were juggling too many things at that time. I guess it was logistically easier to manage properties at home.

"There is a learning curve to going global, but I will consider it seriously.

"It may not be in England, but why not in Afghanistan? We know that at this stage the country is going through upheavals, but things are destined to become stable. I don't know exactly how yet, but we will contribute directly to develop our motherland."

Then I hugged her. "Fatima, you have just given me a new project! I will start working on it right away."

Fatima pursed her lips and just stared. Smiling never fails, so I smiled to salvage the situation. "Correction, Fatima. I will start working on it right away after we finish our romantic ruby anniversary cruise."

Fatima tried hard to suppress her smile but couldn't. "Sheikh Jee, you are too smooth, but remember we are here to enjoy our vacation, not to work—and don't say that you enjoy working!"

So we spent the rest of the cruise making more friends, watching dazzling shows, getting up late, basking in the sunshine, watching beautiful sunsets, and just lazing around and doing nothing in particular.

When we reached home, I hugged her tightly. "Fatima, thank you for the most wonderful forty years of my life. I love you."

Fatima started to cry. "Jee, thank you for the most wonderful forty years of my life. I love you."

NASIB FLIES BACK TO NEW YORK

The next two years passed very quickly. I became extremely busy with the exciting new challenge of investing in overseas property. I did not know how to do that, but in my heart I *knew* I had to do it.

Fatima's health started to deteriorate gradually. She adapted well by doing less herself and leveraging her abilities by mentoring the mentors in the Stexcel organization.

I invested a million dollars as part of a consortium of American-Afghani businessmen in an industrial complex being developed just outside Kabul. I compensated for my lack of knowledge in investing in Afghanistan by joining people who had direct experience but lacked the funds to launch such a big project.

I made sure that my decision was based more on the business viability of the project rather than my emotional need to invest in Afghanistan.

I used the same model to invest in large projects in Kenya, Mauritania, and Bolivia. I never thought I could do that, but progressing step by step made it possible. And there were many more opportunities on the horizon.

The results on these long-term investments are still to be realized, but I feel sure that these will be more profitable than my American investments despite the current political risks in these countries. After all I had made big losses with some of my investments—American investments—and still thrived financially.

Over the years I had learned to love calculated uncertainty!

On her sixty-fourth birthday, Fatima shared some very exciting news. She jumped up and down in her wheelchair. "Jee, this is the best news I have received in nine years. I received an e-mail from Nasib. He is coming home!"

I beamed with joyful relief. "Fatima, I thank Allah! We are going to see Nasib for the first time since he went to Al-Bahar!"

Fatima started to weep with joy and mumbled, "Our life is complete now. We have done extremely well and have all the accolades. I did not realize how much I was missing him until now."

It became evident to me that even though we were disappointed with Nasib, we were only too eager to overlook our past frustrations with him and embrace him.

"Fatima, when is he coming?" I asked her excitedly.

By now she had stopped crying and spoke coherently, "Exactly one month from today, on October 15, 2022. He has already booked himself on flight AM3080 from Riyadh to New York, arriving at ten at night. He is travelling first class. He will be staying with us for seven weeks. Jee, I am so proud of my son!"

I smiled at her comment. As usual the same Nasib became her son whenever she was pleased with him and became my son when she was displeased with him.

I cleared my throat to modify her claim, "Fatima, we are both proud of our son. He will be flying first class on the first American airline to fly the biggest jumbo jet nonstop between New York and Riyadh. I always knew our son would end up doing extremely well."

Fatima was too happy to notice my correction of her claim. "Jee, I think we should cancel our personal retreat to see the fall colors in Vermont."

I countered her suggestion, "But, Fatima, why not do both? We are due to return on the evening of the fifteenth of October. We can go on our one-week retreat as planned, and on the way back we have dinner in a restaurant—in a fancy restaurant in New York—and pick up Nasib from the airport and bring him with us."

Of course, Fatima was very happy with my suggestion. The month seemed to take a long time to pass, but that prolonged our happy anticipation.

Fatima's ailments seemed to disappear, and she became rejuvenated. She planned out what she would be cooking for the seven weeks and what activities we would be sharing with him.

We thoroughly enjoyed our personal retreat. It seemed that the fall colors were particularly brilliant because we were happy that Nasib was coming home.

As we were about to set off to New York in the afternoon, Fatima received an e-mail from Nasib. "Flight delayed due to sandstorm. Will arrive at midnight. Will stay in airport hotel. Don't come to pick me up. Will take cab when I wake up. See you at noon. Will have brunch. Love, Nasib."

Fatima spoke very smugly, "Jee, my son is so responsible. I love him, and I am going to make the same favorite breakfast I made for him when he came home from Afghanistan.

"Now that we do not have to pick him up, we can linger longer by our lakeside villa and then go straight home."

By the time we reached home, it was late at night. So I quickly got the mail for the week on the way in, and we retired for the night so that I could take Fatima to buy some fresh groceries early in the morning for Nasib's long-awaited homecoming.

The phone rang unexpectedly at dawn. I thought it was Nasib.

I did not know at that moment that we were to soon experience the biggest nightmare of our lives!

A man was shouting obscenities and threatening Muslims. "You—Muslims! We are going to kill all of you. All of you are—Islamist terrorists! You deserve to die!"

I was very badly shaken and put the phone down. It rang again. I picked it up with trepidation. The same shrill voice hollered, "I am not— finished with you—9/11 terrorists . . ."

I put the phone down and did not pick it up when it rang repeatedly.

The phone number of the caller was blocked.

By this time, Fatima had woken up feeling very alarmed. "Jee, what is going on? Who is calling again and again?"

I took a deep sigh and replied, "Fatima, I do not know, but something terrible has happened. I think we should watch the news."

It was much worse than we could have ever imagined—a huge airliner had crashed in New York!

The very first image of the breaking news was of some buildings burning fiercely with multiple explosions being heard and a ticker tape at the bottom saying that flight AM3080 from Riyadh to New York had crashed approaching New York airport at half past one that morning.

We looked incredulously at each other trying to deny what we were witnessing.

Then Fatima started wailing, "Jee, that is the flight Nasib was on! Please tell me he missed that flight. Allah! He missed that flight!"

I hugged Fatima and started to weep uncontrollably, "Allah! Please tell us that Nasib missed that flight."

We were both paralyzed by shock and did not know what to do. In between bouts of sobbing, we listened to the news.

It became sickeningly reminiscent of what happed after the 9/11 terrorist attacks twenty-one years ago. All the air traffic in the United States had been halted indefinitely. No flights were landing or taking off.

The newscaster reported of an unknown Islamist terrorist group claiming responsibility for the crash of the American airliner, and a terrorism expert was being interviewed.

All five hundred and fifty-one passengers and crew were feared dead. One hundred people were feared dead on the ground, and many more had been taken to hospitals. The main body of the airliner had crashed into two gas stations and caused huge explosions. The fires were still burning out of control.

We were living the nightmare we never thought could come true.

The newscaster reported that there had been light rain during the night but that the weather was not considered a factor in the crash of the plane. The authorities were treating this as an act of terrorism.

The phone rang again. Fatima was distraught. "Jee, call the police. Call the airline to find out if Nasib was on the plane."

I decided not to call the police because they would be too preoccupied with the crash to do anything about threatening phone calls. When I phoned the airline, there was a recorded message that the passenger list was not available at the time but would be published on the airline's website when available.

We continued to watch the terrible news. There was nothing we could do except to console each other and pray to Allah that somehow Nasib was alive.

Fatima pointed to a large envelope on the table underneath the television where I had put the letters last night. It was from Nasib. I opened it up hurriedly. Inside was a DVD with a note on a sticky paper. "For Mom and Dad only. Insert into your computer. Watch this DVD together. Nasib."

We thought that our nightmare was reaching a crescendo. A jihadist video recorded by Nasib!

Fearful thoughts I had during the hajj came back—a jumbo jet en route to New York being blown out of the sky and Nasib being named as the suicide bomber!

Fatima blurted in a trembling voice and covered her eyes, "Jee, I cannot bear to watch it. I just want to die right now!"

I responded in a choking voice, "Fatima, we have to face the reality that Nasib is presenting to us. We have to be brave enough to face the truth, whatever it may be. He wants both of us to see it together."

With trembling hands I slipped the DVD in the computer connected to our television and sat back to watch it with great trepidation. "Yes, Fatima, let us be brave and face the truth."

I held Fatima's hand trying to comfort her, but she still kept her eyes closed.

The news turned off, and the DVD started to play. Nasib came on the screen and looked straight at us, smiled, and started to speak in a calm and clear voice, "Mom and Dad, I love you. I realize that I have given you a lot of grief in life. I have made this video of apology because I could not face you directly otherwise."

Fatima opened her eyes and squeezed my hand as I paused the video. We were both immensely relieved. She spoke softly while still crying, "Jee, I thank Allah that this is not a jihadist video. Let us continue."

I restarted the video, "Please listen carefully because you will be able to see this video once only. Forgive me for hacking into your computer. I have programmed it so that this DVD will play only on your computer. I have programmed it so that it erases the DVD as it plays. You will understand why I did it this way.

"Dad, first of all I want to thank you for your wisdom and your patience with me. I was too arrogant to even listen. I had already made up my mind on everything. My arrogance was based on my academic, technical, and logical abilities. I now know that logic determines to a very small degree how most things in life work. There are too many intangible variables which logic cannot solve.

"I have made many business plans which look great on paper, but I have found out that actions based on intuition, feeling, and experiences determine results to a very large extent.

"You always raised us with true Islamic values, and I do not know how I allowed myself to be brainwashed during my visit to the madrassa in Afghanistan. Of course I was too arrogant to acknowledge that I had been brainwashed. Instead, I did everything to justify my newly discovered revelations. It was the most disastrous detour I took in my life. You tried your best to make me return to the right path, but I objected every time. I did not listen to my friend Jaffar either. I can only blame myself.

"There were times when I doubted my strategy that the way for preserving Islam was through defeating the enemies of Islam. And I believed the terrorists as to who our deemed enemies were at any given time.

"Now let me tell you the incident that disgusted me so much that I became totally dedicated to restoring glory to Islam through peace and prosperity and not through violence and destruction."

Nasib's calm and clear voice started to falter, and he burst into tears.

We had never seen Nasib crying since he was a baby.

"Mom and Dad, I pray to Allah that you will forgive me. Your friends Muhsin and Mahnoor were murdered by my friend Rashid!

"Remember, his father had been tortured and killed by the Afghan army soldiers. His mother and sister had been raped in front of him. The American soldiers had urinated on his father's face before handing him over to the Afghan soldiers.

"Well, I sent him some money to start his own business, but he used that to plot the terrorist act and exact revenge on the Americans and Afghan army soldiers and policemen.

"After the first suicide bomber killed fifty Afghans and two American soldiers by blowing up the explosive-laden truck outside the police station, it was Rashid who blew himself up to kill more soldiers as they rushed to help their injured comrades. Instead, it was Muhsin and Mahnoor who rushed to help but were killed. I had no idea Rashid would actually do something so brutal, but I feel responsible for his actions. I hope you will forgive me."

I paused the video as Fatima and I shed fresh tears for this tragedy.

We stayed silent for a long time before I restarted the video. "I will not blame you if you don't forgive me. I came to know of Muhsin and Mahnoor's selfless service in establishing the Zebadiyah Foundation. How could we kill such peaceful and purposeful people trying to rebuild our country? I was so full of remorse by their murder that I went to visit the foundation. It is there that I met their son who had come back from England to run the foundation.

"When I mentioned that I had lived in New York, he told me about how fondly his parents remembered the friendship and contribution of Sheikh Umeed and his wife Fatima from New York."

His voice choked again, "I have not told Zebadiyah that my friend Rashid murdered his parents. I have not told Salma about my terrorist past either because I have completely changed my life.

"Mom and Dad, I have adopted the path of peace, and I have dedicated my life to glorify Islam through peace and prosperity."

For the first time Nasib smiled. "I am so happy to admit that I was totally wrong, and you were totally right. You better get used to. me agreeing with you on a lot of things. Dad, I catch myself thinking like you many times!"

Then he became serious. "From the day that I met Zebadiyah, I decided to spend every minute of my life to undo the destruction I had caused and to overcompensate by building monuments to Muslim prosperity. I promised myself that I would minimize contact with everybody until I had achieved that. I became a recluse as far as you were concerned. You must have been anguished as to what I was up to. I hope the progress I have to show will make you forgive the heartaches I have caused.

"I have taken massive action to turn my life around. Allah always gives lucky breaks to anyone who embarks on fulfilling challenges."

Then his face lit up. "Mom, the lucky break that I got was at one of the most difficult times in my life. I had just quit working for Sheikh Zahid and started my own business. My business prospects looked very bleak.

"But my life prospects became very rosy when Salma forgave me and agreed to marry me. Mom and Dad, you now have a very good-looking and smart grandson Hamza who is six and an angel of a granddaughter Parveen who is three. They are already in New York, and I will be proud to show them off to you."

Then he added cheekily, "Seeing Salma, Hamza, and Parveen will make it easier for you to forgive me for not telling you earlier."

Fatima signalled me to pause the video. For a brief moment we forgot about the calamity around us and smiled at each other without saying anything.

I restarted the video. "Salma and I have a very loving relationship—I call her my superwoman, and she calls me her reclusive supernerd. I am very happy because I have been given a passing grade as a loving husband and an excellent grade as a loving father. Dad, now you and I have another thing in common.

"Dad, all the books you had on personal growth on your bookshelf that I used to dismiss—well, I have read them all and put into practice the lessons in them. I have bought CDs and have been to several seminars. That gives a different dimension of understanding. I have read many new ones that even you may not have read. I will share some of those with you. Now I cannot live without continuous personal growth. I wish I had read them twenty years ago.

"As far as being a good son is concerned, I am still on probation. I am working very hard to get an excellent grade."

That made us both cry although we did not stop the video.

"So let me tell you what Salma and I have accomplished in the eight years we have been married—other than raising two wonderful children.

"I implemented the security software system for Sheikh Zahid by leading the engineering team from his company. I trained them to maintain the system. They were an extremely bright group of people and soon expanded the system on their own.

"Meanwhile, with her excellent sales and marketing experience, Salma landed some contracts for our company to write very sophisticated software programs for robots to be used in search and rescue missions after earthquakes. She opened up a branch office in the Silicon Valley.

"I worked day and night developing the software, and it was very successful. Salma hired some other supernerds to help me out. I trained them in my company in Saudi Arabia to work in our branch office in the Silicon Valley.

"Salma noticed that my strength was limited to creativity in programming and that I enjoyed training other people. I would not be able to manage expansion. So she hired a very good manager who ran the head office in Riyadh.

"Salma opened up branch offices in Germany, France, England, Sweden, China, and Japan. We are particularly proud to have a high-tech corporation based in Saudi Arabia and doing international business.

"I can tell you that this is not a back office operation of a Western multinational corporation. We have more than three thousand employees worldwide. I have lost count of the international patents registered by our company. And Salma is the chief operating officer.

"Our annual sales revenues have exceeded quarter of a billion dollars for the last four years, and royalties from our patents are earning us millions of dollars in addition. Salma and I have decided to keep our company privately owned. We have had offers of two and a half billion dollars for takeover, but Salma has even bigger plans."

I stopped the video to summarize what we had heard so far. "Let us thank Allah that this is not a jihadist video. Fatima, our son has truly transformed himself. He found the right purpose in life."

Immediately I admonished myself for assuming the worst. "And let us pray that he did not take that flight and that we continue to benefit from his transformation."

I restarted the video. "Meanwhile, I have freed up my time to collaborate fully with Zebadiyah. Like his parents, he is a very inspiring person. I have the privilege of working with him to perpetuate the legacy of his parents. I have found purpose in life.

"I have used my creativity to patent some algorithms to simulate very humanlike movements for prosthetic arms and legs.

"We have set up a department in Kabul University where we are developing software for prosthetic knees and wrists. Unfortunately, we have all the patients we need to perfect the movements. But the whole world will benefit from our adversity.

"We have selected and trained some extremely bright students from the orphanage itself to become accomplished engineers and doctors. We have funded their education to get degrees from American and European universities. The only condition is that they come and work in Afghanistan for ten years afterward. We guarantee them jobs in our research facility in the University of Kabul. And these jobs are funded by the royalties from the patents of our Saudi Arabian company.

"In ten years time I expect that none of them will need to work overseas.

"Mom and Dad, I would like you to pause this video and answer this question. Do you believe I have done enough for you to forgive me?"

By now we had no tears left. We just looked at each other, nodded our heads, and replied together, "Yes, Nasib, our son, we forgive you. Please come home. Please, please come home, Nasib!"

I restarted the video. "Mom and Dad, I don't know your answer, but I told you that I would overcompensate for my past actions.

"Zebadiyah and I have set up a research company based in Afghanistan. We have partnered with a robotics company in Germany; we have hired some doctors and engineers from the orphanage; and we have patented a machine called Remote Surgery System.

"Up to now doctors in Kabul have remotely performed more than a thousand bone graft operations on gerbils in an operation room in Frankfurt. Other than placing the gerbil on the operating table and taking it off, there was no human intervention. All thousand operations have been performed with a hundred percent success rate!

"You can imagine the benefits of this kind of technology for the world. I can assure you that the world will hear of more and more such developments from the Muslim world. We really have started to shape the destiny of the world in beneficial ways.

"And we have just begun! I remember you saying a few times that the first few steps are even more important than the last steps. Mom and Dad, I am doing my part of your wish—progress through peace and prosperity by the Islamic world.

"Next week I will be internationally recognized for my pioneering efforts in New York. I hope you will forgive me now."

Nasib smiled broadly. "Mom and Dad, ready or not, I am coming home. Your loving son, Nasib."

The screen went blank. Fatima and I held each other and wept inconsolably. "Yes, Nasib, our son, we forgive you. Please come home. Please, please come home, Nasib!"

We wept silently while praying for Nasib to come home. I turned on the television. It had been nearly twelve hours since the crash. There was an official statement from the security agency that they had discounted terrorism as the cause of the crash. They were focusing on some kind of mechanical failure.

For once Fatima and I breathed a sigh of relief.

The door bell rang. I thought of the threatening phone call and carefully parted the curtain of the balcony overlooking the entrance. There was a woman wearing the hijab at the door accompanied by two little children.

I rushed downstairs to open the door. It was Salma, Hamza, and Parveen.

She clung to me, wailing, "Dad, Nasib is never coming home. He was on the flight. The airline phoned me to confirm."

Hamza and Parveen were clinging to each other. The three-year-old Parveen did not understand what was going on and was pestering her mother as to when her daddy would be coming home.

Fatima wheeled herself to the door, and Salma clung to her shoulder. "Mom, Nasib is never coming home. Allah, I love him so much!'

I hugged my grandson and granddaughter for the first time.

All of us hugged each other. Nobody could console each other for a long time.

It was the most difficult truth for us to accept—Nasib would never be coming home.

LIFE CARRIES ON

The next month was the most traumatic period in our lives. Salma, Hamza, and Parveen took Nasib's death particularly hard.

Fatima and I asked them to stay with us as long as they needed to.

This gave us all the mutual support to adjust to Nasib's death.

I had phoned Shahnaaz to break the saddest news of our lives. She was completely distraught but she continued to provide moral support to Fatima. Chris and Shahnaaz phoned every day to comfort Salma.

They were in New Zealand to chair an international conference on sustainable development and had taken Faiza and Jalaal for a few days of vacation afterward.

Shahnaaz wanted to fly to New York right away but could not get any flight due to the mass disruption of flights to the United States.

I persuaded her to finish her conference and book the earliest flight afterward. She agreed reluctantly.

Salma was very withdrawn but gradually opened up. We listened very closely. "Mom and Dad, I never thought that I would agree to marry Nasib after he first broke up with me. I was devastated. But when he invited me to Al-Bahar for some strictly professional consultation, things changed. Neither of us realized our emotional reconnection at that time.

"I finished the assignment and returned to New York. When he proposed to me over the phone one year later, I was not surprised at all. Somehow I was expecting it.

"He sincerely apologized for breaking up in the past and promised to love me and respect me forever. For someone like me who does a lot of technical analysis, it was not easy for me to decide."

Then she smiled shyly. "I listened to my mother's advice. When it comes to the matters of the heart, it is best to listen to the heart. I did not know what that meant but thought about it.

"I mulled over it for a week and was surprised how the decision came about. His apology was very sincere, and I trusted that he would love me and respect me as he had promised. I would love and respect him. We would just make sure that our love would be strong enough to overcome any difficulties in life.

"Just that was enough for me to make my decision. So we got married in a very simple ceremony in Al-Bahar."

It felt very good when Salma addressed us as "Mom and Dad."

Fatima put her hand on Salma's shoulder. "I am so glad you married Nasib. We loved him dearly."

Just talking about Nasib started to make us feel better. Salma opened up more, "Mom and Dad, Nasib was a very good husband as well. By nature he was a very private person, but he was very warm and caring toward me.

"I thought I was religious, but he was even more religious than me. He was bringing up Hamza and Parveen to be very good Muslims. He wanted to do everything to portray Islam in a good light. He was an extremely proud Muslim."

Then she laughed a little. "My biggest challenge was to make him a romantic. After the first year, I gave up. I thanked Allah that at least he was warm and caring."

Fatima nodded and looked up and down at me and started to laugh. "Salma, join the club. Like father, like son! In the case of Sheikh Jee, I persevered and changed him after forty years."

Salma was as smart as she was beautiful! She deflected Fatima's comment. "But he really did respect me. I made some strategic errors in expanding our company, but he never criticized me for it. In fact, he encouraged me. 'Life is like playing tennis. Salma, you fire a lot of aces so just learn from an occasional double fault.'

"And he was a very good father. He was always extremely preoccupied with his work but made sure he took time out to play with Hamza and Parveen. If they needed attention in the middle of what he was doing, he would actually stop what he was doing and attend to them!'

Then she started to laugh. "Life was very unfair in our home. I was the hard-hearted disciplinarian. He spoiled them, and they adored him!"

Then she wrinkled her forehead and continued, "Mom and Dad, like in all marriages, we had a lot of challenges, but we kept one promise when we married—we never went to sleep angry.

"Mind you, that made us patch up things in a hurry. We were always so tired that we wanted to sleep early. There is one thing which I never understood about Nasib. He was never very talkative to begin with, but he became increasingly reclusive after marriage. With the children and me, he was very warm, but with everybody else, he was very businesslike and very brief.

"I often wondered if he was hiding behind some sort of a complex and even offered to help him, but he never had the courage to talk about it.

"I think he got away with it because he was such a technical genius."

Fatima and I glanced at each other and said nothing. Nasib had obviously never divulged his terrorist past. This time it was my turn to deflect the conversation. "Salma, Nasib fired a lot of aces in life and was probably learning from an occasional double fault."

Salma smiled again and agreed, "Yes. He was a very smart and a handsome man. He was a very proud Muslim."

Then she became very serious. "He found his purpose in life. He was worth billions but lived a very simple life. He used his wealth to benefit the world.

"So what if he was antisocial and a recluse? He was a very good father and a very good husband, and I loved him!"

Once again she burst out crying. "Allah, why did you take away my Nasib from me?"

There are no answers for some questions. Fatima and I tried our best to console her.

Each day brought a bit more acceptance of Nasib's death. We were all exhausted by hundreds of calls of sympathy and our relatives and friends visiting us to pay their respects.

Fatima and I got very little time for grieving privately for our son. One morning we got up very early and went to the park and sat by the lake.

We felt very sad but very peaceful. I started slowly, "Fatima, Nasib really did start walking on the path of peace. He demonstrated that by actions. Of course we miss him greatly, but the way he died brings the best closure to his life.

"It has also brought about the best relief to our anguish about what Nasib was up to and what other unpredictable bombshell we would be forced to deal with."

Fatima sighed and agreed, "Jee, for me the biggest relief was that Nasib was not responsible for the airliner crash. I thought it was a jihadist video he wanted us to see. Now that would have been the biggest nightmare of our lives."

Then she shuddered, "I do not want to think about it."

I pointed out other circumstances which determined the best results from a great disaster. "Fatima, let us be relieved that Islamist terrorists were not responsible for this crash. We would all have to relive the backlash of 9/11. The fragile progress being made by Muslims would be set back many years.

"On a personal level of anguish for our family, Nasib may have been killed by some other terrorist group or charged with providing material support to terrorists in the killing of two American soldiers."

This time I shuddered, "Fatima, let us go home. I don't want to even think about it. Let us just focus on Nasib's legacy of peace and prosperity."

When we arrived home, we found Hamza and Parveen playing. Fatima and I had not spent much time with them, but we made up for it over the next few days.

They were delightful children and extremely bright. They reminded us of Nasib and Shahnaaz when they were growing up. It was very unusual communicating with them. Arabic was their first language, but they could speak a little English. Fatima spoke to them in Arabic, and I spoke to them in English. They were very close to Nasib. We bonded very well, and although we had seen them for the first time, it seemed we knew them since they were born. We just knew that they would perpetuate Nasib's peaceful legacy.

At breakfast, Salma shared her apprehension with us. "Today Nasib was going to receive the international award for pioneering the Remote Surgery System. I feel too emotional to accept it on his behalf. I think I will break down. Who else could accept the award on Nasib's behalf?"

Fatima and I replied together, "Hamza!"

We were very relieved that Shahnaaz and Chris were able to rearrange their travel schedule and bring their daughter Faiza and son Jalaal in time for the award ceremony. This was the first time that all our children and grandchildren would have met us together, except that Nasib was missing.

It was a very poignant ceremony. We felt sad and extremely proud at the same time. Hamza felt very overwhelmed with the standing ovation but did very well to receive the award on behalf of Nasib. There was not a dry eye in the audience.

When we reached home, Salma gathered us all together. "Mom and Dad, Shahnaaz and Chris, Faiza and Jalaal, Hamza, Parveen, and I would like to thank you for all your support and encouragement through this most difficult time in all our lives. We know we will be able to count on each of you whenever we need your help.

Then she vowed solemnly, "But I am the one who has to be brave and start planning for the future. I have to be brave for Hamza and Parveen. The foundation that Nasib has laid deserves the most magnificent monument to be built upon it. May Allah give me the strength and wisdom to do that."

We were all very moved by Salma's resolve. We all hugged Salma and Hamza and Parveen. I spoke on behalf of all of us, "Salma, we know you will do an excellent job in raising Hamza and Parveen. We can already visualize the magnificent monument to honor Nasib's legacy."

It has been ten years since Nasib died. We all miss him dearly. Salma and the children continue to do extremely well.

All of us have had many successes and setbacks in our personal and professional lives.

Both Fatima and I have slowed down and we are going through another difficult and unchartered phase of our lives—growing old gracefully.

We are both thankful for what we have been able to accomplish and contribute in our lives. We have learned to thank Allah for the difficulties in our lives.

We still take time to take personal retreats to recharge our old batteries, which now require more frequent and longer durations to recharge.

This time we decided to stay near and revisit Niagara Falls after thirty years. The awesome beauty was the same, but it seemed that we were seeing the falls for the first time.

At sunset, we sat on a quiet bench overlooking the falls. Fatima started the conversation, "Jee, I miss Nasib so much sometimes I start crying and cannot stop for a long time. How much more would he have accomplished if he had been alive today?"

I closed my eyes and took a deep breath before replying, "Fatima, I miss him dearly as well. As you know we were always diametrically opposed in our view of defending Islam. His idea of defense was to attack.

"I had given up on changing his mind. Remember we agreed to follow our own course and stop wasting our energy on changing others. We worked on improving ourselves, and if I may say so, we completely surpassed our own expectations."

Then I became unusually emotional. "If he were alive today, I would have a very affectionate relationship with him like you had with him. He had started to apply his energies to peaceful progress. He made it so easy for me to forgive his past. Yes, I do love him and miss him."

For once it was Fatima who consoled me, "Jee, I understand how you feel."

I continued after composing myself, "As far as how much more he would have accomplished, you may be surprised by my answer. He continues to accomplish a lot through his legacy. The benefits of our actions continue even after we die."

Fatima looked startled. "I never thought of it that way before."

I elaborated by asking her a question, "How much progress have Muhsin and Mahnoor made after they died?"

She nodded her reply. "I see what you are getting at. They did enough while they were alive that their legacy lives on. Now Zebadiyah is building upon what Muhsin and Mahnoor had done. Sheikh Jee, this is very empowering. Do you think we have done enough in our lives for our legacy to live on?"

I paused before replying, "Fatima, let us be humble and thank Allah for what we have accomplished. The Stexcel Corporation would continue on the strength of what you have already established even after you die. Our ego makes us believe that progress will halt when we die."

Fatima responded excitedly, "Sheikh Jee, it is true! Even if we die tomorrow, our legacy will live on. Just look at Shahnaaz, Chris, Faiza, and Jalaal.

"Look at Salma. She is doing extremely well herself and raising Hamza and Parveen without Nasib.

"Al-Bahar is flourishing even after Sheikh Zahid retired.

"There are people in your interfaith forum who are dedicated to continue understanding between Islam and other religions. Allah forbid that you die tomorrow, others will continue.

"My friend Wazeera has not been able to do much since she suffered a stroke. Some of the girls she had taught became teachers themselves and opened five other schools. Yes, her legacy will continue to live."

I felt very pleased that Fatima now truly believed that our legacy will live on after we die.

However, she still looked a bit puzzled. "Jee, I remember both you and Nasib disagreeing on ways to restore glory to Islam, *within our lifetime.*

"Despite all the massive actions we have taken and all the other people in many other Muslim countries we don't even know have taken, are you sure we will restore glory to Islam in our lifetime?"

Fatima always asked demanding questions, and I was ready to answer very confidently but started humorously, "Fatima, yes, I am sure we will succeed within our lifetime. We will just keep on living until we succeed!"

She was not amused and responded tersely, "Sheikh Jee, it is now the year 2032. You are seventy-seven, and I am seventy-four. I am talking within the next twenty years! Will we succeed within the next twenty years?"

I looked up at the sky and stated, "Look, Fatima, as I have always said, Muslims are definitely doing the right things now. There is still an extremely tiny minority who are masking the very significant progress that the majority is making.

"But there is no denying the progress. Progress is never linear. There are always reversals. That is when we need to have faith and persevere.

"Let me give you the example of China. Has it become a superpower? It is on its way. How long will it take before it actually becomes a superpower?

"There are still many obstacles to overcome. There could still be reversals. What is the definition of superpower? Is it to be more powerful than America?

"The point is that China has risen from poverty and powerlessness to exerting very powerful influence in the world during the last fifty years.

"The people had been applying themselves for decades before China got noticed as a powerful nation.

"The same process is happening with Muslim countries. It is just that we have linked the progress of Muslim countries with progress and influence of Islam.

"So there are enough large and small Muslim countries whose people have been working extremely hard, but the progress and influence has not become noticeable yet. The operative word is *yet*, but it is bound to happen. This is guaranteed by principles of how life unfolds."

I stood up and proclaimed, "There will be enough Muslim countries becoming powerful, and through that process, Islam will flourish and be respected by the world.

"And all this will happen because people like you and me have been working hard making peaceful progress.

"Fatima, because we are trying to catch up centuries of lost ground, it may take another forty years instead of twenty. It will certainly happen in our children's lifetime.

"Will you be happy if it happens in our children's lifetime and not in our lifetime?"

Fatima beamed with happiness. "Jee, I will be more than happy."

I continued energetically, "Yes, Fatima. We are definitely doing the right things. Let us have faith! We are in excellent health. We can very easily live another twenty years and then stretch it for another twenty."

Then we hugged each other as the powerful Niagara Falls roared on behind us. We both wished solemnly, "Allah, please let us live to see Islam restored to glory in our lifetime!"

Biography of Sukhvinder Jutla

Sukhvinder Singh Jutla was born in Nairobi, Kenya.

He has an eclectic background. He has an Indian heritage but has lived 13 years in Kenya, 13 years in England and has been living in Canada for the past 46 years. He speaks English, French, Punjabi, Hindi, Gujarati and Swahili.

He got his Electrical and Electronic Engineering degree from the University of Leeds, England and has worked in the electronics, telecommunication and aerospace industries in UK and Canada.

He is happily married and has three children and six beautiful grandchildren. He is very passionate about promoting peace amongst religions and personal growth.

Since childhood he has enjoyed writing books and articles in English and poems in English, Punjabi and Hindi.

Peace through Personal Growth is his latest fictional novel which delivers a compelling message of peace and personal growth through the experiences of anguished parents dealing with a son who has become a terrorist.

www.ingramcontent.com/pod-product-compliance
Lightning Source LLC
Chambersburg PA
CBHW020431130626
46549CB00001B/88